THE PARADOXES OF POSTERITY

THE PARADOXES OF POSTERITY

....

BENJAMIN HOFFMANN

Translated by Alan J. Singerman

THE PENNSYLVANIA STATE UNIVERSITY PRESS
UNIVERSITY PARK, PENNSYLVANIA

Library of Congress Cataloging-in-Publication Data

Names: Hoffmann, Benjamin, 1985– author. | Singerman, Alan J., translator.
Title: The paradoxes of posterity / Benjamin Hoffmann ; translated by Alan J. Singerman.
Other titles: Paradoxes de la postérité. English
Description: University Park, Pennsylvania : The Pennsylvania State University Press, [2020] | First published in French in 2019 by Les éditions de Minuit under the title: Les paradoxes de la postérité | Includes bibliographical references and index.
Summary: "Examines the paradoxes inherent in the search for symbolic immortality, arguing that there is only one truly serious literary problem: the transmission of texts to posterity"—Provided by publisher.
Identifiers: LCCN 2020015281 | ISBN 9780271087030 (cloth)
Subjects: LCSH: Authorship—Psychological aspects. | Authorship—Philosophy. | Creation (Literary, artistic, etc.) | Mortality.
Classification: LCC PN171.P83 H6313 2020 | DDC 808.02—dc23
LC record available at https://lccn.loc.gov/2020015281

Copyright © 2020 Benjamin Hoffmann
All rights reserved
Printed in the United States of America
Published by The Pennsylvania State University Press, University Park, PA 16802–1003

First published by Les Éditions de Minuit
Les paradoxes de la postérité © 2019 by Les Éditions de Minuit
7 rue Bernard-Palissy, 75006 Paris
All rights reserved.

The Pennsylvania State University Press is a member of the Association of University Presses.

It is the policy of The Pennsylvania State University Press to use acid-free paper. Publications on uncoated stock satisfy the minimum requirements of American National Standard for Information Sciences—Permanence of Paper for Printed Library Material, ANSI z39.48–1992.

For my mother

CONTENTS

Introduction: Why Do People Write? • 1

THE PARADOXES OF BELIEF

First Paradox: The Current Concert and the Distant Melody • 21

Second Paradox: The Lottery and the Ruse • 34

Third Paradox: The Renunciation and the Reward • 46

THE PARADOXES OF IDENTITY

Fourth Paradox: The Proper Noun and the Common Noun • 61

Fifth Paradox: The Flow and the Entity • 72

Sixth Paradox: The Distance and the Judgement • 84

THE PARADOXES OF MEDIATION

Seventh Paradox: The Rosetta Stone and Agrippina's Thrush • 101

Eighth Paradox: The Manuscript and the USB Key • 118

Ninth Paradox: The Comet and the Astronomer • 131

Conclusion: Why Do People (Still) Write? • 143

Notes • 153
Index • 169

INTRODUCTION

Why Do People Write?

There comes a time in one's life when it becomes imperative to give a name to the problem around which one's existence has revolved. This act of naming is at the same time arrogant, definitive, and programmatic: it amounts to determining what is most important of all, what is relatively secondary, and what must be given priority in the future. Sometimes it is young people who rise up and declare vigorously that their predecessors had failed to identify the only question of importance. And I think of Albert Camus at age twenty-nine, who begins *The Myth of Sisyphus* with this provocation: "There is only one truly serious philosophical problem: suicide."[1] Brushing off the history of philosophy—Immanuel Kant and his categories, René Descartes's ontological argument—or, more precisely, postponing the resolution of questions that he judged secondary and reduced to what they perhaps are—that is, simple mind games—Camus approaches philosophy resolved to reorder the priorities. At other times it is a retrospective gaze on an existence that has receded into the twilight, a gaze that discerns, through the mass of intertwined experiences, the question that unites the hopes, the errors, the failures, and the throng of passions wound around a life. And I then recall one of the most beautiful opening sentences I've ever read: "The guillotine—more generally, capital punishment and the various methods of meting out death—has been the abiding obsession of my life."[2] With these words, Claude Lanzmann identifies the principal theme whose repetitions and variations wend through and organize his existence, as well as his autobiography.

That a declaration of this kind be made in the heat of a fiery youth impatient to reinvent thought, or that it be the result of the wisdom of a being who, having reached life's end, finally finds himself, briefly, at a vantage point from which he can survey a landscape whose organization finally appears intelligible to him, in both cases introspection and pretention to universality are merged. For this problem is, at the same time, one that each individual has met at every stage of his development, and one that he strives to solve because of the importance that it assumes for everyone. Here, the in-depth examination of an innermost difficulty authorizes the individual to declare a truth for all humankind.

It is by a declaration of the same order that I would like to begin this study. There is only one really serious literary problem: the transmission of texts to posterity. The rest—the modes of renewal of a genre, the uniqueness of a style, and the dialogue between works—we can deal with all that once the contradictions implied by the quest for approval by a virtual public will have been understood.

The reader will no doubt have noted that the "one truly serious philosophical problem" of Camus and the "abiding obsession" of Lanzmann are not unrelated. The first reflects on the reasons why an individual chooses life rather than its opposite, the second on the different manners by which death is administered to us by others. In each case, it is clearly the inevitability of our disappearance that engenders both the works of the philosopher and those of the memorialist My own investigation maintains an underlying relationship with their concerns, for it amounts to questioning the validity of the confidence granted to this form of symbolic mortality that is the inscription of our name, of the memory of our existence, and of the results of our thought in the memory of this anonymous, distant, indeterminate public that we call posterity. For the ambition that consists of obtaining the esteem of the latter is nothing more than one manifestation among others of a need that is profoundly anchored in the heart of all men and women: to identify at least one reason to believe that we are more than animals doomed to disappear and be forgotten.

At the Beginning Is Death

"The worm at the core of the human condition" is how Sheldon Solomon, Jeff Greenberg, and Tom Pyszczynski describe the capacity of each of us to anticipate our disappearance. "The awareness that we humans will die," they write, "has a profound and pervasive effect on our thoughts, feelings, and behaviors in almost every domain of human life—whether we are conscious of it or not."[3] *The Paradoxes of Posterity* are based on the same premise: at the beginning is death. Of course, one will observe that it is also found at the end of our lives, unless we confront this obvious fact—as philosophers have been doing since antiquity—with the no less pertinent fact that, properly speaking, death is to be found nowhere, given that it is a nonevent, the cessation of our experiences and not the last of them. In another sense, however, it is indeed there, from the beginning, anchored in our consciousness when, around the age of three, we learn that we and all of the beings that we love will disappear one day.[4] This revelation is a scandal. Not only do the little beings, who overestimate their objective importance owing to the pampering and consideration of adults who are more powerful than they, suddenly deduce that they are not and never have been the center of the world; they realize also that they are just a perishable fragment of a community that is subject to the same implacable laws. But they become no less conscious, for the first time, that all those they love are also condemned. This experience, common to all humankind, hastens the adoption of what I will call a final value.

By this expression I wish to designate a personal solution to the problem of our mortality. Sometimes we change that solution, but most often, having seen it adopted by an authority figure suffices for us to remain faithful to it until the end of our life. We are going to die, of course, and our grandparents, parents, brothers, and sisters also. But we believe that it is possible to oppose to this annihilation a form of permanence that denies or at least relativizes it by preserving something of ourselves that will not disappear. Perhaps the spiritual part of our person will survive, and earning an eternity of divine grace will become the most important thing in our life. This value is named "God." Perhaps we believe in the permanence of our consciousness during successive lives, so we attempt to transmit to our future incarnations a body of thoughts, words, and good deeds that will guarantee happiness and tranquility in our subsequent existences. This value is "karma." Or we try to bequeath to our offspring not only our name, our genetic and material patrimony, but also principles that will help them in the conduct of their life. This value is called "progeny." That is, of course, unless we transform the thirst for wealth into a quest for the absolute, forgetting that money only has the value we attribute to it, and that it is people's decisions alone that "determine the value of this fetish that masks nothingness, the horizon of their being-for-death."[5] This value is called "money." Or we desire to leave the memory of our person to our successors by accomplishing something that has never been done before: we are the first person to establish a record, or we have created a business, a machine, or a body of work that, like the ambassadors sent by the great Khan, will represent us at the court of future centuries. Diverse in appearance, these behaviors are all determined by the adoption of the same value: posterity.

Entries in the catalog of solutions to render the perspective of our mortality tolerable are scarce, and stating them amounts to an intellectually trivial undertaking given that, at some time or other, we have considered all of them separately, sometimes to adopt them, sometimes to dismiss them—unless we had chosen to simply combine them. These solutions are indeed not mutually exclusive: I can bequeath my fortune to a charitable organization in the hope that it will take my name without giving up my belief in spiritual immortality. But what is less evident is the decisive and concealed role that these values play in the decisions, both big and small, that circumscribe our daily existence and become the purpose we attribute to our existence. Because, regardless of whether we are conscious of it, the idea of death never really leaves us; it is called to mind a hundred times a day: the news on the radio in the morning speaks of the victims of an attack; driving to work we see an animal crushed to death on the side of the road; our colleague has lost his wife, and an occasional pain in our stomach leads us to fear, each time it occurs, the slow growth of a cancer. The very urgency of our physical needs makes us aware that they can only be ignored at the risk of our life.

Faced with these constant reminders that we are going to die, we resort to behaviors whose true purpose only appears to us occasionally. The workers who put in sixty hours week after week are comforted by the thought that their labor is guaranteeing the well-being of their family, but behind this immediate purpose is concealed another—that is, the idea that their very existence is justified by being put in the service of their family. The businesswoman who foregoes marriage and children, who denies herself vacations or leisure activities to devote all her energies to the management of a multinational company, is motivated by ambition, the desire for wealth, power, and prestige—but also by the desire to leave a durable mark on the business with which she has identified herself. The mountain climber who is the first to accomplish a perilous ascent will be hard put, once he has returned to normal life, to explain an unproductive enterprise that could have been interrupted by death at any time. Like Sir Edmund Hillary, he will answer that he climbed Mount Everest "because it was there," or like Reinhold Messner, he will say that he went into the mountains "to live." Behind these cryptic statements, however, the motivation is perfectly clear: these athletes wanted to transmit to their successors the memory of an extraordinary act, for there is no human activity that does not have both its exceptional and its commonplace history, its heroes to live it, and its heralds to sing about it. Thus the value whose adoption allows me to believe that I will not die *entirely* may be called "final," because it is the ultimate justification of my actions, discovered anew each time that I eliminate mentally the secondary values that obscure it in my consciousness.

The problem thus becomes to determine why this value and not another. Why does one choose to try to get around the thought of our mortality through the belief that God will receive our soul in paradise or by transmitting the memory of our person to future generations of which we can know nothing? It is true that responses vary, but what we all have in common is the need to seek a solution to the great problem: why are we living (and this "why" is a questioning of the purpose, not the cause) if it is true that we are destined to disappear? In our quest to solve this problem, we often see others as obstacles. Individuals who adopt posterity as their final value are apt to interpret the attempts of others to leave their mark on the collective memory as a threat. For if there are several of us who covet an athletic record, only the best of us will win first place, thus stealing the symbolic immortality from competitors who had a no less burning need. If several of us wish to mark history by our art, the genius of a competitor is more than a questioning of a vocation founded on a clearly inferior talent; it is a negation of our very person, since it is painfully clear to competent but minor artists that their exceptional contemporary will be the subject of future centuries while they will be forgotten by everyone. In the context of Western society where the affirmation of the uniqueness of each person determines antagonistic behaviors, the ego battles would not be so fierce if the true stake were not metaphysical.

These rivalries between individuals who have adopted the same final value are accompanied by other struggles with those who, on the contrary, have chosen an entirely different one. If I go to mass every week, for instance, and am convinced that obeying a series of precepts handed down from the pulpit will bring me spiritual immortality, what do I have in common with someone who cannot see beyond this life and believes that it will be a success to the extent that it leaves a trace in a history book? What does an artist who works alone have in common with individuals who identify with a certain group whose well-being is their principal concern? And what do all those who have a sufficiently flattering idea of their person to wish that people will be interested in them after their death, have in common with the mass of people who see neither so high nor so far but feel that their life is a success each time a flash of happiness brightens their child's face? We all seek to be worth more than our death, but we go about it in different ways. And whereas this disagreement on the means often inclines individuals toward antipathy and violence, the adoption of a different final value by others appearing as a criticism of the use they are making of their own existence, we would in fact, on the contrary, feel great compassion and affection for others if only we were aware of the common goal we pursue, the futility of the means we adopt, and the ultimate failure of our undertaking.

This mutual compassion and affection are only conceivable if we are able to give up the illusion we choose to harbor. In order for me to accept, authentically, this distinct solution to the problem of mortality that another has chosen, I have to realize that it is no more valid than my own: it is just the manner that person has found to render tolerable an intolerable prospect, and if it proves to be effective for him or her, that is fine. In other words, the ultimate equivalence of final values can only be understood if we have first become aware of their mutual futility. Thus a tolerance founded on the consciousness of a common destiny may only be possible once we have managed to recognize final values for what they are: a means to mask the unbearable whose effectiveness is more or less durable but that, strictly speaking, never yields what we expect from it—that is, complete tranquility at the prospect of death and an immortality that is neither spiritual nor symbolic, but literal.

The Trace of Works and the Network of Memoirs

I have observed that posterity is among the final values to which individuals have recourse in order to tolerate the idea of their disappearance. To declare the foregoing amounts to determining a use of posterity without specifying its significance. So, what do we mean by this term each time we use it throughout this book? It is time to examine more closely a concept whose apparent transparency masks many misconceptions.[6]

To reflect on posterity is tantamount to adopting the role of Oedipus investigating the death of Laius, since we are the posterity of those who came before us. It is a strange concept whose definition leads us to look to ourselves rather than attempt to seize the contours of an abstraction. Not only the public of our contemporaries, we are also the public to which the entirety of our predecessors is speaking. "We": in fact, all of humankind, since the act of publishing a work destines it to everyone unreservedly, an author being able to dream of an ideal readership without having the possibility of addressing it exclusively, and every individual having the freedom to open any work written in the past. Of course, we who represent posterity will die in our turn, and others will assume after us, vis-à-vis our contemporaries who have now become their predecessors, the function of evaluation and recall of works that is currently ours. Posterity is thus recomposed at the same time that it loses its members, much like an organism whose cells are renewed throughout its existence.

As years pass, the responsibility of posterity increases, its moral burden grows heavy, its memory assailed by new entreaties since other candidates for posthumous recognition transmit the fruits of their labors. But what is the nature of this memory in which the authors from the past attempt to make their impression without either "the wrath of Jove, nor fire, nor sword, nor the gnawing tooth of time"[7] being able to destroy them? A work that passes on to posterity is not only one whose copies escape destruction: the words of the deceased author must also be embodied in the mind of a living person; in short, it must be brought to life through reading in order to transcend *potentiality* and be *activated*.[8] If each of us is a parcel of posterity, it is a *network of memories* that composes posterity's mnemonic faculties. And within each of these individual memories, the place occupied by authors from the past varies radically.

Certain authors have transmitted the memory of their work to the quasi totality of humankind. Who has never heard of *Romeo and Juliette* and of the playwright who gave life to this couple? However, while the intimate familiarity of certain specialists with the body of Shakespeare's work extends to the world in which he wrote his oeuvre, other individuals are only familiar with isolated lines from his plays and will never have heard of the titles of his less frequently staged works.[9] Nonetheless, the literature professor at Harvard and the casual reader are both actively involved in Shakespeare's posterity, although, if the playwright has escaped oblivion, he is very diversely present in individual memories. Consequently, a posterity may only be called universal from a statistical standpoint (the memory of a body of work is found in a vast sample of the world population), whereas individuals taken separately will only ever recall a variable proportion of an author's production. We will thus speak of a *memorial imprint* to designate the space, more or less extensive and necessarily fluid, that a work occupies in the memory of an individual. And provided that we change the scale and consider abstractly the network of memories in its entirety, it will appear that the place occupied by the great authors from the past will only ever represent a very tiny percentage of the collective memory that, like a colossal hard disk, is occupied by an enormous contingent of memories, given that writers are far from having a monopoly on posterity—artists and athletes, women politicians like men of action, generals and scientists, all demand their share of posthumous recognition.

Conversely, while a work may not have any current readers, it is nonetheless preserved in a private collection or on a digital platform. One might consider that it is waiting to be rediscovered by one of the future incarnations of posterity: who knows if one day people will not recognize its merits despite the fact that it is on the verge of obliteration? If its memorial imprint is for the moment minimal, reduced to existence in the minds of a few specialists, its potential resurgence will persist as long as there are people who may become interested in it. Published in 1792, immediately banned by the Girondin government, then republished eight years later without provoking the slightest reaction, Claude-François de Lezay-Marnésia's *Letters Written from the Banks of the Ohio* is one of those works that we might be tempted to say did not "pass on to posterity." And nonetheless, as a result of pure chance and a series of individual undertakings, they were republished in 2017 for the first time in two centuries.[10] To be sure, the memory of this work and of its author, Lezay-Marnésia, is only shared by a handful of readers, but the possibility of a growing memorial imprint is now open: how many forgotten works have ultimately joined the canon? Long forgotten, Françoise Graffigny's *Letters from a Peruvian Woman* are now part of the treasured works of the French Enlightenment. It is always possible that as a result of the progressive reorganization of posterity, through imperceptible changes, the memorial space occupied by an author will increase progressively as well. And if the authors who have long held the attention of posterity have a greater chance of seeing their preeminence grow even more over time, any position is at risk of likewise being eroded, renegotiated, or threatened by the evolution of posterity, given enough time.

Finally, within the body of an author's production, the successive forms of posterity are apt to grant posthumous recognition to distinct works. Voltaire's place in posterity is largely owed to texts that he did not view as the principle illustrations of his talent, and those of us who admire the *Philosophical Tales* will perhaps be replaced one day by spectators who will once again applaud his play *Zaïre*. Thus the memorial imprint left by the collective works of an author may retain its scope, whereas the individual works that compose it are apt to receive over the course of time varied attention from the public, posterity granting its esteem to certain of them while preferring others when its membership changes. While the expression "reaching posterity" leads us to think of the transmission of texts as if it were a fateful meeting between a will and an obstacle (authors appear before posterity like travelers stopping before a precipice, not knowing if they will cross it or if they will disappear in its abyss never to be seen again), there are an infinite number of intermediary positions between the poles of universal celebration and complete oblivion, intermediary positions that are never definitively fixed. Moreover, while this expression leads us spontaneously to imagine posterity as an abstract and single entity, it is important to emphasize that it comprises the multitude of current and potential recipients of a work.

It is thus preferable to abandon the "passage" (into posterity) metaphor for what I will call a "cyber" metaphor. Let us imagine posterity as the connection of all the mnemonic capacities of humankind. Taken together, this memory is subjected to a continual variation of its content, given that the appearance and disappearance of the memories associated with the network constantly modifies the store of memories. Each individual memory is occupied in its own way by the memory of a given work, as the example of Shakespeare's readers demonstrates above: an author's posterity is composed of the average of the individual memories that preserve her or his work. This average is in constant evolution owing to a number of factors that may come into play to engrave the recollection of an author's work in additional individual memories: inclusion of a work in the program of a high school or university, a new edition, or the transposition into another artistic form—without forgetting the political events that may provoke renewed interest in a text.[11] Other factors may nonetheless play the opposite role: an author may have become famous for a form of writing that no longer corresponds to the aesthetic tastes of posterity (we scarcely read anymore the twenty-page poems that enchanted the nineteenth-century readership), or posterity may reproach authors for a political position that casts a retrospective shadow on their writing (discovered after his death, the collaborationist past of Paul de Man now weighs heavily on the reception of his works).[12]

Moreover, the cyber metaphor leads to an additional distinction that also applies to the data preserved by posterity: the opposition between saved files and files that are being composed. Indeed, the memory of a computer may be occupied by files that are never consulted or modified, whereas there are documents to which the users return constantly to add new elements or to revise the existing text. It is no different with books, certain of which are the objects of passive knowledge, perpetuated notably by schools, whose persistence in the collective memory produces neither transcriptions in other artistic forms nor rewritings, while other texts continue to stimulate imaginations and bring forth new works that, while distinguishing themselves from their model, bring an additional proof of its existence and constitute an indirect invitation to rediscover it. In this global network of connected memories, it is thus necessary to distinguish between works that occupy part of the memorial space without being rewritten and those that generate the production of new texts.

The cyber metaphor, finally, invites a variation of scale that further destabilizes the representation of posterity as a court of justice possessing only two sentences: the crown of immortality and the condemnation to oblivion. It is in fact possible to imagine a distinction between the trace left by an author on diverse geographical spaces (what is the posterity of François Mauriac in the Bordeaux region as compared to Brittany?), on national communities (what is the mark left by Ryūnosuke Akutagawa on Uruguay?), or on linguistic communities (what trace has Fyodor Dostoevsky left on Italian-speaking populations?). These changes of scale allow us to contest the clichéd representation of the "great writer preserved by posterity," given that there is no posthumous existence whose scope does not vary broadly when spaces as well as historical periods are taken into consideration. Since the network of memories is in constant metamorphosis, posterity is never a reward that is earned once and for all: it consists in a memorial imprint that fluctuates with the flow of time.

The Posterity of Writers

The posterity of writers is the sole subject of the preceding reflections. Nonetheless, it is abundantly clear that the desire to inscribe the memory of a former existence in the network of memories is shared by individuals for whom action in the world, and not writing, is the means to that end. Since antiquity, statesmen and military leaders have been transmitting the memory of their existence to future centuries, and the passion to be mentioned in history books is just as voracious as that which consists in jotting one's name down on the covers of novels or essays. However, the linguistic nature of symbolic immortality turns the investigation of the posterity of literary figures into a query whose conclusions concern all those who seek it, including through their acts. For, ultimately, it is always through a discourse that we are remembered, whether it is the one engraved on the walls of a monument, stated by professors to their students, or printed on the pages of a book. In order not to disappear completely, politicians need biographers who will recount their efforts and measure their impact on the world; once their term in office is over, they often become diarists themselves to add a block to their own monument. Likewise, artists who produce works of art would not be satisfied if nothing but those works remained after their death. They hope that their signature in the corner of the painting will draw attention to themselves, and that their work will be an invitation to discover—in the words of a biographer, a critic, or an encyclopedia editor—the linguistic summary of their life. Likewise, mathematicians who formulate eternal truths in which nothing of themselves is conveyed still associate their name with their discovery: a theorem or a conjecture will be indissolubly bound to their person, and it is once again through language that they will be remembered as the source of this revelation. In short, if it is possible to present a variety of claims to the esteem of the mutating publics that compose in their turn posterity, claims obtained outside literature—in one of those arenas that politics, war, fine arts, sports, and science design around human ambitions—it is patent that future generations will only remember an individual after his or her reduction to a linguistic state.

Consequently, the problems that directly affect writers also concern those whom they evoke in their writing in order to assure the latter that they will not be forgotten in the future. One of these problems is the fragility of languages: I will describe the paradox that is inherent in the activity of a writer who produces a work intended for future centuries while it is nestled in a linguistic system that may not prove to be indefinitely intelligible.[13] This fragility does not constitute a threat for writers alone but rather for the entire body of pretenders to symbolic immortality: if the great exploits of a general are only recorded in a language that has become indecipherable, posterity will know nothing of him. Similarly, the ephemeral character of the material format of texts has repercussions both on the permanence of literary reputations and on the memory of real personalities presented in biographies. When the last copy of the life of a famous woman disappears, it simultaneously destroys a work and the memory of its subject. It results from the preceding that reflection on literary posterity produces both problems and, perhaps, reasons to hope for all of the candidates for symbolic immortality, given that each literary figure is a universal, unique case. Unique because they are all confronted by obstacles that apply to them exclusively (just as the politician or the athlete have their particular adversaries to conquer to prove that they are worthy of remembrance), but universal, too, for these victories belong to all those whose posthumous memory, in the last resort, depends on their use of words.

But we still need to introduce those who enter into the category of men or women of letters. I would like to confer a broad definition on this group, including all those for whom the goal of writing is the achievement of symbolic immortality. It goes without saying that this definition automatically includes practitioners of literature, in all of its diverse generic manifestations. But it is enough to be familiar, even superficially, with specialists in the social sciences to understand that they are, no less than novelists, poets, playwrights, or memoirists, obsessed by the fetishizing of the printed word. This introduction is not the place to muse about the sociology of university professors and even less about their psychology, but a simple fact demonstrates that they are of one mind with writers in the choice of an identical final value. Indeed, the care they all take to list the totality of their written work on their curriculum vitae and on the pages of their websites demonstrates that these publications are at the same time titles to the esteem of contemporaries and to future generations.

Of course, these scholarly publications, articles, editions, and monographs are endowed with immediate, generous, and practical goals. On the one hand, they add to the body of knowledge when they appear and are published with altruistic intentions, whether it be to draw their contemporaries' attention to a particular problem or to a thinker who has been unjustly forgotten and whose works have something useful to offer them. On the other, it is true that they play a role in the career of the professors to the extent that they are a source of job security or of promotion to a higher rank, with the accompanying symbolic and material advantages. However, these goals have their exact equivalent in the realm of literary writing: essayists may well revolt against some injustice of their times without disdaining the comfortable income their works bring them, in addition to present and future glory. I am thus not claiming here that university and literary writing have no immediate and practical goals, but rather that both of them are, in addition, a way to pass on to coming generations the trace of an irreplaceable person and body of thought. To oppose to the universal passage, to the omnipresent ephemerality, the permanence of a text that will not change: this is the dream of all writers and scholars, of all those for whom the book is a last resort.

The Reversibility of Behaviors

There is scarcely any doubt that writers long for posthumous recognition. However, it seems impossible to identify a behavior whose goal would be to guarantee a place in posterity and that would lead to it invariably, any new initiative determined by the quest for symbolic immortality having a chance to succeed, whereas the imitation of an approach similar to one that worked previously may result in failure. Let us take the example of the relationship between celebrity and posterity and of the use of the former in order to obtain the latter. According to Horace there is no gap between current and posthumous fame. When authors have earned the esteem of the experts of their own time because they succeeded in combining the "useful" and the "agreeable," in "pleasing" and "edifying" at the same time, the progressive widening of the circle of their admirers will continue after they have drawn their last breath.[14] On the basis of this thesis, it would be possible to propose a kind of mathematical model in which the postmortem notoriety of authors would depend on that which they had achieved during their life. However, while multiple examples illustrate the idea that literary celebrity may well translate into posthumous recognition, others lead us to assert instead that there is no cause and effect relationship between them, nor even any form of continuity. To be sure, the entombment of Victor Hugo in the Pantheon only followed by a few days the disappearance of this illustrious figure, and the international fame of his works, adapted to stage and screen, has grown incessantly since he passed away. But the case of William Blake demonstrates, conversely, that an author who was unrecognized during his lifetime may be resurrected as a major author after a rescue mission led after his death by a handful of admirers who, through their patient efforts, drew ever greater number of readers to his cause.[15]

Such a disjunction between "celebrity" and "posterity" may be emphasized to the point that we see them as opposites. Historically, the value attributed to the "damned poet" figure during the Romantic period has accentuated the gap between them. If we theorize that posthumous recognition is the reward for radical originality, the emergence of a new voice must necessarily clash with the public that discovers it, and often only the passage of a considerable length of time is capable of fostering its proper appreciation. In the context of this conception of the artistic act, in which the break with tradition produces increased valuation, celebrity is necessarily suspicious: it may indicate a conformity between a certain form of writing and contemporary expectations, thus dooming the authors confined to anonymity beyond the frontiers of their period. To summarize, the behavior exhibited by writers who desire celebrity during their lifetime in the hope that it will be transformed into posterity after their death has as many chances of obtaining the desired effect as does its opposite.

Other behaviors display a similar reversibility. To be embraced by posterity, does a writer have to produce a large body of works or a small one? Insofar as literary tastes may evolve, signing a large number of texts and practicing a variety of genres seems a guarantee of security, the successive versions of posterity being able to choose in the body of works of a deceased writer the texts that best correspond to its fluctuating preferences, values, and concerns. It is not the Jorge Luis Borges of the volumes of poetry that we read most frequently today, but rather the survivor of the terrible accident of 1938, the writer who ventured onto the terrain of metaphysical fiction.[16] Conversely, other authors only ever practiced one genre for the good reason that they only wrote one book: such is the case, for instance, of Jean de La Bruyère and Alain-Fournier, whom we read years, decades, or centuries after their death. While the narrowness of their corpus has not prevented the above writers from inscribing their name in the network of memories, many prolific authors, on the contrary, are regularly suspected of glibness (provoking the uncharitable thought that "they would publish less if they worked more on their texts"), if they are not accused of maintaining a mercenary relationship with literature that deprives them of their legitimacy as an artist. Consequently, the volume published by a given author may just as well be the sign of creative genius as of unfortunate verbosity.

What about the situation of authors in relationship to their peers? To transmit the memory of their work to posterity, is it better to belong to a group (literary school, circle, salon, coterie . . .) or to practice their art in solitude? Since the transmission of a literary work consists in registering it in a mutating network of memories, it is naturally preferable for authors to surround themselves with a large number of disciples whose writings will be additional testimonies to their existence and relays of their aesthetic ideas. Whether the disciples walk in the authors' tracks or end up breaking with them, they will exhibit no less the influence that they have exercised on them, and the more violent their rebellion, the more it will prove the difficulty of the efforts they had to make to free themselves from the yoke of their authority (I am thinking of Huysmans taking leave of Émile Zola). But since reading a book is receiving in one's mind the author's words, the latter does not need to be your contemporary for you to be his or her disciple.

Epicurus had been dead for two centuries when Lucretius became the eloquent propagator of his theses, and while the author of the *Letter to Menoeceus* had imitators during his lifetime, he had many others after his death. Conversely, and according to the time-honored expression, it is always possible for students to overtake the masters and surpass them: in grouping young talents around oneself, you always risk finding a superior genius among them, and your only claim to glory, in the eyes of posterity, consists in having recognized the promise that, in any case, would have blossomed elsewhere and without you (e.g., that is how we remember Leigh Hunt, the mentor of John Keats). Furthermore, an author may choose to live like a hermit, discouraging friendships and making enemies of those who were ready to adulate him; he can travel from one hermitage to another and repulse anyone who approaches him and nonetheless leave his mark on the history of ideas: I am referring, of course, to the extravagant, inescapable Jean-Jacques Rousseau. In short, having connections may be a quality cultivated by authors, and the constitution of a group around them does indeed increase the number of discourses bearing the stamp of their thought, but one can drive everyone away and nevertheless find a legion of admirers after one's death.

Finally, what may we say about the subjective relationship of the individual to posterity? Does it reward those who desire it or those who renounce it? Robert Southey declared that all his efforts were directed toward conquering the esteem of posterity: the latter showed him no gratitude for such constancy. John Keats died convinced that his name would leave no trace; if it is not engraved on his tomb, at least we find it everywhere else. Therefore, although the esteem of posterity is generally coveted by those who write, no one has ever identified an infallible way of obtaining it, and that is the conclusion reached by Heather J. Jackson at the end of a study devoted to authors who, in Great Britain and in the Romantic period, set themselves the goal of conquering symbolic immortality: "Thus, the principal lesson of this book consists in asserting that it is useless to struggle for immortality—there is nothing that a writer, a publisher, or an advertising agency can do to guarantee it—and this lesson applies to the writers of our age as well as to those of the past."[17]

Chance and Posterity

Nonetheless, does this mean that the esteem of posterity is only awarded by chance? An answer to this question comes immediately: there is a correlation between posthumous recognition that honors a work and its literary *merit*. The definition of "merit" varies, of course, in each period, and the genres and works that charm one of the iterations of posterity are not sure to please its following set of members. However, if there is no consensus on the exact nature of literary merit, writers bear within themselves a standard by which they measure their work, since they are the one who determines the moment when, after all the rewritings of their text, no further modification of any kind seems necessary to them—the moment when any further change would be a detriment.[18] But not even they would be able to say, abstractly and in general, what constitutes "literary merit," for they know very well that their own evaluation of works does not necessarily correspond to that of their contemporaries, and they no doubt become indignant, at times, when people call a "masterpiece" a work that they consider mediocre. People who write, however, people who have the liberty to modify and eliminate sentences that they themselves have recorded, are people who are measuring their work against a standard they are unable to define, a standard that has become ingrained in them in the course of their artistic practice, to such an extent that any variation in relationship to this standard produces something like a painful sensation that will only dissipate when the text is amended appropriately. As a result, if it is impossible to establish a timeless and universal norm for literary merit, writers bear in themselves a norm for evaluating their own work and only publish it—unless they are forced to do so by some necessity, in particular an economic one—when it has passed the test of their innermost demands. We conclude from the foregoing remarks that in striving to make the result of their efforts correspond to the undefinable but deeply affecting idea that they have of literary merit, writers are at the same time working on the production of an oeuvre that is worthy of being passed on to posterity.

Indeed, no one believes seriously that posterity's attention is unmotivated: otherwise, all one need do is produce a text, no matter which or how, publish it anywhere, and hope that it will win the prize of posthumous recognition despite the fact that the wager is out of all proportion with its recompense. On the contrary, literary sculpting of an oeuvre is clearly the way to confer on it a superior aesthetic form and thus to increase the chances that it will meet the approbation of future generations. Likewise, if the act of publishing a text surely does not guarantee its transmission to posterity, a contrario, the probability that a work left in a drawer will join the pantheon of literary masterpieces is still weaker. Publishing it, and if possible with a publishing house capable of disseminating it as widely as possible, a house that has managed to create for itself that undefinable aura—prestige—increases substantially the probability of this transmission. And for works to be well received by important publishers, the authors' interpersonal skills, their social position, their connections, their ability to offer in return symbolic or real services are also important, symbolic immortality thus being partially a function of practical virtues that are not directly related to the production of the work itself. Since passing on to posterity is not a matter of pure chance, writing a work with the goal that it be read by future generations is hardly absurd: I will say, more precisely, that it is paradoxical.

Paradox and Posterity

An absurd behavior consists in desiring what we know with absolute certainty we will not obtain: it amounts to pursuing an effort designed to reach an inaccessible goal. Thus it is possible to grant the absurd its dignity when it expresses a revolt against the limits of the human condition. When Cyrano de Bergerac continues to twirl his rapier while death is carrying him away, we are witnessing an absurd behavior that we call "panache." The man who attacks a machine gun nest with a knife likewise accomplishes an absurd act, but this act is characterized as heroism because in choosing to sacrifice himself, he asserts the superiority of his will over the fear of death.[19] Nonetheless, it is rarely in this sublime light that we experience the absurd, which appears to us every time that our actions achieve a result that, far from justifying them, demonstrates their profound inanity. Such is the experience of the worker whose activity does not improve the condition of his or her material and spiritual existence but only perpetuates it. In this game where the winnings are equal to the wager, life goes by without producing anything that transcends it. For their behavior to be authentically absurd, however, authors would have to write novels and, at the end of each chapter, burn the fruits of their labors. Only the destruction of their text would constitute an out-and-out renunciation of the quest for symbolic immortality. But provided that they avoid this extreme and publish their texts instead of destroying them, there is always a possibility, no matter how tenuous, that posterity will revive their thought through the act of reading. Their action thus ceases to be absurd: it becomes paradoxical.

What creates the difference between absurdity and paradox is the possible, eventual, justification of the latter. Absurdity consists in continuing a behavior whose results will never justify it. Such is the etymological meaning of the word "absurd," which designates a dissonance: that which shocks our reason is absurd. The concept of paradox is similar, on its face, to that of absurdity, so these two terms are often used as synonyms: both designate what runs counter to common sense. They are distinguished, however, by the necessity that characterizes absurdity and the potential appearance of contingency in paradox.

An absurd act will forever remain what it always was. The repetition of the same conduct will inevitably produce an identical result, and it is precisely the suppression of the possibility of anything else that leads to the demise of those who have no other perspective than the relentless repetition of the same behavior. A paradoxical act, on the other hand, may well produce an unexpected result, for paradox is what shows itself to be contrary to the general opinion, which is itself capable of being mistaken. Going against conventional wisdom does not in fact mean that one is wrong, and it is possible to maintain a paradoxical thesis that ultimately gains acceptance as the truth. Denis Diderot's famous "paradox of the actor," according to which the actor must not be moved himself if he wishes to move others, is no longer, properly speaking, a paradox: it belongs to the tenets of dramatic art that every budding actor will learn at some moment or other in his apprenticeship (so that it would now be paradoxical to assert that only actors who have experienced the emotions they are acting out are capable of inspiring them in spectators). What characterizes paradox is thus the surprise it provokes at its initial formulation, given that it sets itself against established opinion without appearing to be impossible. Since paradox is linked to surprise, it is inseparable from the philosophical activity that also begins with astonishment; it is precisely because paradox is capable of challenging what we were wrong to take as a given that it functions as a revealer of truth. Conversely, absurdity reveals nothing that we did not know already; it is inseparable from the result whose inexorable appearance is familiar to us even before it occurs.

From this perspective, the behavior that consists in conveying the memory of a work to posterity is not absurd. Indeed, the consideration that we see granted to authors who passed away centuries ago shows that there are exceptions to the rule linking disappearance and oblivion. This proves to be paradoxical, however, insofar as our reason is shocked by the continuation of an effort whose probability of achieving success is minimal. We will therefore find many manifestations of the paradox that haunts the search for posterity, namely the fear that an effort maintained during a whole lifetime will produce nothing durable, and that by trying too hard to achieve posthumous recognition, we will have our life stolen by posterity.

However, the concept of paradox does not only refer to what is considered unreasonable by the general public; it also includes a logical contradiction between the terms of the statement that formulates it. This is the case of the famous liar's paradox: "A man says that he is lying. Is what the man says true or false?" If he is lying, this man is telling the truth. If he is not lying, he is expressing a lie. Logical paradoxes like this one are not the staging of irreparably undecidable situations; they are rather a stimulus for the mind that forces it to find a solution in order to escape the impasse in which its author is trying to imprison us. Since antiquity, there have been a long succession of propositions that attempt to eliminate the apparently intractable logical contradiction between the terms that compose the liar's paradox.[20]

Throughout the chapters of this book I will attempt to identify the paradoxes that the quest for transmission of a literary work to posterity comes up against. These paradoxes may be grouped in three categories, which are the paradoxes of belief, the paradoxes of identity, and the paradoxes of mediation. The paradoxes of belief wrap themselves around posterity when the characteristics traditionally attributed to the divinity are transferred to it: posterity finds itself endowed with functions that belong to God, since it confers symbolic immortality just as God guarantees spiritual immortality. The paradoxes of identity, for their part, result from the tension between the infinite complexity of an individual and the representation—simplified, altered, or out-and-out fictionalized—that posterity makes of her or him after their death. The paradoxes of mediation, finally, show that there is no memory of a work that is not entrusted to intermediaries—cultural, material, and human—whose essential impermanence threatens the sustainability of posthumous memories. This tripartition of the book corresponds to the principal objects of study: "The Paradoxes of Belief" is concerned with the representation of *posterity* by the authors, "The Paradoxes of Identity" with the representation of the *authors* by posterity, and "The Paradoxes of Mediation" with the modes of inscription and preservation of the *works* in the network of memories.

The Metaphysical Thread

The metaphysical preoccupation is never far from reflection on posterity: how many individuals turn their hopes, not toward the immortality of their soul and the resurrection of their body, but rather toward symbolic permanence? Some of them write on Sunday mornings like others go to mass, and they all have their eyes fixed on something in themselves that will last longer than their lives. It is this metaphysical thread of reflection on posterity that I would like to follow in the course of this study, and it is what will lead us periodically to Enlightenment thought. For it is in the eighteenth century that the hope of survival in the memory of future generations established itself in the Western world as a possible alternative to belief in the immortality of the soul, with posterity becoming, according to Michel Delon, a "secular substitute for Christian eternity."[21] The spreading of philosophical materialism in Europe played a decisive role in this substitution by calling into question the belief in the immortality of the soul and by developing, under the influence of scientific discoveries, a completely secular conception of human beings.[22] The quest for a substitute immortality became a way to conceal the terror linked to definitive annihilation, not only of my own person around which the world is organized (since any effort of empathy and curiosity can never change the fact that it is *I* who am accomplishing it) but also of those whom my love endows with a value so irreplaceable that I wish it were in my power to spare them being destroyed and forgotten. Unlike Christian eternity, which only concerns the individual him- or herself (I earn my salvation by my good works, but I am incapable of obtaining it for another, who will have to answer alone for his or her acts on Judgment Day), the secular rewriting of this quest for immortality is endowed with an altruistic side: the immortalizing power that artists solicit in their name is also the power to assign to eternity the memory of their fellow creatures. We will never forget Madame de Warens as long as we read Rousseau, and the memory of Henriette will survive as long as the memoirs of Giacomo Casanova.

THE PARADOXES OF BELIEF

FIRST PARADOX
The Current Concert and the Distant Melody

The first part of this book is devoted to the paradoxes of belief—that is, the paradoxes resulting from the transfer of the traditional attributes of God to the idea of posterity. If posterity is so regularly described as a court for the appearance of people who seek the esteem of their fellow creatures, it is only insofar as it replaces the judgment to which, in the majority of religions, people submit after their passing, and whose verdict will determine their bliss or torment in the afterlife. Following the premise established in the introduction—that is, that the eighteenth century is the historical moment during which this substitution, whose consequences for Western thought are hardly commensurate, occurred—I will undertake the examination of a text written during the Enlightenment in which hope for symbolic immortality stands in for belief in spiritual immortality and is found at the center of the reflection or, more precisely, of the debate around this question. Known both as *The Pros and Cons* (*Le pour et le contre*) and *Dialogue on Posterity*, this work presents the epistolary exchange between a sculptor and a philosopher: Étienne Maurice Falconet and Denis Diderot.[1]

"Fundamental Options"

It is already paradoxical that Falconet pressured Diderot into agreeing to the publication of their correspondence, which ran from December 1765 to February 1767. Falconet exhibits in his letters a complete indifference toward posterity, and one would have expected him to have no objection to the disappearance of an exchange of letters in which he and Diderot clash over the influence of the mental image of a future public on the activity of a creator, before blundering into a fastidious discussion on classical painting that resembles another "Quarrel of the Ancients and the Moderns." The sculptor strives to demonstrate that the former were in the infancy of an art that greatly matured over time, while the philosopher defends them passionately by invoking the authority of Pliny and Pausanias. But far from being satisfied with the pleasure of the discussion or agreeing, philosophically, that these missives would only be read by their intended addressee, Falconet pursued for years the project of publishing them, which he proposed to Catherine II in March 1767 when he was in Russia and had just sent the final letter of the volume to Diderot.[2] The following spring Diderot expressed concern about this editorial venture that he had never encouraged and that he mistakenly thought had been completed successfully when he finally got wind of it:

> Well then, when will we receive this pamphlet that you were so furiously intent on having printed? I really would have preferred to revise the whole thing, especially those first little rags that were scribbled on the end of the table. What is being published may be so ragged, so lame, so cold, so bad that I will never pardon you for showing so little regard for your friend's glory. Woe to you if you get the upper hand in this quarrel. You have to make better statues than me, but I have to write better than you.[3]

Learning that, contrary to his fears, their "dispute" had not yet been shared with the public, Diderot requested a copy of the manuscript from Falconet in order to make corrections. He received it in September 1767, but the philosopher took months to get to work on it. The task proved to be colossal, since both men had weaponized countless quotations whose sources now had to be verified. Years went by as Diderot undertook his review of the text ("I'm clarifying a charming dispute," he wrote to Sophie Volland),[4] which, in the end, he nonetheless abandoned.

The explanation of this behavior was to be found in his assessment of the literary quality of the manuscript and of the qualification of this dispute on posterity to be destined to said posterity. This assessment varies from letter to letter: if the missive quoted above describes disdainfully his correspondence with Falconet as a collection of "little rags," another finds it, on the contrary, rather charming owing to the spontaneity of their exchange. "If you'll take my advice," Diderot wrote Falconet, "you won't delete anything in those pages. You risk, in polishing them, to lose an impression of negligence that is always appreciated by the readers; that's the characteristic of works that are done with ease, without artifice, without pretention."[5] Despite these moments of indulgence concerning their verbal joust, Diderot ultimately condemned this friendly quarrel whose tone is sometimes bittersweet, for these texts that discuss the role played by the idea of the current and future public as regards the action of individuals were not written for either public. Their origin, if we are to believe Falconet, was a conversation begun at Diderot's home, followed by an exchange of notes and then letters.[6]

To retouch these letters in order to make them worthy of being passed on to contemporary readers and future generations would have risked depriving them of what, in Diderot's eyes, represents their principal quality—that is, this "appearance of negligence that always pleases"—and embarking on a complete reworking, since it would have been necessary to give them a literary organization that is totally lacking, the discussion between the two men resembling a dialogue of the deaf,[7] leaving them both spinning their wheels, which Falconet notes himself at the end of the volume.[8] Diderot will thus refuse, nearly fifteen years after the beginning of this epistolary joust, to authorize Prince Dmitri Alexeievich Gallitzin to include it in the complete works of Falconet: "We are so poor, so petty, so ragged, so sloppy, so boring, and so scattered everywhere that it is pitiful."[9] Accordingly, Falconet never got satisfaction during his lifetime, as the first publication of *The Pros and Cons* dates from 1828.[10] As for the fate that awaited him in this first edition, it would no doubt have put to the test his renunciation of "future consideration" if he had been aware of it, since his letters were eliminated from the volume.[11] The publisher justifies this exclusion in the following terms: "The manuscript that I have includes the letters from the sculptor and from the philosopher, but since Falconet virtually never offers anything but cold sophisms devoid of the magic of style, while Diderot, in his replies, reproduces the arguments of his adversary with their full force in order to attack and destroy them, I only published the latter, and I am certain that readers will be grateful to me for it."[12] As Emita B. Hill remarks, however, the publisher had no right to impose this condemnation, since he had never seen the letters of the sculptor.[13] His criticism of Falconet's style is just a rote repetition of that by Jacques-André Naigeon a half century earlier.[14] As for Diderot, he would perhaps have been indignant at the inclusion in his collected works of missives that he thought poorly of and that he had never revised thoroughly.

In short, Falconet's actions were not consistent with the positions he takes in the *Dialogue*, which are thus discredited. This denigrator of posterity toiled with great perseverance to pass on to it the expression of his indifference. For Diderot's part, he exhibited greater faithfulness to his principles when he rejected a work that he did not consider worthy of being read by future generations. To whichever correspondent one turns, it is easy to find reasons to spare oneself the reading of their common work. Nonetheless, the emulation that motivates them is the source of both the tediousness and the grandeur of a text that is critical to the subject we are treating here.

There is no lack of tedious passages, both men attempting to sting the ego of the other. Given the difference in their respective intellectual backgrounds, the learned quarrel was no doubt bound to become acrimonious. While Diderot received a solid classical education at the prestigious Lycée Louis-le-Grand and at the Sorbonne, Falconet, "married early and weighed down with children to feed,"[15] was the son of a journeyman carpenter and a true autodidact who taught himself a bit of Greek and a lot of Latin, and who had no intention of allowing Diderot to lord it over him when it came to knowledge of antiquity. He thus resorted to an abundance of quotations to show the philosopher his familiarity with classical literature, accompanying them with detailed and offensive commentaries when they are borrowed from Pliny, whom he had made into a personal enemy owing to the mass of errors he accuses him of pedaling.[16]

Diderot reacts with shock to Falconet's iconoclastic comments on his beloved classics and seeks to promote a thesis that is particularly dear to him: the right of the man of letters to express his opinion on the fine arts. The author of the *Salons* indirectly defends his own role as an art critic when he flies to the rescue of Pliny and Voltaire, with Falconet having accused the latter of heaping ill-advised praise and blame on artists of the century of Louis XIV owing to his complete ignorance of painting technique.[17] The sculptor wished to be recognized by the philosopher as a distinguished humanist, while the latter expected his friend to accept his authority in art criticism. Perhaps they would have found some common ground if they had not attempted, simultaneously and in a contradictory manner, to assert the intrinsic superiority of the activity in which they had respectively excelled. Their exchange thus gave rise to a quarrel about the prioritization of the fine arts and of literature and provoked numerous twists and turns in the course of a conversation that one would have preferred to see more centered and focused on its initial subject.

There is, nonetheless, no lack of grandeur in *Le pour et le contre*, the epistolary dispute leading Diderot and Falconet to bring to light a considerable number of difficulties related to the concept of posterity and in such a fertile manner that an analysis of their correspondence is an ideal starting point for this investigation, which will return regularly to the problems formulated by the two men throughout 1766. The passion with which Diderot expresses himself drives Falconet to surpass himself, and the sculptor succeeds time and again, with solid reasoning and implacable composure, in putting the philosopher ill at ease. In this struggle between the two men, Falconet resembles "solid Mayot," the chess player whose exploits at the Café de la Régence are so admired by the narrator of *Rameau's Nephew*.[18] But the richness of their debate may be explained above all by the critical importance that the idea of posterity holds for them; for Diderot and Falconet, this is not simply one controversy among others. It is not a vain pretext to exhibit a rhetorical virtuosity that could have been exercised by grappling with any metaphysical problem, such as the role of experience in the forming of ideas or the innate character of moral conscience. Posterity is at the heart of a dispute devoted to "fundamental options."[19] The form of existence they imagine for posterity has profound resonances in their innermost being; it is directly related to the practice of their art and, ultimately, to the meaning of their lives.

For and Against What?

This dispute is called *The Pros and Cons*, but in fact, for and against what? In order to understand, we must return to the debate that precipitated the correspondence between Diderot and Falconet, and whose subject recalls the type of questions posed in contests organized by the scholarly academies in the eighteenth century: "Whether the image of posterity leads to the finest actions and produces the best works."[20] This question combines two distinct problems: the first concerns the anticipation of the nature of posterity's judgment, whereas the second is related to the potential of this image to stimulate the search for virtue and artistic excellence. This "image" of posterity is in fact problematic. Are we speaking of a representation that remains confined to the mental state or one that is extended to the sensitivity of the individual as well? And is this representation capable of driving people to seek in advance the applause of posterity, unless other forms of encouragement prove to be more effective in enjoining them to surpass themselves? The debate between Diderot and Falconet is thus both metaphysical (what is the relationship between the mental image of posterity and the body of the person who conceives it?) and ethical (is this image the stimulus that brings out the best in a person?).

As Marc Buffat observes, a "sound metaphor" runs through *The Pros and Cons* and is picked up by the two letter writers, permitting them to oppose "the posthumous glorification that is music—chord, concert, or harmony—to the current denigration that is noise—disharmony, cacophony."[21] From the very first letter of Diderot, posterity is in fact equated with a concert: "Although it is sweet to hear during the night a flute concert being played far off in the distance, the few scattered sounds reaching my ears knit together by my imagination, aided by the finesse of my hearing, into a complete melody that delights it all the more since it is largely its own creation, I believe that the concert that is played close by also has its charms. But would you believe it, my friend, it is not the latter but rather the former that intoxicates us."[22] These concerts that Diderot compares represent two distinct publics, the current public and the future public. The concert that is played close by is the one we hear easily, because it is performed by our contemporaries, whereas the one whose harmony reaches us from afar is played by our successors. The only difference between these two concerts, Diderot asserts, is their intensity.[23] We easily perceive the first while we have to strain our ears to appreciate the second, whose chords are sometimes on the verge of the inaudible: "My ear, more vain than philosophical, even hears at this very moment some *imperceptible* sounds of the distant concert," observes the philosopher.[24] The difference in intensity results in recourse to imagination in the case of the distant concert, whereas this is superfluous when it concerns the one where we are the public directly concerned. We owe it indeed to our imagination that we are able to create the link between the scattered sounds that reach us between two interruptions and compose in our mind a continuous musical passage.

While the concert produced by the contemporaries is perhaps easier to hear, it is sometimes troubled by discordant voices that threaten the harmony with a criticism or an offensive remark, be it only the expression of a reservation. Moreover, the pleasure that it can produce may always be compromised, if not entirely spoiled, by the supposition that it could die out as soon as the current musicians disappeared. How many brilliant reputations have not survived those who had deserved them? On the contrary, although the concert of posterity comes from farther away, it is arranged in such a manner in the listener's mind that the enjoyment caused seems unparalleled. The praises it comprises is in large part the work of their beneficiary, inserted by him or her between the silences of this interior melody in order to prevent its interruption.

This preference of the concert of posterity over the praises sung by contemporaries is directly attacked, nonetheless, by Falconet in his response to Diderot's first letter. "Your comparison of concerts is sweet, agreeable, and charming," the sculptor concedes, "but for it to be accurate, you should have said, I hear a concert, and I believe that there will be another one after I am gone." In fact, he goes on, striving to establish a distinction between a real sensation and the mental image of a future sensation, "one strikes my ear, producing sensations that are unequivocal; the other will perhaps be well played, but I wouldn't bet on it."[25] Falconet will subsequently voice additional criticism of posterity, reproaching it in particular for repeating praise and blame that is often unwarranted, because posterity is misled by intermediaries who do not have the competency (particularly in the area of artistic technique) necessary to mediate between a creator and his or her future public. However, the core of his opposition to Diderot is to be found in the disagreement that focuses on the sound metaphor: the current concert is real; it is composed of praise whose precise nature and sources can be identified. On the other hand, the praises of the future may never be uttered; they are only the mental image of an unreality that time may never vindicate.

In formulating the reasons for his skepticism, the sculptor nonetheless gives Diderot ammunition that the latter hastens to use. Indeed, the philosopher ponders, "What is a sensation that is not equivocal?" If we unpack the premise of Falconet, who does not go to the trouble of clarifying his terminology, an "unequivocal" sensation is provoked by a real experience. For example, an artist feels in the course of his or her labor a dissatisfaction that indicates that the work is not yet complete. On the other hand, an "equivocal" sensation is produced by a purely imaginary cause such as the mental image of praise from a concert of admirers who are not yet born. In other words, if we follow Falconet's logic, it is possible to establish a distinction between sensations based on their cause.

However, his adversary finds this opposition unconvincing. What then would an "equivocal sensation" be? Would it be a sensation whose reality an individual may doubt or a sensation whose intensity is less than that of a sensation that we will call "unequivocal"? Falconet does not make the distinction, giving Diderot the opportunity to defend the aptness of the sound metaphor: "The concert comparison is not only agreeable, it is accurate." In fact, he continues, "What concert is more real than the one I hear, and whose melody and all the accompaniments I am able to sing? Note that well. Even if it is only the sweetness of a beautiful dream? And is the sweetness of a dream nothing? And nothing a sweet dream that lasts my whole life and keeps me in a state of ecstasy?"[26]

According to Diderot, there is no reason to distinguish between the sensations provoked by the current concert and the imaginary concert. Whether the concert is perceived directly by the senses of the subject or anticipated in his mind through his imagination, that changes nothing as regards the nature of the sensation felt in his body. The argument used by Diderot to respond to Falconet is based on the notion of the continuity between mind and matter: it is in the very sensitivity of the subject that the agreeable impression produced by the future praise of posterity is felt. The references to the body and to the sensations that affect it agreeably (the "sweetness," the "ecstasy") emphasize the fact that this impression is not confined to the mental being of the individual. On the contrary, and consistent with materialism's theses, it extends without interruption into a person's physical being.[27] Indeed, Diderot adds, "There is no pleasure we feel that is chimerical. The imaginary invalid is truly ill. The man who believes he is happy really is."[28] So, although the two concerts are perceived by different faculties (the first is heard while the second is constructed by the imagination), they nonetheless produce in the subject sensations that are completely identical.

It is thus on a metaphysical plane that Diderot and Falconet first join combat, the philosopher demonstrating that the direct perception of praise by our contemporaries or the imaginary representation of praise by posterity are at the origin of a similar satisfaction, felt in the very flesh of individuals who know or believe (it is the same thing) that they are admired for their works or their actions. His following argumentation flows from these premises: the natural ambition of artists leads them to crave more the admiration of future generations than the approval of those who surround them. And if it is reasonable to nourish such ambition, it is not only the immensity of time that they aspire to conquer but the infinity of space as well: "My friend, if our productions could go to Saturn, we would like to be praised in Saturn; and I have no doubt that if they were capable of traveling to the farthest reaches of the universe like they can to all the points of our planet, and reach infinite time itself, it would be no different in this sphere; and the artist's ambition would extend to the immutable, immense, infinite, and eternal space just as to a single point in this space."[29]

In this cosmic thirst for universal recognition, we perceive an accent of excess comparable to that of Don Juan dreaming of other worlds in which he could pursue his amorous conquests: for the infinity of human desire the limits of the earth seem too narrow.[30] Born by this desire of praise that knows no temporal bounds, if they are forced to recognize the physical limits of our planet, it is natural for artists to covet the admiration of the countless generations that will follow. If one has to choose, it is better to be praised after one's death rather than only during one's life: it assures a longer period of veneration. We thus understand that the "thought of posterity," based on this thesis, can drive individuals to surpass themselves. It would even be, according to Diderot, the most effective force to arouse the desire to accomplish memorable actions and to sign masterpieces.

A Gap in the Dispute

However, there is an objection that Falconet does not make as regards Diderot's argument—which is regrettable, for had he raised it, perhaps he would have succeeded in pushing the philosopher to his limits and forcing him to admit that the rational foundations of his belief in posterity were not as solidly established as he thought. To formulate this objection, we need to return to a metaphor that does not work as well as it first seems: the distinction between the sounds actually perceived (the "flute concert" whose scattered sounds reach our ears) and the work of our imagination that reestablishes a melodious continuity interrupted by the spatial distance representing metaphorically the temporal remove. Well, what does establishing the continuity between scattered sounds imply other than inserting the sounds that are lacking? The fragmented melody needs to be completed by the notes I introduce into the blank spaces.

The problem with the sound metaphor used by Diderot is the implicit distinction it establishes between sounds emanating from a source that is exterior to the listener's mind and sounds inserted by the listener's imagination into the gaps in the melody. This distinction in fact separates homogeneous elements, for the notes of the distant concert are just as much a product of the listener's imagination as are those that she or he introduces into the melodic flow: the anticipation of posterity's judgment necessarily implies the role of imagination, given that said judgment has not yet been delivered. Strictly speaking, Diderot cannot claim that the distant concert is "in large part" produced by the people who seek to perceive it: it is *entirely* the product of their imagination since it is impossible to establish a clear distinction between unformulated accolades that are granted greater or lesser reality. So, it warrants emphasis, the scattered notes of the distant concert are just as imaginary as those that are integrated by the listener into the musical flow. There is no doubt, however, that this mental image may produce genuine satisfaction, felt in the very flesh of the person concerned, and Diderot demonstrates this eloquently through his observations on the subjective reality of both an imaginary ill and an assumed happiness. We may, on the other hand, wonder what authorizes the philosopher to anticipate the praise of a posterity that does not yet exist. This is a question that he notably avoids asking, and this is precisely what is missing in this dispute, for it implies an *act of faith* that is not recognized as such.

To fill this gap in the debate between Diderot and Falconet and to identify the source of the "distant concert," we might risk suggesting that the future judgment of posterity is anticipated by means of a probability projection. Since I receive praise during my life, I may legitimately believe that additional tributes await me in the future. The current concert would only be the prelude to a later concert, even more fabulous because it will reverberate infinitely throughout the centuries. In fact, however, Diderot is not indulging in a supposition about the future based on a favorable present; on the contrary, he is betting on the saving grace of posterity. While we may be dragged through the mud by our contemporaries, we may always hope that a time will come when our merit will be recognized at what we consider to be its true value, a time when the admiration of future generations will compensate a hundredfold for the insults (or simple indifference) of those around us. For Diderot, the belief in posterity is inseparable from the hope that individuals, persecuted by their contemporaries, have in the superior judgment of their descendants, a hope that is in accord with the optimistic belief of the Enlightenment in the progress of the human race over the course of history.

Diderot defends this thesis fervently, praising those who, facing a painful alternative, decide their course based on the praise they know they will deserve from posterity even if they are sacrificing the esteem of their current public: "It is characteristic of the most heroic souls to be supported and encouraged in difficult circumstances by the most disinterested means of all, the indispensable reflection and comforting thought of a clear mind that sees what things will become in the future; it is the catechism par excellence of the patriot."[31] It is revealing, in this respect, that Diderot identified throughout his life with Socrates, a philosopher condemned by his contemporaries but whose sacrifice won him the admiration of future generations.[32] He, too, sought consolation in the thought of the judgment of posterity: "I protest with all the sincerity of which I am capable that in the midst of the persecutions I suffered, it was comforting for me *to be sure* that my luck would change one day."[33]

Among those "persecutions," Diderot is no doubt including the three months of imprisonment he endured at Vincennes during the summer of 1749. His confidence in the judgment of posterity is the flip side of the mistrust he bore his contemporaries for an incarceration that taught him an unforgettable lesson about the "choice of audience" and the "ways of distributing a text."[34] Understanding that anonymity is not sufficient protection when publishing a libertine novel like *The Indiscreet Jewels* or a bold philosophical text like *Letter on the Blind*, Diderot adapts the method of distribution of his subsequent books to their subversive potential, "organizing his work in concentric circles, from writings destined to the public of his time (*Encyclopedia*, bourgeois dramas) to works kept to himself in the hope of a posthumous publication (*D'Alembert's Dream* or *Rameau's Nephew*)."[35] Convinced that posterity would give him his due, the philosopher resolved to reveal to his contemporaries only a selection of a far greater body of works. Others will come, he muses, who will take stock of his genius in discovering the entirety of his writings. His faith in posterity is not reduced to an abstract principle but also determines the publication strategies he adopts for his works. How bold a bet whose success will only be determined after the death of the person who wagered all, both his existence and the meaning he grants it . . .

This confidence exhibited by Diderot in the salutary power of posterity rests, however, on fragile foundations insofar as nothing can be known in the present of the judgments that will be rendered by future generations. After all, how can we be sure that these judges not yet born will not be every bit as unjust toward us as those who summoned us before them in our lifetime? In *Rousseau, Judge of Jean-Jacques* (1780, 1782), the citizen of Geneva exhibits an extreme mistrust toward a "public" that hatches dire plots against him, and this suspicion prevents him from envisioning posterity as an appeals court. Posterity, too, is by definition a public, and that suffices to lend it malicious intentions from the outset, since it is composed of individuals who will form an opinion of the dearly departed Rousseau based on slanderous, false, and deceptive testimony, bequeathed by those who will claim to have known him while in fact being ignorant of the true nature of this incomparable heart. "Faced with reports of a public in bad faith, fascinated by false images and rumors, lost to reason, he only weakly called for a future rehabilitation," observes Antoine Lilti.[36] Why would posterity be above the jealousies and incompetence that so often characterize judgments by the public on individuals that are currently under its gaze? There is a far greater probability, on the contrary, that the misunderstanding between them will grow with time.

However, far from seeing in posterity an extension of the current public, subject to the same faults, victim of the same preconceived ideas, Diderot perceives it as the unique court in which to seek vindication of one's actions and texts. At least he is convinced of this at the time of his dispute with Falconet, before being assailed by doubts when writing the *Essay on the Reigns of Claude and Néron* (1782).[37] As Yves Citton remarks, Diderot's belief in the future recognition of an artist's merits is perhaps "one of the only dogmatic instances of his thought, which is elsewhere flexible, prudent, mobile, hesitating, and evasive. In the correspondence with Falconet from 1765 to 1766, the philosopher seems to subscribe to a mindless optimism, driven by a *blind and irrational need*."[38]

If the disagreement between Diderot and Falconet persists throughout their exchange, despite the considerable argumentative efforts deployed by each of them, it is ultimately because it bears on a point that is all the more difficult to demonstrate since it is one of these convictions that is deeply held *before* being supported with arguments, a reality that Falconet finally recognizes in the last third of the correspondence: "Our discussion of posterity is a *matter of sentiment*: we each have the right to adopt the one we feel."[39] The confusion between "real sounds" and "imaginary sounds" in the musical metaphor used by Diderot indicates that the certainty of future recognition by posterity is not even in question: it is a given for the philosopher, who is less concerned with giving it a rational justification than in demonstrating its power to stimulate people to surpass themselves.

At the base of this belief in the favorable judgment of posterity we thus find, as we do in the case of belief in the existence of God, an act of faith that assumes not the suspension but the postponement of rational activity. This is what is implied by the distinction established by François Quesnay in the article "Evidence" of the *Encyclopedia*: "There are two kinds of certitude," he writes, "faith and *evidence*," adding, "Faith teaches us truths that cannot be learned through rational processes. *Évidence* is limited to natural knowledge."[40] Faith is thus the consent given by the mind to a proposition in which reason has at first no part before, in a second stage, producing arguments that confirms its validity. Consequently, if faith is not alien to reason, at least the latter is not strictly indispensable to the former; reason serves as a redundant confirmation of what we knew by other means: "Although faith does not *enter us* through reason," writes Edme-François Mallet in the *Encyclopedia*, "it may nonetheless be founded on all the elements of which we've just spoken [the senses, physical evidence, authority], because it is not necessary for all the truths related to faith to be absolutely and indispensably obscure."[41] It is possible that the senses (which perceive the spectacle of a complex world ruled by immutable laws), evidence (which asserts itself through the contemplation of correspondences between microcosm and macrocosm, like these swirling galaxies that form on the surface of a cup of coffee), or authority (that of the church fathers) bring reasons that can be communicated to others to prove the existence of God. But the certitude engendered by faith can only be reinforced by our reason and not determined by it.

Whether the object of faith be the existence of God or the honoring of an individual by a public not yet born, in both cases such faith is only demonstrable to the extent that is it considered certain without any demonstration. It is nonetheless necessary to ponder the source of one's faith or, to use Mallet's expression, the manner in which it *enters* the mind of a person. The belief in the favorable judgment that posterity holds for him may have accompanied Diderot his whole life, without posterity itself appearing at any given moment: neither revelation nor Pascalian "night of fire" are indispensable to provoke a profound belief in posterity's favor. Perhaps this belief was rooted in an absolute confidence in his own genius: this concept is in fact linked to that of posterity insofar as both presuppose an *exception* (the genius occupies a special place in his own time, one that posterity conserves for him after his death).[42] According to Diderot, creative genius distinguishes itself by the *confluence* and *coordination* of three distinct faculties: "We have three principal means: observation of nature, reflection, and experiments. Observation gathers the facts, reflection combines them, and experiments verify the result of the combination. The observation of nature must be diligent, the reflection profound, and the experiments precise. We rarely see these means brought together. As a result, creative geniuses are not very common."[43] Genius is therefore not a faculty in its own right with which certain people and not others are endowed, no more than it is the expansion of a single faculty (intelligence, creativity, imagination . . .). Diderot defines it as a specific use of three faculties that all beings generally possess and by the ability to marshal them harmoniously in a creative effort. Consequently, it is by the conviction that one belongs to this rare race of "creative geniuses," a conviction reinforced by a body of work that projects one's own uniqueness, objectively, to the rest of the world, that one may gain the profound certainty that he or she will be chosen by posterity.

Nevertheless, an individual's faith in this particular honor by posterity may also have its origin in a kind of ruse consisting in the refusal to entertain a thought whose examination would destroy the sense of one's own life. Certain goals lead individuals to orient the essential of their efforts toward them and at the same time to abandon other objectives that could only be pursued in detriment to their principal aims. The intensity of this quest, the magnitude of the sacrifices it entails, requires a commensurate reward: the admiration that individuals desire in return would not be adequate if it were only expressed during their lifetime, especially since they must normally persevere for many years before their uniqueness is recognized by their contemporaries. They demand even more: the praise of posterity and the symbolic immortality it offers.

But if these individuals were to lose faith in the posthumous proclamation of this praise, just as it is possible to lose one's faith in God, their efforts, their sacrifices, their very life would appear to be in vain: inspired thought becomes a dead letter the moment one presumes its addressee absent. Consequently, belief in posterity is only defended with such fervor by Diderot because it plays a dominant role in the justification of his mission in life, which is, among other things, to bequeath to the future the best of universal knowledge, condensed into a single book.[44] It results from an act of faith that protects it from any challenge by reason, for if faith does not enter the mind of an individual through rational activity, such activity is incapable of dislodging it subsequently. In short, writers only believe in posterity to the extent that they wish to continue to believe that they have put their life to good use. Faith in posterity is a sort of blind spot in the mind of creators who thus escape an inquiry that could call into question their reason for living, and specifically living in their particular manner. If Diderot argues *for* posterity in his debate with Falconet, it is because arguing for it is also a way of arguing *for himself*. We thus discover at the root of religious faith, as of faith in posterity, the subconscious desire to guarantee the survival of a certainty without which the individual would have to adopt a different final value—or agree to live without one.

When all is said and done, the analysis of the debate between Diderot and Falconet yields a first paradox that is inherent to the concept of posterity: a paradox of belief. Posterity is the public that produces a discourse about people who no longer exist as it speaks. But it is impossible to discuss the faith of these individuals in the future production of a discourse on their subject. We are dealing with a deeply rooted conviction that may possibly be justified a posteriori in a rational manner by basing it on objective virtues but, above all, with a certainty that is critical to the creator because it satisfies a profound need. We thus need to keep in mind that belief in posterity presupposes an act of faith all the more precious to the individuals who invoke it as it is a justification of the use they are making of their life.

SECOND PARADOX
The Lottery and the Ruse

The correspondence between Diderot and Falconet treats posterity from the viewpoint of *emulation*. Is the idea of a future public alone capable of stimulating creators to surpass themselves, or may other images provoke an aspiration to excellence just as intense? The philosopher and the sculptor seek to measure the impact of the idea of posterity on artistic activity rather than to determine the best way to show oneself worthy of the approbation of a future public. In their abstract reasoning, they proceed from posterity to the artist and not from the artist to posterity. Nonetheless, if posterity is indeed the secular equivalent of God, determining what one must accomplish to gain symbolic immortality is a problem that is similar, in its implications, to that facing Christian philosophers seeking the means to obtain grace.

Although divine judgment of a person's life remains unknowable (isn't a person capable of mending her ways as long as she is still living?), it always presupposes a form of rationality, be it only the commensurability between a crime and its punishment or between merit and reward. In other words, it is not pure chance that decides the postmortem destiny of individuals but a *legality* whose operative rules are communicated to believers by means of their sacred texts and their spiritual guides. Indeed, there are no religious beliefs without rules, whose respect determines a future compensation, whether it be the Christian paradise or the form that the subsequent existence of Buddhists will take. It is not the same for posterity, which renders its judgments according to criteria that literary figures are in no way sure of knowing and does not delegate to them any reliable intermediary (the literary critic does not have the same function for the writer as the priest does for the Christian: one would be more likely to suspect him of getting it wrong than credit him with telling *the* truth). In this second chapter, I will therefore ask the following questions: How can one—to the extent that this is possible—deserve the high regard of posterity? And how can one be sure that it will even concern itself with you when its judgments are impossible to anticipate with any certainty?

"Buying a Lottery Ticket"

Comparing posterity with a lottery has been done so often that it has become a cliché. We find it notably in the writings of Stendhal, whose desire to speak to the readership of the twentieth century is well-known.[1] It is therefore worthwhile to return to this analogy, briefly evoked in the introduction, to explore it further and to establish if posterity, like a lottery, involves events that are impossible to know before they happen. It is true that the results of games of chance share with the judgments of posterity a fundamental unpredictability. In particular, it is impossible to deduce the future of a work on the basis of its current reception by the public. The past has provided abundant examples of glory that has vanished after the death of an author (who still reads Sully Prudhomme, despite the fact that he received the Nobel Prize in Literature in 1901?). Nonetheless, it is impossible to establish any necessary relationship between the current obscurity and the future acclamation of a text.

On the one hand, such obscurity may well come from the absence of merit of a work whose mediocrity will appear just as clearly to posterity as to its first readers; on the other, the exponential proliferation of texts since the revolution of the printed book places each author in the overwhelming company of contemporaries who also exercise the profession of writing. Immersed in this enormous crowd, writers remain obscure during their lifetime while future generations threaten to spill other truckloads of books that will bury all the more deeply their own. Calling for a posthumous rediscovery amounts to crying out from the depths of a mass grave: already minimal, the chances of rescue dwindle even more at each moment. Finally, the criteria of appreciation by posterity are as difficult to anticipate as the general movement of history, and the latter influences the former. Modern society had to evolve in the direction suggested by George Orwell for *Nineteen Eighty-Four* to be considered a premonitory masterpiece. On the other hand, a text like the *Voyage en Icarie* (1840) by Étienne Cabet is seen today as a literary curiosity because the ideal society he depicts there, founded on the abolition of private property and inspired by the "Christian communism" of Sir Thomas More, failed to materialize in the twentieth century.[2] It is thus the future that acts retroactively on the status of literary works, turning some into prophesies and others into utopias. And if authors who imagine the future strive to see it as clearly as possible, it is completely beyond their control whether posterity describes them as brilliant visionaries or as simple dreamers.

If the unpredictability of the judgments of posterity stems from diverse causes of which it would be superfluous to make an exhaustive inventory, said judgments may nonetheless never be ascribed to pure chance, which seems to discredit the comparison with a lottery. Indeed, if posterity's edicts were issued in an entirely arbitrary manner, they would cease to have the slightest value, and the authors, abandoning their dreams of posthumous rehabilitation, would consider pleasing the current public to be the only criterion for success. On the contrary, this lottery follows rules, but unknowable rules that the participants simply assume to be equitable. If it is impossible for them to anticipate the result, it is not because the lottery designates its winners for no reason, but because the laws that determine its decisions remain mysterious. Although unpredictable, posterity is nonetheless considered rational. In this respect, it lends itself to a kind of metaphysical belief that has all the characteristics of faith: it is like God, whose mysterious motives might seem to be capricious if we did not attribute them to a rationale that exceeds our intellectual faculties. These analogies between the creator and posterity are responsible for the sliding from one to the other in the mind of many artists: they hope to find eternal life in the collective memory and not in a beyond that seems even less plausible to them.

While not guaranteeing it, one practice at least seems generally capable of increasing the probability of surviving into posterity: the exclusive dedication to the production of a body of work. That dedication may involve an unconscious attempt to move cruel posterity to pity: "Look how I have suffered to please you!" It may also indicate the adaption of a capitalistic logic to the domain of art: the quantity of my temporal investment will increase the benefits it will yield to me in the future. In the two cases, the underlying logic is the same: the time of a human existence, so short in relation to the infinite succession of future generations, must be devoted in its quasi totality to the production of a work if that work is to have a reasonable chance of escaping oblivion. Joachim du Bellay says nothing else in his "Defense and Illustration of the French Language": "He who wishes to take flight by the hands and mouths of men must long remain cloistered in his room; and he who desires to live in the memory of posterity must, as if dead to himself, sweat and tremble again and again and, while our courtly poets drink, eat, and sleep to their fill, endure hunger, thirst, and long sleepless nights."[3] Alas, a rational lottery but a lottery all the same, posterity does not obey a criterion that is so easy to manipulate. The poet Théophile de Viau, for his part, issues a warning to laborious fellow poets who would like their dedication to asceticism to be a sufficient basis for symbolic immortality:

> I know some who [. . .]
> Wish to persuade us that what they are doing is beautiful,
> And that their fame will survive the grave,
> For no other reason than their whole life
> Was consumed by a little piece of work,
> That their verse will remain precious to the world,
> Because in writing it they've grown old.

The spider likewise, in spinning out its excretion,
Uses up its whole life and makes nothing that lasts.[4]

Du Bellay and de Viau do not only take contradictory stands concerning *talent* in literature, the former asserting that it must be supported by extremely hard work while the latter considers it the preserve of people with superior natural gifts.[5] The two men likewise lock horns as regards the type of artistic activity that is most apt to draw the homage of posterity. However, the practices they designate still have a point in common: posterity is explicitly the goal of the author, whether he tries to earn its approval through a long effort (like du Bellay) or considers the spontaneity of the creative act as the best way to produce an immortal object ("A good mind always produces its object with ease," de Viau proclaims).[6]

Conversely, do not certain authors attempt to reach posterity by affecting indifference to it? Is this indifference an authentic renunciation of the temporal extension of one's life beyond the grave, or is it rather a wily ploy whose goal really consists in gaining the favor of future generations? Giacomo Casanova, a great gambler before the eternal—and it is perhaps not superfluous to recall that he was codirector of the lottery of the Royal Military School—makes his existence the subject of a work that is lived *with no intention of writing it*.[7] In the next part of this chapter, the example of Casanova's *The Story of My Life* will help us to determine if posterity is the reward obtained through an unpredictable lottery or if it is possible to manipulate its judgments by means of a ruse.

Casanova's Wager

1789: the French Revolution sounds the death knell of the Old World, and Casanova is old and is going to die soon. At Dux in Bohemia, where he has taken up residence as the librarian of the Count of Waldstein, he has become a mere shadow—worse, a caricature—of his former self. The Prince de Ligne is the witness of this final dereliction and mocks the declining adventurer cruelly. Casanova—the citizen of the Republic of Venice, the escapee from the Plombs prison, the adventurer admired by all of Europe, a continent he has crisscrossed over and over again—appears to him like a grotesque puppet, a cadaver living on borrowed time who still wants to be a playboy.[8] With the fairer sex much less accommodating than in the past, the hostility of the public was an additional source of sadness for the Venetian, who had always adored fine company. So he began to write, for writing, he says, is still conversation; all he had to do was imagine an elegant circle—one of those in which he had so often shone—to find the right tone, the right word. Thirteen hours a day, he announces in a letter, he worked at the composition of *The Story of My Life*, which allowed him to insert, between his gaze and the grayish reality of the Bohemian castle, the luminous visions that arose from his flamboyant past.[9]

In the preface written in 1797,[10] eight years after having begun his memoirs and just a few months before his disappearance, Casanova begins a meditation on the relationship between his life and his work: "Worthy or unworthy, my life is my material, my material is my life. *Having lived it without ever thinking that the desire to write would come to me*, it may have an interesting character that it would perhaps not have had if I had lived it intending to write about in my old age, and, moreover, to publish it."[11] If Casanova asserts that the life most worthy of being related is the one that is the least concerned to be told, it is because the anticipation of the memoirist project imposes on its author a responsibility as regards his future literary image and a concomitant limiting of his current liberty. The person who, in the course of his existence, is already imagining its retrospective narration seeks to be worthy of the image he intends to give of himself one day: to know that one is the protagonist of a future book is already to wish to be its hero. This future memoirist may be tempted to avoid adventures in which his honor, fortune, and dignity may be compromised; to avoid certain actions that he knows ahead of time he will have trouble justifying to his readers. Everything considered, he is, of course, as free to act as to relate his actions in the future: no one other than himself prevents him from behaving however he likes and then burying in silence what he wishes to disappear with him. But a memoirist knows that he is never taken at his word, and that a day will come when the truth of his version of the events will be examined. The Casanova devotees have demonstrated this eloquently, with a meticulousness bordering on the fastidious, by tracing the footsteps of their hero, checking one by one every detail related in *The Story of My Life*. Thus the authorial freedom of the memoirist bears a responsibility similar to that of the historian whose work is submitted to a colleague for verification. Of course, he is free to arrange the facts, to conceal some of them, but he knows that such falsification risks being denounced by the biographer, his reticent admirer.[12]

Led with no intention of being related, this life would thus be more interesting—let us agree for the moment—but more interesting for *whom*? In other words, who is the reader that *The Story of My Life* presupposes? The rest of the preface indicates that it is a textual representation of the "good company" that formerly received the Venetian so graciously.[13] But the readership imagined by the author as he writes is not the one to which he intends to present his book: he is referring to an ideal interlocutor but not an authentic addressee. On the one hand, at the very moment at which Casanova is working on his memoirs, the Revolution is working on the destruction of the aristocratic and gallant society at whose table he formerly sat. And on the other, Casanova knows that he is in the twilight of his life and presents himself as a dead man with the gift of speech: "*vixi*" (I lived), he writes in the preface.[14] The words of the memoirist are already posthumous; they are not bequeathed to posterity through the intermediary of his contemporaries but directly to it. The voice of the person who is already no longer is speaking from the grave to those who do not yet exist, Casanova's prose evoking François-René de Chateaubriand's ahead of time. The public that the Venetian targets by the tale of his existence is thus none other than posterity—his "neighbor," as he calls it in a booklet of the same year.[15] In an elliptical manner, it is the logic of a wager that Casanova sets out in the 1797 preface, one concerning the strategy a memoirist has the choice of adopting with a view to seducing future generations. This wager may be formulated in these terms: it is to the extent that one is not concerned with posterity that it will grant you its favors. "Wager that you are going to lose everything, and then alone will you be saved." However, should we believe Casanova when he asserts that he has lived his life with no intention of writing about it? For several decades he supported his adventurous life by gambling and never hesitated to "correct chance" when it threatened to turn against him.[16] After finding the means to guarantee himself the good graces of Fortune, did he succeed in obtaining the favors of Posterity through a ruse, too?

A Project Long Cultivated

The writing of *The Story of My Life* coincides with Casanova's last years. Residing in Dux in 1785, he wrote a first version between the end of the summer of 1789 and the summer of 1792. This first version covers the period from the year of his birth to 1772. As for the last part of the memoirs, which finish just before his return to Venice in 1774, it was "probably written beginning in 1794, with subsequent corrections."[17] Before *The Story of My Life*, Casanova had already produced two autobiographical texts: *The Duel* and *The Story of My Escape from the Prisons of the Republic of Venice*.[18] Published respectively in 1780 and 1787, these narratives are late works whose appearance does not directly contradict the preface of 1797 and its declarations concerning a life lived with no intention of relating it.

However, *The Story of My Life* itself provides numerous proofs of the slow maturation of an autobiographical undertaking that, contrary to what the preface asserts, was never absent from the Venetian's thoughts throughout his life and was in no way the result of a late emergence. It was rather an "old project, constantly in Casanova's mind."[19] On the one hand, he had practiced for many years a singular autobiographical genre: the oral autobiography. This practice is showcased in *The Story of My Life* where Casanova regularly depicts himself captivating an audience: he was only sixteen when he was already charming the Senator Malipiero with the story of his breakup with the beautiful Juliette Preati.[20] Among all the autobiographical fragments with which he fascinated his contemporaries, his two purple passages are the stories of his escape from the prisons of Venice and of his duel with the Polish Count Branecki. He recounted them verbally time and again to satisfy the curiosity of elegant groups who delighted in these tales from a European celebrity.

This practice of oral autobiography preceded the memoir writing, bequeathing to it numerous characteristics, in particular "the taste for lively dialogue reproduced word for word and the need to maintain contact with the reader."[21] Casanova was sometimes inclined to consider the oral version of his stories superior to their literary transcription: "My reader knows this story," he remarks about his escape from the Venetian jails, "but it is much less interesting written than when I tell it in person."[22] More interesting or not, this version nonetheless proves that Casanova was accustomed to being the main protagonist in autobiographical tales well before the writing of his memoirs. The escape in question took place in the night of October 31, 1756, three decades before he began *The Story of My Life* on the friendly advice of O'Reilly, an Irish physician living near him.[23] There is little doubt that Casanova held forth to live: his stories opened the door of elegant circles where he found his dinner and, certainly more important, a feast of praise that his ego adored all the more since it was lavished by social groups from which he normally would have been excluded. But perhaps he also lived *in order to* narrate, his numerous discourses thus becoming so many opportunities to work on his narrative effects in front of a live audience before transmitting them to posterity.

Many textual details reveal in fact the premeditation in Casanova's preparation for the future composition of his memoirs: "Well before his retreat to Dux, Casanova also noted the events of his life, the people he met, his travels, and his conversations in notebooks that he called his 'capitularies.' He conserved his papers throughout his life, depositing them in safe places when he could or carrying them with him in his travels, at the risk of shocking a customs official, like he did in Barcelona in 1768: 'I open my trunk, and this man is astonished to see that it was at least two-thirds full of notebooks."[24] Begun "around the age of sixteen,"[25] these voluminous "capitularies"—dossiers in which he gathers pell-mell his correspondence, excerpts of conversations, and impressions from his travels—exhibit a clear desire to accumulate materials designed to compensate potential lapses of memory. Enriched and conserved throughout the years, despite the numerous vicissitudes of an itinerant existence, they demonstrate the patience with which Casanova prepared the transcription of his existence into a book. The absence of premeditation in his memoirist project, finally, is belied by the texts he published during his long career as a writer on diverse and varied topics. Even subjects that apparently lend themselves the least to a direct intervention by the author exhibit a surprising autobiographical compulsion on his part. When he attempted to refute the *History of the Government of Venice* by Abraham Nicolas Amelot de la Houssaye in a text from 1769, Casanova revealed fragments of his own story.[26] The same phenomenon is repeated in another work that, a priori, did not lend itself either to an insertion of the authorial figure. In his *History of the Turbulence of Poland* (1775)—an essay devoted to the dividing of a part of Poland between Austria, Prussia, and Russia—Casanova indulges in new digressions of which he is, personally, the principal subject.[27] It is thus hardly surprising that a novel (a genre whose affinities with memoir writing are much more evident than political history) also turns into implicit autobiography. Édouard, the hero of *Icosameron*,[28] narrated in the first person, is the author of prodigious acts that recall those that Casanova claimed to be capable of, appearing hence as a fantasized double for the Venetian, a "demigod, legendary founder of a race, a civilization, and of a world that function according to his pleasure and his profound wisdom."[29] With Casanova, everything—history, novels, journalistic writings—tends toward autobiography.

Consequently, far from having lived his life without ever believing that he would want to write about it—to use the words in the preface of *The Story of My Life*—Casanova, on the contrary, had prepared its composition so far ahead of time that it is a safe bet that an experience, at the very moment that he was living it, already appeared to him in the form it would take in his future memoirs—supposing, of course, that he had not decided to undertake certain experiences precisely so that they would enrich with yet another adventure the future text of his story. For what reasons, however, did he refuse to admit that the plan to write the story of his life was there all along?

Eluding the Fault

Casanova claims he did not conceive his autobiographical project until the end of his life because, in admitting the opposite, he would have had to assume the complete responsibility of adventures undertaken solely to be included in his book. "I began to make of myself a *literary being*, someone who sees things as if they were to be written one day," notes Annie Ernaux after relating the circumstances in which she wrote her first book.[30] Casanova is a "literary being" in the two complementary senses of this expression: both "he who lives in the anticipation of writing his work" and "he who controls the content of his future work by deciding to live what he intends to narrate in the future." The literary being is thus the individual who, by never losing sight of the future metamorphosis of his life into a text, is unable to plead irresponsibility regarding the decisions he made based on the aesthetic or novelistic potential they presented. Well, throughout his existence, Casanova pursued the enjoyment of a transgression (contesting authority) free of both punishment and remorse. This project of "subversion without revolution"[31] exerted its influence to various degrees over Casanova's autobiographical undertaking, playing the role of organizing principle of a work that first presented itself as a collection of disparate and fortuitous adventures. It likewise determined the goal attributed to the memorialist narrative insofar as this text is not an act of self-justification before a "reader-judge"[32] but figures instead as a means of enjoying a memorial pleasure that the reader of *The Story of My Life* is invited to share—on pain of being identified by the Venetian with one of the many "fools" he has duped.[33]

In this respect, one of the first scenes related by Casanova prefigures the terms of a problem that, time and again, he had to later face—namely, how to violate a moral norm while escaping the experience of culpability, or, in other words, without being recognized by others as responsible and without feeling any remorse? Recounted in the first pages of his memoirs, the theft of a crystal object belonging to his father reveals a fantasy of innocent transgression: the young Casanova steals the paternal instrument and lets his brother take the punishment.[34] Throughout *The Story of My Life*, Casanova strives to maintain the fiction of a lucky irresponsibility that, if we are to believe him, was the consequence of his submission to powers constituting a personal pantheon, deities similar to celestial bodies that exercised on his will a more or less irresistible influence.[35]

Providence, the divine will that remunerates the good and bad acts of an individual following an immutable system; Fortune, which renders problematic the principle of causality by rewarding folly with happiness and a measured action with misfortune; Destiny, which decides for all eternity the existence that an individual must lead without his or her being able to change anything; and the "combinations," the concatenation of events that imperiously dictates directions on lives: to various degrees, all these exterior and uncoordinated forces bring to bear on the liberty of the hero of these memoirs a weight that quashes it or at least restricts it severely. They play a direct role in the plot twists and reversals that give its particular rhythm to the narrative of *The Story of My Life*. In short, they infuse this autobiographical narration with the picaresque character typical of an early modern novel. For example, here we have Casanova embarking for Constantinople solely because he pronounced the name of this city during a discussion with a cardinal: the sudden inspiration is equivalent to a commitment because it seems to express the will of an internal "Spirit" that indicates to him what direction he should give his life.[36] Sometime later, Casanova resolves to return to Venice when a Greek merchant, by suggesting it to him, appears to him to be an intermediary through whom God is speaking.[37]

These forces, to which the hero of the memoirs pays close attention, are directly responsible for the sudden lurches of a behavior marked by surprising twists and turns. By following their inspiration, Casanova purports to obey an authority from which he cannot free himself, and that thus bears the entire responsibility for his breaches of morality and laws:

> Fortune, which as a synonym of chance I should disdain, becomes respectable in that it seems to wish to appear as a divinity in the most important events of my life. . . . It only seemed to aspire to exercise on me an absolute empire in order to convince me that it was rational and master of everything. To persuade me of this, it employed striking means designed expressly to force me to act and to make me understand that my own will, far from declaring my liberty, was just an instrument it was using to make of me what it would.[38]

Had he admitted that the plan to write his autobiography had existed his whole life, Casanova would have at the same time ruined the fiction of the carefree irresponsibility that he attempts to maintain throughout *The Story of My Life* in depicting himself as a plaything in the hands of higher authorities. The cause of his submission to their sudden inspirations would have been immediately revealed, namely the desire to lead an adventurous life likely to attract the interest of future generations that we now know to be the public that the author was targeting when he was near death. I do not mean to suggest that Casanova did not sincerely believe in the influence of these various deities on his will, but rather to assert that he only chose to believe in this to the extent that he foresaw that his submission to said deities prepared the future transmutation of his life into the most novelistic of autobiographies.

At the heart of the Casanova pantheon is thus revealed an additional divinity that he names "immortality" in a letter from 1785 to Maximilien de Lamberg, a missive in which he announces that he has conquered this grace by the publication of *Icosameron*: "At the end of this work, which will be divided into two in-octavo volumes of five hundred pages each, I will say like Ovid does of his *Metamorphoses*: Here is a work that will deliver me to immortality."[39] Casanova, however, did not conquer this symbolic immortality by his memoir novel but by his novelistic autobiography; that is, he did not obtain it with the text that he devoted explicitly to this goal but rather with the one that he presented as a plan that he adopted late in life. The chiasmus between the two texts exhibits the ruse employed by Casanova to obtain the favors of Posterity, an additional feminine deity within his personal pantheon. Casanova seduced this divinity like a woman in whom he pretended to have no interest. We know that an old law of seduction consists in saying that in pursuing an object of his desires, the seducer risks being judged irksome, whereas acting indifferent toward her is more apt to excite her interest. Casanova behaved in a similar manner with Posterity: while he dreamed of conquering it and gathered for this purpose a considerable amount of narrative material—the events of his life, that were conserved in the notebooks that he destroyed as he transformed them into a literary masterpiece—he pretended to have no other goal than to enjoy the present. But this enjoyment itself was oriented by the desire to preserve it in the form of a book; it was not what it pretended to be, namely the choice of mortality over eternity, agreeing to disappear with no hope of leaving the slightest posthumous trace. On the contrary, it aspired to an intensity sufficient to render its recounting capable of captivating future generations.

Despite appearances, Casanova's quest for a passage to posterity was not only a constant preoccupation but the cause of much pain. It is true that it did not lead him to sacrifice his life to a work, as do many men of letters who, according to Diderot, purchase their survival in the collective memory by a complete dedication to their art: "We hear within ourselves the praise that they [our fellow men] will give us one day, and we sacrifice ourselves. We sacrifice our life, we cease to exist now in order to live in their memory."[40] Contrary to Diderot, this "immolation" of the individual in the name of his future veneration had no charm for Casanova, who was likewise not inclined to embrace the monastic existence advised by du Bellay in the excerpt quoted above. Casanova refused in fact to "remain in his room" (unless he found himself there in charming company) and didn't believe that to survive for posterity he had to "die to himself and tremble often." As opposed to the voluntary confinement of the artist who keeps at his task tirelessly, Casanova chose to lead an adventurous existence with the express goal of transforming it into an autobiographical narrative. Casanova thus seems to gain on the planes of both existence and literature. To the insolence of a flamboyant and happy life he would add that which consists in surviving in the collective memory by obtaining a recognition—in the form of critical editions and scholarly work devoted to his texts—that we usually reserve for authors who seem to have deserved it by the sacrifice of their life to their work. Despite initial misunderstandings (for a while his work was only known in a redacted version, and the myth of the unrepentant seducer long overshadowed the stunning virtuosity of a highly versatile writer), Casanova has succeeded in joining the pantheon of major authors not only of the eighteenth century but of French literature in general.

However, the Venetian agreed to sacrifices of quite another order to attain posterity, depriving himself, for instance, of the happiness embodied by a loving and beloved woman whom he nonetheless chose to leave, as if he were prey to a curse that he could not recognize. "How could I thus become my own torturer?" he wonders when breaking up with the beautiful Marcoline, whom he adored and who adored him, bringing them both to tears as he decided to separate for reasons that remained mysterious to him. "I did a hundred things in my life that I've regretted, each time driven by an *occult power* which I took pleasure in not resisting."[41] These farewells to happiness that he pronounced in losing a cherished mistress—the beautiful Marcoline but also the mysterious Henriette, the tender Manon, the studious Esther, and the youthful Gabrielle[42]—may be interpreted as something other than a simple desire to multiply female conquests, an interpretation that would identify Casanova as a Don Juan, of whom he was indeed the very opposite.[43] The "occult power" to which he alludes consists rather in a desire that drove him to wish to live more: a new adventure, a new love, a new act of madness, for fear of not having done enough for the future story of his life to fascinate posterity and convince it not to forget him. Casanova thus served eternity behind the mask of the present, and his pleasure was never its own goal but rather a means to conquer at the same time the admiration of centuries to come. In his manner, he illustrates a new paradox of belief: indifference toward posterity conceals a behavior calculated to gain symbolic immortality.

THIRD PARADOX
The Renunciation and the Reward

The example of Casanova shows that achieving recognition by posterity may be orchestrated by an author who pretends not to be concerned with it, the Venetian deploying a seductive strategy toward a feminized and deified image of "Immortality." This deity joins a diverse and personal pantheon, with Casanova cultivating a particularly amusing form of polytheism if we remember that he undertook theological studies and became a Catholic clergyman for a time.[1] Since the paradoxes of belief result from the transfer of attributes of God to the idea of posterity, it is important to move from a polytheistic conception of this posthumous court to a different conceptualization that derives from monotheism. I will study in this chapter the discourse on posterity by Jean-Paul Sartre, in his own works and through the evidence provided by Simone de Beauvoir. Sartre announced his farewell to posterity, which does not mean that he gave up hope of achieving it all the same, in the form of a reward commensurate with the sacrifice that was required for it. I will take, as a departure point for this third chapter the year 1945, at which time Sartre experienced a metaphysical crisis concurrent with the totally unexpected and immense fame he suddenly enjoyed.

Farewell to Posterity

A long passage in *The Force of Circumstance* (*La force des choses*) helps us to identify the causes and paradoxical implications of the farewell to posterity that Jean-Paul Sartre announced in the period immediately after the war:

> He gained throughout the world an unexpected audience: he felt that he was being denied that of future centuries. Eternity had collapsed; the men of tomorrow had become those crabs to which Franz speaks in *The Sequestered of Altona* [*Les Séquestrés d'Altona*]: impervious, hermetic, radically other. His books, even read, would not be those that he had written: his oeuvre would

not survive. This was really, for him, the death of God, who until then had survived beneath the masque of words. Sartre owed it to his pride to assume such a total catastrophe. He did so in the *Presentation* which, in October, was placed at the beginning of the first issue of *Les Temps modernes*. Literature had stripped off its sacred character, so be it; henceforth he would place the absolute in the ephemeral; locked in his era, he would choose it over eternity, agreeing to perish completely with it. This resolution had several meanings. As a child, as an adolescent, Sartre's favorite phantasm was that of the damned poet, misunderstood by all, struck by the lightning of glory beyond the tomb or, so that he could nonetheless enjoy it a little, on his deathbed; once again, he was betting on turning failure into triumph. Inordinately honored, in gaining everything he had lost everything: agreeing to lose everything, he nourished the secret hope that he would get everything back. "*The refusal of posterity was supposed to give me posterity.*"[2]

Let us begin by establishing *who is speaking* in this passage. At first glance, these reflections on posterity yield the perspective of Simone de Beauvoir and not the ambivalence of Sartre himself as regards posterity. The publication of Simone de Beauvoir's memoirs beginning in 1958 nonetheless served as an "official chronical of the literary, intellectual, and political path of the couple," such that Beauvoir's work belongs to the "Sartrian autobiographical constellation." Indeed, "in the intellectual and affective economy of the Sartre-Beauvoir couple, no text of the one could appear without the imprimatur of the other; this means not only that Sartre agreed to Beauvoir's memorialist project but that he accepted in advance to recognize himself in her comments and analyses, that he necessarily embraced."[3] Consequently, the above passage from *The Force of Circumstances* is more than the external reconstruction of an intellectual journey: it appears with the sanction of the very person it concerns. The implication of Sartre in these reflections on posterity is also expressed by the comment "unpublished notes" accompanying the quote in italics at the end of the text: it is a fragment sent by Sartre to his companion to be included in her work. This combined authorship shows that the intellectual itinerary traced by Beauvoir is the result of a mutual reflection: the voice of Sartre echoes that of his companion in order to assent to what she is saying about him.

It is thus a kind of delegated autobiography that we read in these remarks. On several occasions Sartre tried out this shift of the autobiographical voice, as is demonstrated by the oral biographies that appeared in his declining years.[4] Among the latter, we include *Sartre by Himself* (*Sartre par lui-même*), "Self-Portrait at Seventy" ("Autoportrait à soixante-dix ans"), and "Conversations with Jean-Paul Sartre" ("Entretiens avec Jean-Paul Sartre"), recorded by Simone de Beauvoir in 1974 and published seven years later in *The Farewell Ceremony* (*La cérémonie des adieux*).[5] But to understand the causes and issues of Sartre's metaphysical crisis in the postwar period, it is more revealing to compare the excerpt quoted from *The Force of Circumstances* to the text of *The Words* (*Les Mots*), the only Sartrian autobiography in the classical sense of the term. On the one hand, *The Force of Circumstances* was published by Beauvoir in 1963 and *The Words* came out the following year: these two autobiographies were thus developed simultaneously by Sartre and Beauvoir. In addition, *The Words* undertakes a demythification whose goal is the sacralization of literature and all of its corollaries: the figure of the "great writer," the "genius" that is revealed in the course of seminal experiments, the "genesis" of an "artistic vocation" presaged by unmistakable signs. Nonetheless, while the mourning of the passing of the sacredness of literature is *already* accomplished in *The Words*, in which a sometimes playful account, toying with self-parody,[6] is marshaled to bury definitively the illusions that Sartre had long abandoned, it is the suddenness of this mourning that is described in *The Force of Circumstances* through the evocation of a bygone age: the time when the realization of a disappearance—the disappearance of posterity as the reward for the long labors of the "damned poet"—pierced a consciousness that was now going to undertake the task, so difficult, of acknowledging it, substituting a new belief, and integrating this new belief into a new system of values.

What event is at the origin of a metaphysical crisis that Simone de Beauvoir compares to "the death of God"? It is the experience of worldly success that hides from Sartre the hope of posthumous glory; or, in other words, it is fame in the here and now that forces him to renounce posterity. The passage quoted in *The Force of Circumstances* refers to the immediate postwar period and comes after a description of the sudden celebrity in which Jean-Paul Sartre was bathed from 1945 onward. This fame was illustrated notably by two consecutive events: the lecture he gave on October 29, 1945, to a huge crowd, engraved in people's memories as an "unprecedented cultural success";[7] and the publication of the text of this lecture under the title *Existentialism Is a Humanism* (1946), which garnered a wide audience and established itself as a breviary of Sartrian philosophy. Sartre and his thought were omnipresent in the postwar press, which lavished constant praise or criticism on him, while the general public adopted the word "existentialism" and progressively emptied it of its substance. "The incredible hype, the constant hammering of his name, his works, and those of his close fellow writers in the French literary world"[8]—in short, the extraordinary vogue of existentialism in general and of its figurehead in particular—was a cultural phenomenon for which Simone de Beauvoir offered two explanations.

The first consists of a transfer of national pride to the belles lettres. Having become a second-rate power, France exalted literature to compensate for its inability to deal with the two postwar giants as an equal. Just as the colonial enterprise, after the defeat of 1870, had embodied the pursuit of national glory outside the European space dominated by Germany, after 1945 it was literature that picked up the baton by becoming the intangible territory in which the national genius distinguished itself. An enthusiastic celebration of French literary products thus appeared in the postwar era, a celebration that included mediocre works whose only merit was to be written in the language of Molière at the right time and whose glory—undeserved in Sartre's eyes—seemed to sully his own works by granting them the same distinction. Ironically identified with the "French soil,"[9] existentialism became a French product for exportation in the same sense as high fashion, perfume, and, two decades later, "French Theory."[10]

The second explanation of this fame of which Sartre is the reticent beneficiary consists in the concordance of the contents of his philosophy and the expectations of the postwar audience. Simone de Beauvoir observes that Sartre's readers had lost their faith in immutable progress and universal peace: "Existentialism, in attempting to reconcile history and morality, authorized them to assume their transitory condition without abandoning a certain absolute, without ceasing to confront the horror and absurdity while maintaining their dignity as human beings, without giving up their uniqueness. He seemed to offer them the perfect solution."[11] However, this initial enthusiasm masks a misunderstanding: in fact, Sartre was inviting his readers to surmount their petty bourgeois condition, as he had done, and to assume the sometimes difficult responsibilities of their liberty. Beauvoir sums up the ambiguity of Sartre's success by declaring, as regards his readers, "They came, they returned to him because he was asking the same questions that they were asking themselves; they fled him because his answers wounded them."[12]

A famous definition of celebrity, offered by Nicolas Chamfort, consists in saying that it is "the advantage of being known by people who do not know you"[13]—that is, by a public that forces you to recognize yourself in an inauthentic portrait of yourself. Nonetheless, rather than simply a paradox of "knowing" (*connaissance*), celebrity also exhibits a paradox of *recognizing* (*reconnaissance*). Following Sartre's example, we might thus complete Chamfort's epigrammatic definition by saying that being famous is also the privilege of being recognized for reasons whose legitimacy you do not necessarily recognize yourself. Contrary to how it appears to us in general today, celebrity is not a globally enviable situation for which we only have to pay with occasional obligations. For Sartre it was an unwelcome distinction that, being awarded to him sooner than he had anticipated and owing to a misunderstanding, forced him to redefine both his relationship to literature and, ultimately, the project that oriented his use of his liberty.

It is true that Sartre's malaise regarding his sudden fame is a bit surprising, given that this central figure of the postwar had despaired for a decade his lack of public favor. As an adolescent Sartre foresaw celebrity at the age of twenty-eight at the latest and had no doubt that his writings would not only be published but that they would bring him immediate fame. Well, the 1930s were a long period of failures and disappointments that undermined the absolute confidence in his lucky star that he had enjoyed when he was younger. Dreaming of teaching in Japan, he found himself in Le Havre; anticipating glory for his books, he had to recover from the successive rejections of the manuscript of Nausea (La Nausée), then titled Melancholia.[14] The glory of the postwar period, fervently desired by the brilliant child become an obscure teacher in the depths of the detested French provinces, should have provoked in him a feeling of triumph all the more ecstatic since it had been denied to him for so long. It is thus impossible to understand the feeling of curse and catastrophe with which Sartre met his celebrity unless we relate it to one of the mythologies about the artist's condition as it was conceived in the course of the nineteenth century.

In the excerpt quoted from *The Force of Circumstances*, we are faced with a specific phantasm: the damned poet. Beauvoir gives an intentionally ironic description of the artist who pays with his lifelong labors for a posthumous glory that he nonetheless enjoys in advance, for a brief moment, on his deathbed. Thus his death is not accompanied by regrets and anguish but by the sweet certainty of having finally won the game, just as the repentant sinner catches a brief glimpse of the gleam of paradise that the priest allows him to deserve in extremis in receiving his confession. As clichéd as it is, this image of an artist whose suffering is the necessary ransom of genius still marked Sartre's concept of the condition of the man of letters, because Sartre the child had transmitted it to the forty-year-old adult he had become after the war. Born in 1905, Sartre was not so far, at the time of his first readings—a period he describes precisely in *The Words*—from the great poets of the preceding century whose destiny had illustrated the transformation of misery into glory. To the greatest of them—Baudelaire—he was to devote a biographical essay that appeared in 1947 and was thus contemporaneous with the brutal arrival of fame that Beauvoir describes in *The Force of Circumstances*. "Educated in the old manner,"[15] Sartre cannot see in the figures in his literary pantheon—the author of *The Flowers of Evil* (*Les Fleurs du mal*), but also Stendhal, Stéphane Mallarmé, and Franz Kafka, to name but a few—any example of a glory received in their time; it is necessarily the mediocre writers, the inferior talents, who receive the approval of contemporaries, who are always suspected of stupidity or philistinism. As for the tiny elite that alone is capable of recognizing the superior artist during his life, it nonetheless sees its judgment confirmed by posterity. This is, at least, the standard narrative of redress that the *doxa* repeats without ever seeking an explanation of the sudden rationality exhibited by the judges of posthumous glory: how do they come to honor the artist that they ignored when he or she was still alive?[16] By a reversal that fame forces him into, Sartre concludes that his worldly success is a guarantee that his work will be forgotten after his disappearance: immediate recognition could only be a sign of future scorn.

If we follow this logic, we can only conclude that the greater the immediate recognition, the less likely the embrace of posterity. As Beauvoir depicts him in *The Force of Circumstances*, Sartre experienced a shock provoked by modernity that recalls the famous analysis that Walter Benjamin devotes to Charles Baudelaire.[17] Whereas Baudelaire is described by Benjamin as the witness of mass industrial society, of commodification, and of the loss of the aura of cultural goods, Sartre is presented by Beauvoir as the contemporary of a new phase of capitalism featuring the increased speed of transportation, the emphasis on international exchanges, and the completion of globalization. These global transformations had a direct impact on the author of *Nausea*, for they abruptly and spectacularly broadened the specter of the celebrity that was honoring him. Not content with being recognized in his own time, Sartre was suddenly recognized by an international public that he had never hoped to reach so quickly: "While he had desired the approval of posterity, [Sartre] never expected to reach anything but a very limited public during his own lifetime: a new fact, the appearance of *oneworld*, transformed him into a cosmopolitan author; he had imagined that *Nausea* wouldn't be translated for a long time: thanks to modern techniques, to the speed of communications and transmissions, his works appeared in twelve languages."[18]

The existence of an international readership and of literary celebrities who transcend the borders of their homeland have become commonplace in the twenty-first century. It is true that owing to the persistent resilience of the sacrificial logic that had marked Sartre ("one must suffer during one's life to be recognized by posterity"), we are also inclined to look condescendingly on works whose literary qualities seem a priori suspect the moment they meet broad public success in the country of the author, and a fortiori on the international stage. Nonetheless, the globalized character of celebrity to which the film industry has accustomed us now belongs to the expectations of contemporary writers, who can dream of being quickly translated and celebrated throughout the world. For Sartre, this broadening of the audience of the authors and the increased speed at which their writings were distributed around the planet were new phenomena, facilitated by technical means that did not exist in the age in which his literary idols had produced their works, nor in that of his own intellectual upbringing. A witness of a new era of capitalism, Sartre is also its victim: it gave him too early, too quickly, and too broadly a notoriety that he had only hoped for once he had been transformed and ennobled by a posthumous recognition.

The result of this unwelcome fame is a type of chiasmus: whereas failure was an indication of triumph, triumph could only be a sign of failure. Sartre decided to accept the consequences of this inversion of terms. Conforming to the Stoic tradition that encourages us to desire what is impossible to change, Sartre renounced symbolic immortality and chose the present *over* posterity. As we saw in the excerpt from *The Force of Circumstance* above, "Literature had shed its sacred character, so be it; henceforth he would see the absolute in the ephemeral; locked in his age, he would choose it over eternity, accepting to perish entirely with it."[19]

In this excerpt, however, Simone de Beauvoir distorts the vocabulary employed by Sartre in the "Presentation of the *Temps modernes*." The expression "perish entirely with it" is found there, indeed, in an identical context: the men or women of letters take their responsibilities in their own period and, when all the battles have been fought, agree to disappear with it.[20] However, the term "eternity" is used by Beauvoir as a synonym of "immortality," whereas Sartre is careful to distinguish between these two terms in the "Presentation of the *Temps modernes*." What are the reasons for this conceptual distinction, and how does it help us to better understand the Sartrian paradox of posterity, a reward that is sacrificed with the hope of obtaining it *nevertheless*?

From Immortality to Eternity

If we are to believe Simone de Beauvoir, the "Presentation of the *Temps modernes*" is the text in which Sartre draws the necessary conclusions of the desacralization of literature and of the inherent limits of the human condition. For recognizing the "death of God" who "until then had survived under the mask of words," amounts to accepting the finiteness of man, the finiteness of an animal endowed with consciousness who, after burying the idea of transcendence and its corollaries (in particular, the belief in the immortality of the soul and the possibility of resurrection), resolves to disappear *entirely*, without expecting to last beyond the period in which the simple chance of his birth had assigned him to live. It is thus the employment of an existence without future, completely enclosed within a given period, that Sartre describes in this 1945 text, contemporaneous with his sudden celebrity.

Sartre begins by demonstrating that the man or woman of letters, for at least a century, had exhibited a regrettable "temptation of irresponsibility" (9). Establishing a parallel between two movements that one would tend spontaneously to contrast owing to the pronounced differences between their aesthetics—Art for Art and Realism—Sartre asserts that both promote an ideal of detachment that distracts writers from the combats of their age: "The disinterestedness of pure science is like the gratuitousness of Art for Art" (10). Sartre nonetheless asserts that writers are always actively involved in the issues of their time: they are irremediably "in on it," whether they want to be or not. Silence has repercussions, and passiveness is a negative commitment: saying nothing is a form of agreement with the order of the world as it is. Since it is impossible not to take a position, Sartre maintains, you might as well take yours in a voluntary and fully conscious manner. There is, however, according to him, a particular turn of mind that dissuades writers from becoming involved in the battles of their period and thus reinforces the "temptation of irresponsibility." This turn of mind consists in directing one's writings not to one's contemporaries but rather to posterity:

> No doubt, certain authors have concerns that are less current and views that are less short. They pass through us as if they weren't there. So where are they? With their great-nephews, they look backward to judge this bygone era that was ours and of which they are the only survivors. But that is a miscalculation: posthumous glory is always founded on a misunderstanding. What do they know of these nephews who will fish them out from among us! Immortality is a dreadful alibi: it isn't easy to live with one foot beyond the grave and the other on this side. How can you deal with current business when you are looking at it from so far away! How can you engage passionately in a combat or rejoice in a victory! Everything is the same. They watch us without seeing us: we are already dead in their eyes—and they return to the novel they are writing for people that they will never see. They are allowing immortality to steal their lives. (14)

In this passage from the "Presentation of the *Temps modernes*," Sartre anticipates one of the principal questions of *What Is Literature?*(*Qu'est-ce que la littérature?*) (1948). He reminds us that this question—"For whom does one write?"—may be answered: "For posterity." Well, choosing your great-nephews and -nieces and not your contemporaries as your addressee reinforces in an author the "temptation of irresponsibility" evoked above. By addressing this future readership, writers fix a prematurely retrospective gaze on the period to which they belong. This period thus no longer appears to them as *their* period, the one in which they are completely immersed, the one whose battles concern them and engage their responsibility: they see this period, which they observe from a distance, as if it were already bygone—when they do not simply choose to ignore it completely to devote themselves to abstract principles in their books.

The reasoning of Sartre is based on an idea that we have not met anywhere yet, an idea notably alien to the correspondence between Diderot and Falconet. Of course, Sartre develops in passing a traditional argument that we found earlier in Falconet's writings: posthumous glory is always based on a "misunderstanding," because it is awarded on the bases of criteria that are impossible to foresee and by individuals we can know nothing about, since they do not yet exist. Nonetheless, the brunt of the criticism Sartre addresses to the idea of posterity does not consist in saying that it is a mental image devoid of substance (which was the principal argument of Falconet) or in demonstrating that it is a lottery that we never know who will win (as Stendhal puts it). It comes to bear rather on the psychological dispositions regarding the present fostered in writers by the idea of posterity.

In this respect, the concluding sentence of his comment above—"They are allowing immortality to steal their lives"—does not mean what we might tend to think he is saying—that is, that the writers who are turned toward their great-nephews and -nieces make the error of devoting their existence to the production of an oeuvre whose transmission to those who will come after them is highly uncertain. It has a different sense in the argument developed by Sartre, for whom writing for posterity is tantamount to traversing as an indifferent witness the period whose combats and turmoil are represented prematurely in the past form they will take in history books and not in the urgency and immediacy of current struggles that concern the writer first and foremost. By appearing to him as it will be conceived by the members of future generations, the world that surrounds him has no more consistency in his eyes than the still disembodied future toward which he casts his gaze. If writers turned toward posterity have their life stolen by immortality, it is because they are living between two phantasmic times without belonging to either: the one of which they are de facto contemporary, but which they erroneously see as an a posteriori representation; and the other, following their death, which will never exist for them other than in the form of another product of their imagination.

To the question "For whom does one write?" Sartre chooses to answer: "For one's contemporaries and for them alone." The immediate consequence of this decision consists naturally in a loss of interest in posterity's judgment of an author and his works: Sartre renounces any hope of "posthumous rehabilitation" and claims that the only victories of any value are those that the author achieves during his lifetime. However, if the writers who engage passionately in the combats of their age do not do so in order to earn the approval of their "great-nephews" they touch, through their involvement in the issues of their time, on values that go beyond its limits:

> Thus, in taking stands in the uniqueness of our age, we meet, ultimately, the eternal, and it is our task as writers to reveal the eternal values that are innate to these social or political debates. But we aren't interested in going to seek for them in an intelligible heaven: they only hold interest for us in their current state. Far from being relativistic, we declare loudly that man is an absolute. But he is an absolute in his time, in his milieu, on his earth. ... It is not by running after immortality that we become eternal: we will

not be absolutes for reflecting in our works a few emaciated principles, void enough and null enough to pass from one century to another, but because we have fought passionately in our time, because we have loved it passionately and agreed to perish completely with it. (15)

It is the separation of immortality and eternity that Sartre intends to achieve. Immortality is the permanence of an author and of his oeuvre in the network of memories. According to Sartre, eternity is a concept of another nature: it is the sum of immutable values that traverse each age in its turn. Even if men ascribe to these abstract values—we hear them speak in favor of "Justice," "Liberty," and "Equality"—it is always in the context of particular circumstances, of *situations*, that they seek to implement the ideals they promote. When they are contemporaries of Sartre, we hear them confront each other "about the disarming of the FFI or about the aid that should be given to the Spanish Republicans" (15), or else about climate change and the overpopulation of prisons in the United States if they are living in the age of Noam Chomsky—and each of them will strive to promote these values in their actions, their words, and their commitment. Sometimes, of course, their successors may decide that they did disservice to the value for which they claimed to fight: thus the exceptional measures implemented during the Terror did less to defend the cause of Liberty than to suspend it in favor of immediate political and military objectives. In other circumstances, it is their dedication to one of these values that may lead them to flout another: one may go against "Equity" in the name of "Honor," as the judges of Captain Alfred Dreyfus proved in refusing to void his first condemnation by a military tribunal. Doing nothing that might stain the French army seemed preferable to them to freeing an innocent man. Immutable, these values run through successive generations, but the combat in their name always takes on different forms, because it is the work of individuals whose situations are constantly different. When all is said and done, the concepts of eternity and immortality are so distinct in Sartre's language that they become virtually antinomic. For if eternity may only be acquired in one's own time, one must forego writing for immortality, which distracts writers from an engagement in the battles of their era. We thus arrive at this contradiction, which is only apparent since Sartre gave a specific meaning to the terms that compose it: it is only insofar as one gives up immortality that one becomes eternal.

The Sacrifice of Abraham

However, the use that Sartre made of his examples actually undermined the most radical consequence of his reasoning—that is, the symbiotic relationship between an author and his or her time that condemns the former to disappear as soon as the latter is past. Everything happens, in fact, as if giving up posterity were precisely the way to obtain it, a type of experience of renunciation that, provided it is absolute, is reversed to give to the author exactly what he had agreed to lose. Sartre takes in particular the example of Descartes to clarify his distinction between the "absolute" and the "relative": "The absolute is Descartes, the man who escapes us because he is dead, who lived in his time, who reflected on it day after day with the means at hand, who developed his doctrine from a certain state of the sciences . . . ; what is relative is Cartesianism, this wandering philosophy that we carry with us from century to century and in which each person finds what he puts into it" (15–16). But a very simple objection comes to mind: in whose eyes is Descartes this "absolute" if it is not posterity's? Indeed, Sartre demonstrates without wishing to that Descartes did not perish "completely" with his time, since he, himself, three centuries after his disappearance, recognizes the irreducible uniqueness of a philosopher who took his reflection as far as he could with his own inner resources and in the state of scientific knowledge in his age.

In a similar way, while he was distributing praise and blame to his predecessors, Sartre assumed toward them the function of the posthumous tribunal that he claimed to forego for himself. For the great writers of the past are summoned by Sartre, who distinguishes between them according to the nature of their commitment. We have seen that commitment was an element inseparable from the writer's form of existence; if pure noncommitment was impossible, there are nonetheless both conscious and involuntary commitments, commitments for which one takes responsibility as opposed to commitments by abstention. When Sartre writes, "I hold Flaubert and Goncourt responsible for the repression that followed the Commune because they did not write a line to prevent it," or when he salutes successively Voltaire, Émile Zola, and André Gide for having, "in a particular circumstance" (13), taken responsibility as writers, he shows precisely, by his praise and his blame, that a writer's battles in the issues of his or her time have repercussions in the future, and that posterity is there to evaluate retrospectively the consequences of a commitment that is inevitable at the moment in which they are exercising their trade. And how could he not hope that one day a successor, a "great-nephew," would play the same role regarding his own memory that he, himself, adopted toward the great writers of the past? There would surely be someone to recall his defense of Henri Martin, just as there were descendants of Voltaire and Zola to praise their writings in favor of Jean Calas and Alfred Dreyfus. And just as Flaubert had Sartre to re-create his life, *something* of the latter writer survives in the monumental biography of Annie Cohen-Solal.

Although Sartre assumed the traditional role of posterity for others while refusing it for himself, he nonetheless redefined, implicitly and slyly, its rules of access. Traditionally, acceding to posterity is conceived as the fruit of a long dedication: it is the idealized image that had engraved itself in the mind of the young Sartre, as Simone de Beauvoir demonstrated in *The Force of Circumstance*. Sartre rewrote the rules of the game governing the passage into posterity: it is by foregoing it that one ultimately gains it. This feigned renunciation recalls Casanova's sham indifference that concealed a behavior designed to win the admiration of future centuries. However, there is a crucial difference between Casanova's attitude toward posterity and the one adopted by Sartre: his predecessor adopts a conscious ruse, as would a professional gambler, whereas Sartre's renunciation must be authentic to be transformed into a reward. While one is in fact a professional gambler, superstitious and cunning, the other is a man raised in the knowledge of the Bible, who confirms, albeit reluctantly, the sacredness of literature even if he seems to doom its products to oblivion.

Sartre's renunciation of posterity is modelled on the sacrifice of Isaac by Abraham. To please God, Abraham must agree to this sacrifice with absolute obedience, but since it is a father's sacrifice of his own son, Abraham's submission is accompanied by the underlying hope that the act is in fact superfluous, and that the apparent willingness to agree to it will be sufficient. Nonetheless, it is this very hope that Abraham must deflate, because it belies the submission that the Almighty demands: you cannot trick He who knows all and sees in everyone's heart, and Isaac's father will not save him by mimicking the act of sacrifice. Thus Abraham must exhibit an *authentic* obedience to prevent the sacrifice of Isaac and make God's will his own without hoping for anything beyond that: the angel who stops his hand returns his son to him precisely because he has agreed to lose him.

Sartre transfers this religious logic of renunciation transformed into reward when he imagines posterity. Of course, of all the modern writers he is the one who "will have done the most to chasten, in himself but also in us and, in any case, in his contemporaries, the very idea of an oeuvre seeking, on appeal, its final verdict."[21] But this "chastening" is incomplete at the time of the creation of *Les Temps modernes* and cannot entirely destroy the hope for the survival of the texts and of their author in the collective memory. No one who devotes himself entirely to books and thought could consider without horror—despite the affectation of detachment—that books will, in the end, have "no place on this earth," that they are speaking of "nothing that interests us directly," and that, when all is said and done, they will crumble and collapse with nothing remaining except some "ink stains on moldy paper."[22] This morbid complacency in the depiction of the death of books is the equivalent of the submission of Abraham: a farewell as definitive as possible to prepare the reunion. In 1945, Sartre was betting on "the transformation of failure into triumph" and nourished the irrepressible hope that the "refusal of posterity" would, in the end, bring it to him.[23]

Later, at the end of his life, Sartre would go back on this paradoxical renunciation of posterity. In his last autobiographical texts, he claimed to feel "no fear" before the judgment of posterity and, while not being convinced that it would be good, to hope that "it would take place."[24] Or, in "Self-Portrait at Seventy," he could declare to Michel Contat, "I hope that people will still be reading me a hundred years from now—although I'm not too sure of that."[25] Outside testimony brings new proof of this ultimate return to the most traditional concept imaginable of posterity as a means of escaping the anguish of death by the perspective of symbolic immortality. John Gerassi maintains, for example, that "Sartre claimed not to fear death, because his writings guaranteed him immortality."[26] These comments and testimony come several decades after the immediate postwar period, the brutal onslaught of Sartre's celebrity, and the metaphysical crisis he experienced in 1945 as related by Simone de Beauvoir. It is nonetheless remarkable that at the very moment that literature seemed to have a merely transitory value for him, a time when his current fame appeared to deprive him of posthumous glory, he was incapable of foregoing entirely the hope of posterity's embrace. The example of Sartre thus allows us to formulate this final paradox of belief: as vigorous as it may be, there is no renunciation of posterity that succeeds in dispelling the hope of being saved by it *nevertheless.*

THE PARADOXES OF IDENTITY

FOURTH PARADOX
The Proper Noun and the Common Noun

Through the examination of the paradoxes of belief, we have tracked the consequences of the adoption of posterity as a final value by writers, some of whom accept it willingly (like Diderot), while others claim not to (like Casanova and Sartre). By substituting itself for the deity in the minds of writers, posterity determines in them a series of behaviors whose goal is to obtain its goodwill, behaviors that transfer to the secular realm the reverence and calculations of a believer before the deity or, more precisely, that endow Literature with a comparable sacredness by substituting Posterity for the Almighty. The faith pledged to this new deity becomes all the more difficult to question by the very people who claim to have foregone it, as it confers a metaphysical significance on their existence when it has not already replaced in their value system the God that the church of their time enjoined them to venerate. For lack of anything better, and in the absence of a valid alternative to what already represented an alternative, there is nothing else to do but continue to believe in Posterity rather than resign oneself to believe in nothing.

This search for symbolic immortality presupposes, however, a certainty whose legitimacy we have not yet examined: the certainty that it is indeed the creator himself that posterity remembers in speaking of him. What artists seek *in the first place* is never certain. Is it to satisfy a need to express themselves whose result, provided it is aesthetically successful, will permit them in passing to transmit to posterity the memory of their existence? Or is it rather the desire for a symbolic survival that first leads them to create, the oeuvre being the means to reach this metaphysical goal? In both cases, what is never questioned is the identification of the creator with the individual whose existence is inscribed in the web of memories. It is the paradoxes surrounding the notion of identity that will be the subject of this second part—that is, the contradictions that result from the tension between the complexity and mutability of an individual in the course of time and the simplification, the distortion, indeed the fictionalization of what is retained of her or him by posterity. Given that the identity of a person is inseparable from the name that designates her and distinguishes her from others, it is to the author's name that I will devote this section in order to ask if the referent that is associated with her remains identical regardless of the uses to which it is put by the successive members of posterity. In particular, I will ask if the nature of the individual existence identified with the name retained by posterity varies with each new generation.

An Exclusive Club

The creators who aspire to celebrity after their death have no doubt that the first beneficiaries of the "passage into posterity" will be themselves, whose persona will be carried by their oeuvre like passengers on a ship, and who will be the subject of the discourses of future generations—yes, themselves, authors of an oeuvre and authors of their life, both of them designated by the intermediary of this arrangement of letters that they use to state their identity: their surname. Determined, no doubt, by the underlying implications of the metaphor "passage into posterity," which gives rise to the contradictory and simultaneous images of victorious crossing and a fall into limbo, literary people imagine posterity as an exclusive club to which one belongs and whose doors remain closed, with no intermediary positions between the two states nor any evolution of status following admission. However, is the discourse on posterity still about the creator him- or herself, or are we dealing with a reinvention of this persona? Having "passed into posterity," is one's memory spared by the passage of time, or does the author's name progressively come to designate a different person—if not, perhaps, multiple distinct persons—from the one who used it during their lifetime?

In order to study whether time acts on the memory transmitted by those who have, in any case, gained the approval of posterity, it is useful to analyze an example that is both distant and famed. The distance between the present time and the period from which this example is taken will permit us to determine if the action of time leaves intact the memory of those who have survived into posterity; as for fame itself, it will be the sign of a successful passage into posterity, whose public has effectively preserved the memory of an individual long dead. Among the innumerable examples I could have chosen, because they also fit these criteria, the name of Molière must be invoked, not only because he meets the two criteria I have just specified but because the symbolic immortality he enjoys seems virtually unequalled.

"The language of Molière": by the clarity of its meaning, this cliché expresses the capacity of the author of *The Misanthrope* to represent a quintessential form of success. Molière has made the French language so much his own that it is designated by his name: now there you have a success as difficult to equal as to challenge once it has been acquired. Moreover, the numerous forms of institutional recognition that Molière continues to receive—such as the inclusion of his works in school curricula, transforming the knowledge of his plays by past, current, and future students into elements of national unity—are guarantees of the permanence of his name. These undeniable facts regarding Molière's place not only in literary history but also in the construction of the French identity are significant in and of themselves, for they express a loose and spontaneous consensus in which intelligence scarcely plays a role anymore—which, paradoxically, is perhaps the highest form of posthumous recognition an author can ever achieve. But what does this name, so famous, still designate? What remains inside, in the secret of its syllables, of the flesh and blood person who had, in fact, borne it one day? In the *Encyclopedia*, Diderot establishes an identity between "immortality" (understood as "the type of life that we acquire in the memory of men") and the permanence of the name. As he explains, "Names would disappear with empires were it not for the voices of the poet and the historian that pass through times and places and teach them to all centuries and all peoples."[1] If the analogy established by Diderot between the transmission of the name to posterity and symbolic immortality is generally accepted, it is still essential to determine what remains of the individual in the name by which he or she is remembered.

The Name of the Author and Its Referent

At first sight, the example of Molière seems poorly chosen to examine the evolution of an author's name over time, given that, properly speaking, "Molière" is not a name but a pseudonym whose bucolic resonance calls to mind the surnames adopted by numerous actors in the time of Louis XIV (Montfleury, Floridor, Bellerose, etc.). This linguistic creation is comparable to that of the names "Scapin," "Tartuffe," and "Alceste," different only in that it is not a linguistic being that Jean-Baptiste Poquelin baptized in this manner but a very real individual: himself. Nonetheless, the name "Molière" was used by a person whose birth name was known by both his contemporaries and by posterity, so we are faced with a transparent mask that readily reveals the identity of the man wearing it.[2] To account for the variety of cases subsumed under the category "author's name," it is thus less useful to oppose the "family name" to the "pseudonym" than to adopt a different criterion: referential transparency.

By referential transparency, I mean the variable intelligibility, in the eyes of posterity, of the relation between an author's name and the individual it designates. It will be called maximal when the author's name refers to the individual who has employed it continually from birth to death, using it on the covers of his works as well as on official documents (marriage certificates, contracts, receipts, etc.) that are traces of an individual journey left for future generations. The use of this name in the private and public writings of the contemporaries of an author provides posterity with additional evidence that permits it to attest to the existence of the person who bore that name and to verify what it believes it knows about him based on his own words. Among innumerable examples, let us consider Victor Hugo, whom one can hardly accuse of hiding humbly behind his oeuvre. The degree of referential transparency of a surname is scarcely superior to that of a pseudonym, assuming that the latter was openly used throughout a literary career. To the example of Molière, we may add that of Voltaire: in both cases there is no doubt concerning the person designated by the freely adopted name; only a type of intellectual note is made necessary by this transparent pseudonym (Jean-Baptiste Poquelin, aka Molière; François-Marie Arouet, aka Voltaire). On the other hand, the referential intelligibility is clouded in the event that the relationship between the person and the name is troubled by any uncertainty surrounding the identity of the one who has adopted it.

For one thing, it is possible for an individual to adopt a pseudonym without ever admitting it. In this case, the connection between the real person and the author's name is ambiguous in proportion to the difficulty—indeed the impossibility—of relating the pseudonym to the real person who signed the works. The person hiding behind the name "Elena Ferrante" did everything possible to never be discovered—and despite the revelations of an indiscreet reporter, she continues to maintain the secret.[3] But on the other hand, it is equally conceivable that the traces left by the author are scanty and his or her biography full of holes: in this case, the referent of the pseudonym is not ambiguous because the author is hiding behind it, but because the individual to whom the pseudonym refers is himself mysterious. Such is the case of the pseudonym "Count of Lautréamont," clearly adopted by Isidore Ducasse, whereas the biography of Ducasse remains fragmentary. Here, the referential transparency dims because the pseudonym, although it may refer correctly to a given person, identifies someone whose history is not well-known: the connection between the name and the author is a source of uncertainty, for we are too unfamiliar with the individual to whom the name is attached.

Finally, the referential transparency becomes even more opaque when the name of the author designates a subject that it is impossible to identify unambiguously. Does the word "Homer" refer to a blind man or to a Sicilian poetess whose self-portrait is the Princess Nausicaa—or is it just a linguistic way of designating the anonymous bards who, collectively, performed the writing of the *Iliad* and the *Odyssey*?[4] Anne Dacier, the translator of these two poems, refuses to try to settle the question: "Nothing is more natural than the desire to know the life and adventures of a great poet like Homer [. . .]; but, unfortunately, this is a curiosity that will never be satisfied; the most famous of men will always be the least well-known."⁵

Degrees of Referential Transparency: A Typology

Degrees of Referential Transparency	Examples
Crystal Clear: the surname is the author's name.	Victor Hugo
Clear: the surname and the author's name are distinct, but the referent of the pseudonym is known to contemporaries as well as to posterity.	Poquelin / Molière
Cloudy: the surname and the author's name are distinct, and the referent of the pseudonym is hidden by the author.	? / Elena Ferrante
Cloudy: the surname and the author's name are distinct, and the biography of the latter is not well-known.	Isidore Ducasse / Lautréamont

The brief inventory above does not attempt so much to exhaust the possible relationships between the author's name and its referent—it would be possible to enrich this typology with intermediate cases—as to emphasize the very variety of these relationships. Nonetheless, the multiplicity of conceivable relationships between an author's name and the person that it designates in no way prevents an identical and universal evolution: whatever may be the intelligibility of the link between the author's name and its referent, in the course of time and its successive incarnations the author's name becomes a common noun and its biographical referent a fiction continually reworked by the members of posterity.

The Minimal Narrative

Let us return to the name "Molière," which, we have seen, exhibits a paradoxically high degree of referential transparency, despite the fact that it is a pseudonym. The person referred to by this intermediary is perfectly identified and his biography well-known. Whole works have been written on Molière, works that leave gray zones—the opposite would have been surprising—in the life of this man born nearly four centuries ago, but that are no less capable of tracking his existence from his first steps to the day of his disappearance. So I say "Molière," and a digest of my knowledge about him immediately comes to mind: "*son of one of the king's tapestry makers, alienated from his family, traveling the roads of France to amuse the people with his farces; then, back in Paris, he wins favor with the king, becomes the adversary of the religious zealots and the author of masterpieces before dying at the end of a performance of* The Imaginary Invalid." Of course, this *minimal narrative* is still too vast for those who hardly know that Molière was a playwright: I passed through crowds in Asia where perhaps not a single person knew *Tartuffe*. And for the Molière specialist, this rapid tableau is, conversely, irritatingly crude, a portrait executed before the invention of perspective that, compared to the wealth of knowledge that he possesses on this subject, scarcely deserves to be titled "Molière." However, this minimal account embodies the statistical average of the knowledge conserved by posterity, and it is a reduction to this quintessential state that any candidate for the memory of future centuries may envisage as the only reasonable objective.

Posterity, it has been said, has ever more souls in its care. It is the public that collects and transmits to its successive reincarnations the discourse on all of these dead people whose number is constantly growing. Luckily for it—that is, for the community of the living who are, at a given time, the posterity of all those who came before them—in comparison with the number of those who die, the number of individuals who leave objective reasons to be remembered is far lower. Newcomers, however, still come regularly to add themselves to the already interminable list of those, men and women, for whom we are responsible. Thus each generation pulls the wagonload of former centuries whose weight constantly increases, and this Sisyphean voyage is not relieved by the promise of anyone getting off: our only perspective is the increase of both the task and the seriousness inspired by a greater responsibility.

Taken in the broad sense of the expression, institutions of learning are given a leading role in the production and diffusion of posterity's discourse. It is they who share knowledge about those they judge worthy of the memory of new generations. It is they who, in their higher tiers, produce the knowledge that the lower levels synthesize and distribute to the younger. It is they again who, through constant evaluation and ranking, determine the degree of priority to be granted to the memory of one dead person relative to all those who are vying for the attention of the living. This prioritizing is constantly discussed and challenged, both by the production of original research on the deceased and the irruption of newcomers who necessitate the rewriting of literary or intellectual history. These are not vain titles of glory that are distributed to those who, by definition, are no long there to enjoy them; it is, much more radically, variable degrees of posthumous existence that they are granted or denied. A literary figure whose oeuvre is judged secondary by posterity will only be accorded a minor place in the books written after his death. An article of around ten pages will be devoted to him or her, one in which their obscure name will be cited alongside that of more illustrious contemporaries, or we will find that author relegated to the narrow space of a footnote. The ink used by posterity to evoke a past existence is the ritual instrument of an invocation: it is in proportion to the quantity of ink sacrificed to them that the dead are brought back to a greater or lesser spectral life.

Whatever the amount of ink actually sacrificed to deceased authors, however, the most famous of them will never occupy more than an absurdly small portion of the global memorial space possessed by posterity. Even if Molière occupies a place comparatively vaster than that enjoyed by Gédéon Tallemant des Réaux or Jean-Louis Guez de Balzac, the memory of his existence and that of his works is only a tiny fraction of the memory for which posterity is responsible. If the memory of an author is ultimately reduced to the form of a "minimal narrative," it is because this narrative embodies the statistical average of the ignorance and expertise held in common by all those who, at a certain point, constitute the posterity of all those who precede them. This concept is inseparable from that of "general culture," in the two complementary senses that we may give this expression: the culture that a given individual possesses concerning the world in general and the culture that the general public possesses concerning a given subject. Taken separately, the individuals who form at a point in time the group called "posterity" have variable degrees of knowledge and interest regarding a cultural object. The memory of an author will be conserved like a lively flame by some, while her or his works will only evoke in others some vague associations of ideas, and even for the former, this memory is liable to decrease, fade, and join in the same obscurity those writers that we only know *by name*.[6]

Taken collectively, on the other hand, these variable degrees of expertise and ignorance merge into an average. Of an author and his or her works, if we consider all their possible legatees, there remains a kind of condensed legend, or common knowledge, in the best of cases held vaguely by everyone (Who knows absolutely *nothing* of Shakespeare? The Uros I met years ago on Lake Titicaca, *perhaps*), but more often preserved by a minuscule number of guardians of the torch. Consequently, being recognized by posterity never means, for authors, leaving an exhaustive memory of their works and existence to the group of individuals that constitute future generations: that would occupy an excessively large memorial space. If they address this memory to those who collectively survive them, an overwhelming majority of those individuals will respond with indifference.

Here, however, we may foresee an objection. Is not the minority in question in fact the very heart of posterity that authors are specifically addressing? If the memory of their oeuvre and life is similar to an open letter to all the conceivable addressees of future times, do they not know that among the latter, only the small group of those interested in books in each period will hear their appeal and preserve the memory of their passage on Earth? Rather than universal notoriety, do not certain people prefer the esteem of a small community, the *happy few* to whom Stendhal was speaking? But what, in truth, is the memory preserved at the heart of these small societies? Is it still the author, in his or her indomitable uniqueness?

From the Proper Noun to the Common Noun

As a person who exists, I undergo a succession of experiences that are linked seamlessly; I can, of course, distinguish developments and turning points, but it is nonetheless true that possible adventures are capable, at each instant, to cast new light on the meaning that I give to my past. I can decide, for instance, to become involved in politics after exhibiting toward it a complete indifference. This commitment will lead me to reevaluate the meaning that I formerly assigned to past experiences; thus the indifference I had exhibited in the past for public affairs will no longer appear to me as the logical consequence of my dedication to superior ideals (the search for truth or for aesthetic perfection). I will henceforth interpret it as a kind of regrettable egoism I am pleased to have cast off. As long as I am still living, the unpredictable orientation of my future will suspend the determination of the meaning I can give to my past. But those who survive me have the task of organizing my former existence within a narrative of their making; they have to determine what event was "foundational," what other one was a "break" or a "turning point"; and the production of this discourse on my life will generate in turn other discourses that are positioned in relation to the former, such that from volume to volume my existence becomes what others make of it from the moment I am no longer there to answer them and pursue my mutations. This is what one calls a "biography": the fossilization of a life that hardens ever more with each of the new discourses devoted to it. Not content with assuming the right to write my existence, my successors appropriate my works as well: those that I liked the most are liable to appear inferior to those that I, for my part, considered to be simple recreation. Voltaire wanted to be an author of epic poetry: other than a handful of specialists, who has finished reading *La Henriade* (1728)?[7] This disagreement between an author and his or her posterity regarding the ranking of their works does not necessarily demonstrate the wisdom of an outside judgment. In other words, posterity does not necessarily exhibit a rationality that is superior to that of the author, and its opinion of an oeuvre does not become more objective over time. Posterity is, after all, only a public, a public with its prejudices, its unconscious favoritism, its assumptions—and passions that are just as ardent when provoked by the deceased as by one's contemporaries.[8] It is quite possible that the consensus it expresses toward writers known as "classic" indicates less the clarity of vision produced by a progressive distancing from the object being judged than a form of intellectual laziness consisting in the adoption, without daring to question them, of judgments rendered by predecessors. Likewise, literary modes evolve, taste changes, genres formerly considered minor are now the most prestigious: the novel was a vulgar form of entertainment in the seventeenth century; today people hardly read anything else.[9]

Thus the life and works of an author are bequeathed to posterity, who does with them what it will. Naturally, it was necessary for *someone* to live for the texts to come into being, but the discourse produced on the person and her or his writings frees itself progressively from its supporting material and becomes the equivalent of a work of fiction. Because fiction—everyone knows—is also founded on truth. To write a novel, an author has to meet a large number of authentic individuals, and very often fuses together these diverse personalities to create with these heterogeneous fragments the monster called a character. Posterity does nothing different with an author: it seizes some biographical material—or, at least, the knowledge it succeeds in gathering about an author's billions of experiences, thoughts, and sentiments, often contradictory—before organizing it into a narrative. This fictionalizing of biography is never as clear as in the works that represent the writer among his or her characters: Jean de La Fontaine is staged beside the lion and the rat; Lewis Carroll chats with Alice's rabbit; Molière masquerades as a certain Tartuffe and frequents a Monsieur Jourdain, who does not know how to declare his love to Célimène.[10] In their very fantasy, these works bear witness to the typical action of posterity: a process of appropriation in which the biographical narrative is revealed to be a fiction because it is mixed up in the inventions sprung from the mind of an author.

It is true that said authors are capable of anticipating the narrative that posterity will produce about them and orient it in a direction of their choosing. In their public writings, they present themselves in the guise of the persona they wish to embody for the eyes of future generations: that of the committed intellectual, the itinerant writer, the prince's counselor, the aesthete in his or her ivory tower, the universally misunderstood individual, the Balzac-like laborer. This list could be extended, but, in all truth, by only a small number of models: the roles that an artist aspires to espouse are not so numerous, on the one hand because there are only a limited number of mythologies to adorn the art of writing and, on the other hand, because young authors inherit these postures and forge an ideal from them that, if it does not prevent them from producing variations from it in the course of time, perhaps diverts them from inventing completely new ones. There is no doubt that in their private writings authors may reveal less heroic individuals, less worthy of the admiration of future centuries than those they were composing for that purpose; whence the interest that specialists evince in texts that they were not intended to read (personal correspondence in particular), and that give them the impression that they have gained access to the *inner* truth of that person.

However, these private writings may by subjected to a posteriori treatments that serve the interests of the author. On the one hand, authors may request the return of letters, which they may burn to conceal secrets that otherwise would have fallen into the hands of the inquisition led by successors. On the other, it is always possible to rewrite letters to invent evidence that supports the legend under construction: with posterity in mind, Voltaire modified after the fact his Prussian correspondence, in the hope of presenting himself in a favorable light in his disputes with Frederick the Great.[11] In other words, in a histrionic manner accompanied by a staging—indeed a falsification—of documents, authors are capable of inventing a persona with which they wish to be identified by future generations. But despite their ability to formulate in advance the discourse that posterity will accord them, to bequeath to it the very words and images they wish it to use in speaking of them, authors never leave of themselves anything but a fiction. It is a fiction of which they are, of course, partially the creators, but in the knowledge that it dissimulates their internal contradictions, their flaws, sometimes their vices and the fear that haunts them when they reflect that they are perhaps not worthy of the legend that they are inventing for themselves. Their very success may be a burden for them, for it locks them up in the golden but narrow frame of a full-length portrait in formal dress. Alphonse de Lamartine, quoted by Pierre Michon, had urges to break the image that he had nonetheless worked to construct: "The good public believes that I spent thirty years of my life making rhymes and gazing at the stars. I didn't spend more than thirty months doing this, and poetry was only a form of prayer for me."[12] Too bad: it is as a smartly dressed poet, melancholically gazing at the water of a beautiful lake, that he will be remembered. Sometimes an author anticipates his or her legend, sometimes his successors invent it for them, but it is always in this inauthentic and simplified form that he or she *passes into* posterity.

Whatever may be the referential intelligibility it exhibits, strong or weak, supported by multiple corroborating testimonies or, on the contrary, depending on a history so lengthy that it is filled with uncertainties, the author's name is virtually always subject to a similar evolution: for posterity in general it is the vessel of a minimal narrative that passes over the essential content of a life, and for that part of posterity that is actively interested in books, the name is nothing but the title given to this narrative called "biography." Thus the name of an author who has disappeared eventually no longer designates her or him: the proper noun has become a common noun. A common noun in the normal sense of the term, because through metonymy it is possible to view it as a synonym of a thing: "I read a Balzac," "the Virgil on the mantel." A common noun in the figurative sense as well, for its referent is no longer a person but the collective invention of that person, the *common* oeuvre of posterity with which the author concerned would most often have only found a vague resemblance with himself.

Thus the quest for posterity presupposes this insurmountable paradox: posterity consists, for authors, in transmitting the memory of their existence by means of language, but, in the end, they are themselves reduced to language, such that their life is no longer anything but the medium of a collective invention—what we call legend. This is why everything, absolutely everything, is literature: there are only stories built on stories. Humanity tells itself stories about those who composed it, and people who expect praise from future generations offer their existence as the material for a collective rewriting. By dint of living among books and being constantly concerned with them, authors becomes the victims of an Ovid-like metamorphosis: they become books in their turn.

FIFTH PARADOX
The Flow and the Entity

In the preceding chapter, I tried to highlight one of the contradictions implied by the quest for symbolic immortality: while literary figures yearn to transmit the memory of their existence to future generations, the latter only ever remember their fictional double, if not multiple doubles whose identity varies according to the person who remembers them. *Someone* is embraced by posterity, and symbolic immortality, as such, is not challenged since the memory of an existence is effectively perpetuated, but the discourse accorded that existence is constantly reconfigured in the course of its shaping by posterity, such that its referent ends up largely erased. It is rendered enigmatic by the superimposition of words that claim to know it, like a portrait covered by so many sketches of the same subject that the original image, disappearing under numerous palimpsests, becomes over time indiscernible. In other words, the *reinvention* of the person who wishes to be remembered *authentically* reveals a paradox inherent in the search for symbolic immortality.

Yet more radically, I will now ask if the belief in the existence of an individual likely to be remembered by posterity is not itself the product of an illusion. It is no longer a matter of determining if it is possible for posterity to remember a creator in a way that does justice to the complexity of that individual, but if there ever was a subject that future generations could in fact remember. The wavering of belief in spiritual immortality and the concomitant spread of belief in symbolic immortality are major events in Western thought whose emergence I placed in the eighteenth century, under the combined influence of a challenge to traditional religious authorities and the development of philosophical materialism. This remarkable turn in the history of beliefs is witnessed by the cult of "great men" and the glorification of those who have been useful to humankind.[1] While avoiding an overly radical distinction between "Western thought" and "Eastern thought"—one of whose pitfalls consists is underestimating the ultimate overlapping of certain of the conclusions of their particular thought, as well as neglecting the convergences revealed by the translation of texts representative of their respective traditions—I would like now to show that the belief in symbolic immortality presupposes in the Western world a conception of the person that is contrary to that cultivated by Eastern thought, and Buddhist thought in particular. The questioning of the existence of the subject, as it is spontaneously understood by everyone, is not just one dimension of Buddhism among others: it constitutes a necessary precondition for the realization of the spiritual journey that it advocates. It is thus obvious for us to seek in Buddhism, rather than any other Eastern religion, arguments in favor of the conventional and ultimately erroneous concept of the subject.

With the goal of revealing a new paradox of identity, I will compare the definition that is given of this concept in the Bible to the teachings of the Buddhist tradition. The choice of these references may be explained, of course, by the immeasurable influence they have exercised in the West and the East, but also and especially by the desire to follow what I have called the "metaphysical thread" of this investigation into posterity. The belief in the latter involves nothing less than the justification of an existence and belongs to the final values that an individual is likely to embrace; through posterity, we are dealing with the idea that individuals conceive of their destiny after death. To question the idea of posterity in the West and in the East in the light of both the Bible and Buddhist tradition will help us determine how belief in symbolic immortality is affected by the spiritual and cultural context in which it develops. It will also lead us to explore a question that this book has only barely touched on for the moment, that of the ethical value of the search for posthumous recognition. While there is scarcely any doubt in the West that this quest is legitimately desirable—we have seen with Diderot that the very anticipation of the judgment of posterity stimulates a desire for grandeur in the person concerned—this aspiration, with all the egoism and metaphysical presuppositions it implies, is a major obstacle to spiritual awakening according to Buddhist thought.

Uniqueness of the Person and Faith in Resurrection

I will pass rapidly over what I call belief in the uniqueness of the person, because what I understand by that is what we understand conventionally—that is, the conviction that there exists an irreplaceable, autonomous, defined, and durable if not eternal subject, a subject that we designate by the personal pronoun "I," recognizing that it evolves over time without our ever losing the ability to identify with it. We say, "I am the same," thus asserting the stability of a principle that perseveres despite the modification of our body, the variation of our states of mind, and the gain and loss of symbolic attributes (power, fame, reputation, success, etc.). And even if we say, "I changed," we always recognize that a particular subject remains beneath these alterations. While the predicates of this substance may vary, the substance itself stays intact.[2] This spontaneous conception of a subject as the holder of an identity, a name, and a unique existence is based on the Bible in the West and is prolonged in the faith in resurrection, as Cardinal Godfried Danneels reminds us.

Author of a pastoral letter written in 1991 for the Easter celebrations and reproduced seven years later in the periodical *Questions actuelles*, Cardinal Danneels evokes certain fundamental principles of Christian dogma in order to contrast them with the Buddhist belief in reincarnation.[3] He presents that belief as one of the possible responses to the problem of the postmortem destiny of individuals, the two others being the Christian response of resurrection and the materialist response of definitive annihilation. Quoting statistics, he announces that faith in reincarnation is making headway in the Western world, not only outside the Christian community but in the very ranks of its faithful.[4] He finds two possible explanations for the increasing growth in the Old World of this "Eastern" belief. On the one hand, the church did not speak enough "of the beyond, of the sense of injustice, of the difficulty of accepting the brevity of life." The excessive discretion of the Catholic priests on these themes would thus be at the origin of a metaphysical void that Buddhism was conveniently filling. On the other hand, the very people who claimed to believe in reincarnation did not distinguish it properly from resurrection, such that the proliferation of Buddhism did not indicate so much a colonization of Western souls by an exogenous religion as a simple semantic misunderstanding. To clarify the distinction between reincarnation and resurrection and to reaffirm that the Christian response is the only one that adequately describes the fate of individuals after their death, Cardinal Danneels recalls several fundamental principles of Christian dogma: "After our earthly life—which is unique and cannot be reproduced—God will resuscitate us, each of us personally, as He did for his Son. For He loves each of us individually, and in his eyes we all bear a unique name. We are not a pearl on the necklace of rebirths constantly occurring to constantly result in death. Death was vanquished by Christ once and for all. We are thus liberated from death and from any reincarnation."[5]

It would be possible to suggest a critical reading of this letter for two complementary reasons. On the one hand, it contains a certain number of inaccuracies in the version that it produces of the belief in reincarnation. Cardinal Danneels asks if Buddhism is not wrong to use this term, given that it denies the very existence of a *subject*.[6] In so doing, he is in no way demonstrating an error of terminology, and even less an inherent contradiction in Buddhist thought, but rather an incorrect understanding of the belief in reincarnation, since Buddhism claims the continuity of existences without implying the permanence of an entity that constitutes a subject.[7] What we thus have here is just one example among others of the deformation of Buddhist thought by the defenders of Christian dogma that was so typical of the writings of Pope John Paul II.[8]

On the other hand, Cardinal Danneels does not subject belief in resurrection to the systematic questioning he imposes on faith in reincarnation. Citing the work of Ian Stevenson—a professor at the University of Virginia who investigated hundreds of children throughout the world whose memories were attached to a deceased person[9]—Cardinal Danneels observes that the doctrine of reincarnation cannot claim to be a scientific explanation, and that there exists, ultimately, no "binding conclusion in favor of reincarnation."[10] On the one hand, Stevenson's work is based, of course, on facts, testimony that he very carefully documents, and that he subjects to a rigorous critical examination. This testimony exhibits a level of truth comparable to that which historians use to produce a discourse on events that they could not experience personally: to deny it the status of proof is tantamount to calling into question any pretention to truth developed from the words of others, therefore undermining the foundations of a large part of the social sciences. On the other hand, there is a certain dishonesty in noting the absence of any "binding conclusion" in favor of the belief in reincarnation. Stevenson admits quite clearly, in fact, that the cases he is analyzing *suggest* the truth of the phenomenon of reincarnation: if certain of them seem more convincing and decisive than others, none of them has the value of a proof that he would consider definitive.[11]

In order to reestablish the balance between Buddhism and Christianity, it would be equitable to turn Cardinal Danneels's question around and ask him what "binding conclusions" he can offer in favor of the resurrection of Christ. Although Cardinal Danneels's letter prompts us to contest the legitimacy of certain of his refutations, it is less its polemical content that interests us than his insistence on two elements of prime importance in the Christian faith: that a human being only has one life, and that this unique subject will be resuscitated, through Christ's love, at the Last Judgment. It is said in Hebrews (9:27), "Men only die once, after which there is a judgment," and it is notably on this text that the Second Vatican Council based its reaffirmation of the uniqueness of human life in the face of the growing faith in reincarnation.[12]

The concept of a subject entity possessing a unique existence is taken up by the very people who replace the hope in spiritual immortality with the search for symbolic immortality. Even if I were to refuse to believe in the existence of a creator who will embrace me in the afterlife, I will no less continue to identify myself with an entity whose existence is the sole opportunity to realize a unique potential. In other words, the secular rewriting of the purpose of human existence as the diffusion of the memory of an existence in the network of memories retains two metaphysical presuppositions that the Christian faith constantly reaffirms: that there exists a subject entity, and that this entity only has one life. This rewriting demonstrates the propensity of a body of critical thought to retain, despite itself, the metaphysical presuppositions of the doctrine from which it is striving to dissociate itself.

But what happens when we change the culture of reference? More precisely, what happens when we renounce the belief in a subject entity as well as in the uniqueness of existence by referring to the fundamental teachings of Buddha? In particular, does this not transform our conception of the ethical value of the search for posterity?

The Five Aggregates of Attachment

Twenty-five centuries ago, when the prince Siddhartha Gautama attained his Awakening after a long labor, he resolved to share with the human race the wisdom he had acquired. But the truths he had conceived were so subtle that he doubted people would be capable of understanding them. He thus reflected on the means to formulate teachings that could be understood by everyone and would succeed in guiding beings, step by step, on the path of liberation. This progressive education began in the Sarnath Deer Park and was delivered to the five ascetics who had accompanied him at the beginning of his quest. In his first sermon, Buddha sets out "Four Noble Truths" concerning the human condition. These are the truth of suffering in the conditioned world; the truth of the cause of suffering; the truth of the possibility of putting an end to suffering; and the truth of the path that leads to the end of suffering.[13] They constitute the "structural framework of all of the more advanced teachings of Buddha" and are in fact a corollary of the medical practices of his time: "1. Establish a diagnosis of the sickness; 2. Identify its cause; 3. Determine if it is curable; 4. Determine a means to treat it."[14] The first of the Noble Truths describes both the impregnation of human existence by *dukkha* (a Buddhist concept combining the idea of the inherent painfulness of life with its lack of satisfaction) and the composite character of the person: "Birth is dukkha, old age is dukkha, sickness is dukkha, death is dukkha; sorrow, lamentations, pain, grief and despair are dukkha; association with what one dislikes is dukkha, separation from what one likes is dukkha; not to get what one wants is dukkha: *in short, the five groups (as objects) of grasping (which make up a person) are dukkha.*"[15]

Of what are we speaking when we use Buddha's expression "the five groups of grasping," also translated as the "five aggregates of attachment"? An "aggregate" (*skandha* in Sanskrit) is a group of mutable elements whose interaction with other similar groups is improperly confused with a unique, autonomous, and durable entity. Gérard Huet observes that the term *skandha* may be translated by the expression "constitutive factor of the ego," adding that the teaching of Buddha advises us to "liberate ourselves from them by becoming aware of their vacuity."[16] The five aggregates are the corporal form, sensation, perception, mental formations, and the discriminating consciousness. Before undertaking the analysis of the five aggregates, and in order to clarify their meaning, we must establish the reason they are qualified by the term "attachment." Each of these groups is, by itself, the object of a subjective investment on the part of the person concerned, as if it were a defining component of that person's very substance. I say "my body," "my sensations," "my perception," "my character," "my conscience," but if, as we shall see, there exists, according to Buddhism, no permanence either in the elements composing these groups or in the reciprocal relations of the latter, or even in any abstract entity that would combine them, where does this "I," whose existence I claim as mine, reside? Nowhere, replies Buddhism, for whom the concept of "I" is the result of an erroneous mental construction.

I must make here another preliminary remark, concerning the role played by the development that is going to follow in this reflection on posterity. If, as Buddhism maintains, the existence of an autonomous and durable "I" is an illusion, then any action whose goal consists in satisfying the imperious demands of the ego reinforces the strength of this illusion by provoking a moral suffering that Buddha attempts, on the contrary, to eliminate. In this respect, the desire to inscribe in the network of memories the memory of the existence of a subject would be the result of an inadequate understanding of the nature of the person as well as the source of self-inflicted suffering. In other words, it would be both false from an ontological viewpoint and detrimental from an ethical viewpoint. To demonstrate this, it is necessary to establish clearly the composite and mutable nature of the person, which is possible to accomplish by describing the five aggregates of attachment distinguished by Buddhism.

The first aggregate is the matter that constitutes the body of a sentient being. This aggregate consists of four elements that interact: solidity ("earth"), fluidity ("water"), heat ("fire"), and movement ("air"). When a person dies, these elements dissolve one after the other.[17] In its very constitution, the body is not the same for a single moment: the cellular renewal demonstrates its intrinsic mutability. Formed of one hundred thousand billion cells that are divided into two hundred and fifty different types, the human body loses twenty billion cells every day, while twenty million of the cells that compose it are multiplied by two every second. With the exception of the neurons and the cardiac cells, whose renewal is slow or nearly nonexistent, all our organs, our tissues, and our cells are regenerated in the course of our life. These myriad and incessant changes demonstrate that the illusion of corporal unity conceals the inconspicuous truth of an exorbitant impermanence.

The second aggregate is composed of the group of sensations and emotions that arise from the contact between the world and our senses. These emotions are never monochromatic; every one of them is mixed and tends to be reversed. Buddhism remarks, in fact, that the experience of desire is permeated with a suffering that continues, multifaceted, diffuse, and mental, even when its object has been reached: possessing what we desire does not mark the end of the lack but the rise of regrets, worries, and new desires. Thus our emotions never have the purity we hope for, or only for moments that are so fleeting that their very disappearance is a new source of suffering.

The third aggregate—perception—refers to the group of intellective activities that permit us to know, recognize, and interpret physical or mental objects: it is through our perception that we identify whatever we are confronted with, in both the physical and mental spaces. When an object is revealed to our senses, perception intervenes and characterizes it as this person that we have already met; when an emotion arises in our consciousness, perception is there to say, "It is fear," or "It is a great joy." It accomplishes its work incessantly at varied and simultaneous levels, since its activity bears on the changing material objects that strike our senses at the same time as it deals with ideal objects it identifies in our consciousness.

The fourth aggregate combines the mental formations—that is, the psychological dispositions that determine the actions of a person and the nature of their karmic repercussions.[18] Certain of them are named "virtuous" (such as humility) by reason of their capacity to bring happiness to an individual in this life and in the ones that follow, whereas others (like malevolence) are called "non-virtuous" because they result in one's current and future misfortune. As for "neutral" formations, they combine the mental states that are capable of engendering both virtuous and non-virtuous acts: thus regret is virtuous when it promotes spiritual progression and becomes non-virtuous when it tends toward mortification.

The last aggregate—the "discriminating consciousness"—is the cognitive process resulting from the group of psychological phenomena. One of the basic activities of the discriminating consciousness is the production of knowledge about the contents that are communicated to it by the senses. If the discriminating consciousness acts on the other aggregates, it is influenced by them at the same time: it is thus not a reigning faculty that controls the others but the receptacle of mental phenomena whose emergence is provoked by the other aggregates. While certain of its contents change from one second to the next, others tend to appear on a recurring basis and thus to be perceived as the "character" of a person.[19]

It is impossible to extract anything from Buddhist thought that is not connected to other elements in its system. In addition, this system is so subtle and demanding that each of its concepts should be the subject of a detailed commentary to do justice to both its multiple nuances and its relationships with the rest of the doctrine. What precedes is thus far too rapid in at least two respects: because it should have clarified the links between the description of the five aggregates and other aspects of Buddhist thought, in particular the theory of the interdependence of phenomena or "conditioned coproduction"; and because the explanation I devoted to each of the aggregates only gives a summary idea of the composite elements they include and the complementarity that characterizes their functioning.

This presentation is nonetheless sufficient to suggest in what sense the conception of an entity called "subject" is mistaken in the Buddhist perspective. "What we call a 'person,'" Peter Harvey sums up, "is a rapidly mutable collection of mental and physical processes in interaction that lead over time to the reoccurrence of character traits. Only partial control may be exercised over these processes, with the result that they frequently change in an undesirable manner and lead to suffering. Since they are impermanent, they cannot constitute an immutable Self."[20] According to Buddhism, not only does the subject entity not exist, but cultivating the belief in this idea is at the origin of suffering that it would be possible to avoid by eradicating, at its root, the illusion that causes them.

Posterity in the Light of the Noble Truths

If we proceed to a reevaluation of the concept of personal identity inspired by Buddhist teachings, to the point of recognizing the conventional character of any expression indicating the existence of a subject entity, what are the consequences for the meaning given to the quest for posterity? In particular, does the ethical value assigned to the inscription of the subject in the network of memories change the moment it is questioned in the light of the second of the Noble Truths, the one that identifies desire as the cause of all of the suffering permeating human existence?

"The first sermon identifies three types of desire: the desire for sensual pleasures, that for existence, and that for non-existence. The second category includes the pursuit of personal interest, of reinforcement of the ego, and of eternal life after death as one's *self*," Harvey observes.[21] In the Buddhist perspective, the search for posterity is revealed in several complementary senses as the origin of an increase in suffering in the conditioned world. This search entails suffering at a fundamental level, because it is the result of a desire: since it is said that desire leads to action and action to suffering, the quest for symbolic immortality cannot avoid infusing in the existence of the individual who pursues it an underlying suffering.[22] However, it is not only because it responds to a desire that the search for posterity is a cause of suffering but because the very existence of the object whose lack it laments is problematic. For even if desiring an object occasions inevitable pain (if only the pain inherent to a decision that quashes any alternative possibility), the existence of this object is not put into question by the person who obtains it. I can recognize, of course, that a new car is not bringing me the joy I was expecting from it, that it is even becoming the cause of new concerns that I did not envisage formerly; its reality, the fact that it is there in front of my eyes, is nonetheless indisputable—unless I choose to adopt a form of idealism refuted by certain Buddhist thinkers, such as Chandrakirti (ca. 600–650), that casts doubt on the existence of objects outside of my consciousness.[23]

This is not the case with posterity, which is the desire of an object whose attainment will always remain uncertain. The obscure writers are no more assured that their work will be remembered in the future than the most famous authors: the disinterest that greets the works of the first may well be perpetuated, and the celebrity of the second die with them. Moreover, the web of memories is in perpetual reorganization, such that the search for posterity presupposes the permanence of the memory of a changing, composite individual through the intermediary of a community that is itself heterogeneous and mutable. Thus the desire to be one of posterity's chosen is the cause of incessant subjective suffering, for people who nourish it can never know for certain if they will obtain satisfaction, and even if a period of posthumous attention were granted them, who can tell them that this notoriety will not be succeeded by complete obscurity?

Still other reasons may be added to the above to demonstrate that the quest for posterity entails multiple forms of suffering that, from a Buddhist perspective, would justify suspending it in the interest of the person who is pursuing it. This quest presupposes, in fact, the existence of an individual entity whose uniqueness I exalt: it is not only because I believe in the existence of a substantial self but also because I affirm the uniqueness of his productions that I proclaim the legitimacy of the transmission of both his works and the memory of his existence to those who will come after him. Nourished, reinforced, this belief in the existence of the self brings about an escalation of suffering in this life: any questioning of the possibility of the transmission of my work to posterity adds to the pain experienced by a "self" that loves itself sufficiently to wish to persist after its death. As Matthieu Ricard observes, originality—a concept based on the belief in the absolute uniqueness of an artist—does not constitute an aesthetic value in countries where, like Tibet, the teachings of Buddha have since the seventh century permeated the consciousness, mores, and entire mode of life:

Moreover, the notion of "novelty," the desire to invent constantly in order not to repeat the past, is in my opinion an exacerbation of the importance accorded the "personality," the individuality that should at all cost express itself in an original manner. In a context in which one tries, on the contrary, to dissolve this attachment to the all-powerful self, this race to originality seems at the very least superficial. The idea, for example, that an artist must always strive to liberate his or her imagination is of course alien to a traditional art, a sacred art, which is a support for meditation or reflection. Western art often seeks to create an imaginary world, whereas sacred art helps to penetrate the nature of reality. . . . There exist magnificent expressions of sacred art in Tibet; the artists devote much heart and talent to it, but their own personality disappears entirely behind the work. Tibetan painting is, by this fact, essentially anonymous.[24]

In the light of these reflections, it appears that the search for posterity is opposed to the prescriptions of Buddhism for three complementary reasons. On the one hand, this search grants value to the affirmation of a creative uniqueness, whereas Buddhism emphasizes the interdependence of beings within the conditioned world. On the other hand, it exhibits the insatiable pride of individuals who seek the admiration of their fellow creatures after their death, whereas Buddhism considers humility to be a virtuous mental predisposition. Finally, it adds to the suffering of individuals by subjecting the metaphysical significance of their existence to the approbation of a public that is yet to be born, and whose judgment of their work remains unknowable.

From the viewpoint of the personal ethics it requires one to cultivate, the search for posterity is likewise contrary to the recommendations of Buddhist thought. As the Dalai Lama reminds us, we all hope to be happy and avoid suffering.[25] In this respect, there exists between ourselves and all those we meet a congruity of aspirations indicating our membership in one and the same community, whose members only succeed in attaining happiness by working for that of others. Conversely, the ambition of artists who strive to inscribe the memory of their names in the network of memories leads to the development of an adversarial attitude toward their peers. The space in this network being limited by nature, a struggle for posthumous recognition is engaged between candidates for the memory of future centuries and all their contemporaries who seem to desire, at their expense, the same thing. And in the event that one of them might exhibit a greater probability of postmortem fame, jealousy and hate of this superior genius, and the accompanying hate of oneself, are the ordinary consequences.

However, the most striking contradiction between the teachings of Buddhism and the search for posterity is revealed in the examination of faith in reincarnation, that very faith that Cardinal Danneels attempted to refute through the authority of the Bible. In the West, the uniqueness of existence assigns to individuals the duty to realize in their current lives their creative potential: subjects have only one life to bring to fruition the talents they have been granted. From the Buddhist perspective, what are commonly called "subjects" do not accept the uniqueness of their current existence: they know that other lives will come after their own. Moreover, I say "their own," as if there existed a permanent entity experiencing its successive lives, while properly speaking it is not "they" who remain in changing bodies but a dynamic continuity of consciousness joining in the end a new corporal vehicle. Ricard clarifies for us the concept of reincarnation by distinguishing it from this other concept with which it has been improperly confused since the introduction of Buddhist thought in the West—that is, metempsychosis: "To begin with, it is necessary to understand that what we call reincarnation in Buddhism has nothing to do with the transmigration of any kind of 'entity,' nothing to do with metempsychosis. So long as we reason in terms of entities rather than functions and continuity of experience, the Buddhist concept of rebirth cannot be understood. It is said that 'no thread passes through the pearls of the necklace of rebirths.' There is no identity of a 'person' across successive rebirths, only the conditioning of a flow of consciousness."[26]

The Western belief in the existence of a subject entity—a unique, autonomous, durable substance—is opposed to the Buddhist conception of the person: an aggregate of aggregates, a union of psychic and physical materials of an impermanent nature and with variable interactions, which becomes after death a flow of consciousness that, at the end of a sojourn in this intermediary state between the last breath and the next, named *bardo* by Tibetan Buddhism, is transmitted to a new body carrying with it the silt of karmic debts and the golden threads of virtuous actions. In this perspective, the anguish associated with the irreparable disappearance of the person is not a determining cause of creative activity: other lives will come, and perhaps the artistic apprenticeship, like the spiritual improvement that requires hundreds of existences to lead to nirvana, is the result of an evolution that began well before the birth of the current incarnation. One is not born Proust, but rather becomes him, after innumerable lives.

Thus the belief in the cycle of reincarnations radically modifies the ethical significance of the quest for posterity. If I am called to be reborn after the conclusion of this life, the preservation of the memory of this one has no value any more essential than that of previous and future lives: it is not the unique existence of an irreplaceable entity but rather one of the multiple spaces in which a flow of consciousness works toward its perfection. "I" no more exists than this life exists in the conventional sense of the term—that is, as the stretch of limited time beyond which nothing has been nor will ever be any longer: other lives will come that will be the complementary space in which the constant reorganizations of this impermanent flow that I call "me" will take place. Perhaps one of these ulterior "me's" will discover the works written by its preceding incarnation and will find in it an encouragement, a knowledge, or a consolation without knowing *who* had *really* obtained it for him or her. Just as the search for posterity testifies to a poor understanding of the nature of the individual, it exhibits an inaccurate appreciation of the nature of existence, an existence constantly begun again, infinite as long as the cycle of reincarnations has not been broken. It is not a question of diminishing the value of this life by submitting that it is only, after all, one of those that a mutable flow of consciousness will experience. Much to the contrary: since it is the space of a progression toward spiritual perfection, it is infinitely precious. But we must consider it as an existence among those, innumerable, during which our spiritual journey is accomplished, sometimes in the sense of a greater wisdom, sometimes in a retreat toward the ignorance of the ultimate nature of things.

It is said, "If one were to were to pile the ashes and bones of oneself burnt in this everlasting transmigration, the pile would be mountain high; if one were to collect the milk of mothers which he suckled during his transmigration, it would be deeper than the sea."[27] Following the precepts of the Buddhist doctrine, the preservation of the memory of a life could not constitute a final value as is the case in the West, given that it is only one existence among many others. And the very fact that we tend to identify with the person who experiences this existence and wish that she be remembered in the future indicates that we are ignorant of the mutability of the "self" and aim to reinforce its importance instead of deconstructing it by meditating on its composite, dependent, and fluid nature. A new paradox of posterity emerges around the Buddhist conception of the nature of the subject: there can be no transmission of the memory of what, properly speaking, never existed.

SIXTH PARADOX
The Distance and the Judgment

The examination of the fifth paradox demonstrated that the intention to transmit the memory of a past existence to posterity is contrary to the principles and goals of Buddhist thought. This undertaking presumes a belief in the stability of the individual and a desire for posthumous celebrity that Buddhism considers to be just so many causes for suffering that it is essential to eliminate in the interest of the very person who nourishes them. If Western culture, on the contrary, makes this attempt at transmission legitimate, it is not only because there exists among its members a consensus regarding the permanence of individuals and the uniqueness of their existence but also because the evaluation of their merit, both personal and artistic, is delegated to posterity as the most competent judge in this matter. Whereas the "damned poet" with which Sartre identified during his youth disappeared without anyone ever recognizing his or her genius,[1] that very genius nonetheless revealed itself gloriously in the eyes of a vigilant posterity, better advised than the distracted or malicious entourage of the now deceased creator. However, a problem immediately arises upon examining this clichéd scenario that features the blindness of the contemporaries and the retrospective lucidity of the successors. Posterity is a public composed of the same individuals whether they observe living authors or those who have just disappeared. We are thus faced with a simple question: for what reasons would we assume the infallibility of this public when it judges deceased authors after having suspected it of incompetence when they were still living?

In this chapter, I will analyze a new paradox of identity by studying the tension between posterity's pretention that it can adequately recognize the *merits* of writers and the likelihood that posterity will be influenced by the same passions that affected a creator's contemporaries. The concept of "merit," we shall see, cuts across three distinct categories. First, it touches on the problem of *literary quality*: to say that posterity alone is an adequate judge of authors is tantamount to saying that it is not mistaken about the aesthetic value of their works. Nevertheless, the problem of *individual merit* is likewise integrated into this posthumous evaluation, for it is the author that posterity claims to judge to the extent that its interest cycles constantly between the creation and the creator, the trace left by a writer in the network of memories also being the recomposed memory of an existence subjected to the evaluation of its successors. Finally, the questions of aesthetic merit and individual merit are united in the eyes of posterity, which evaluates the *coherence* between them: to judge authors is also to make an evaluation of the consistency of the principles expressed in their works and the manner in which they lived. And in the event that the behavior is contrary to the principles, the latter would be put into question, considering that the discrepancy between what is said and what is done may be interpreted as a legitimate reason to doubt their respective value.

Time and Passions

We spontaneously understand posterity as an abstraction, since the meeting between it and an artist is only conceivable in the form of a mental image: it is, by definition, what will come after him or her. However, these are indeed authentic individuals who constitute posterity, artists being survived by contemporaries who embody their posterity after having composed their public. There is thus no ontological difference between readership and posterity but only a difference relative to the object they are judging: contemporaries of the artists, the same individuals become their survivors. It is also evident that posterity will ultimately be composed of men and women who have never personally known the author whose works they are discovering and did not even tread the earth in the same period. These individuals, however, receive a double and paradoxical characterization: while we readily recognize that they are capable of being mistaken in their judgments when they are dealing with their contemporaries, we endow them, at the same time, with a superior faculty for arbitration when they decide on the merits of authors of the past. This brings us to the following question: Why do authors have to be dead before their talent is granted an adequate evaluation?

In truth, it is less that we give our confidence to posterity's judgment than we refuse it to the judgment of contemporaries. In other words, it is only relative to the denigration from which the latter suffer that the judgments of the former seem acceptable to us. For we all know, before making public our opinion of a work, we will have to face the vengeance of the living if we judge them severely. Authors are sure to be praised by their contemporaries when they are capable of either helping them or doing them harm. Provided that their symbolic position in the literary world permits them to do favors or to hinder careers, there will always be writers to sing their praises and present said praises to those authors as the first harmonies of the "distant melody."[2] Conversely, critics feel secure when they enjoy a more enviable position than those whose works they are evaluating: the judgments, for example, of a prestigious reader committee, a great newspaper, or an academy on the author of a first novel. Faced with this newcomer, still too weak to be able to harm them, those who occupy these high positions can indulge in the pleasure of intransigence, give free rein to their ill humor, or enjoy the slightly acid satisfaction of a symbolic execution that will elevate them a little without costing them much effort.

On the other hand, this struggle becomes hideous in the case of the confrontation of two authors of equal force whose moral, aesthetic, or political positions have become irreconcilable: this is when we witness one of these "miserable quarrels" that provoked the rupture between Rousseau and Diderot[3] or between Sartre and Camus, in which the adversaries feel strong enough to strike their blows without fearing those they may receive in reply, in which they show themselves to be wise enough to recognize in secret the immense qualities of their adversary without being sufficiently judicious to forego the glory of triumphing over him or her. Thus the works of others are evaluated on criteria that are often only distantly related to their objective qualities and depend far more on the nature of the personal relations between the critic and the author: one admires in order to be admired in one's turn or because one has been admired; one denigrates to appease old resentments, and the books are only instruments of an irreconcilable battle of egos concerning less the equitable opinion one should form of them than the personal superiority that an individual is striving to establish at the expense of others.

Theoretically, once authors have disappeared along with those who had reasons to try to harm them through their writings, the moment has come to *really* speak of literature. The dead person whose works you are discussing can be of no use to you nor do you do them a disservice of any kind, and even if she or he has heirs who would stand up for them, their rancor will not be as strong as it would have been had you challenged the merits of *their* writings; after all, this matter concerns the symbolic immortality of relatives, and no matter how close they were, it is still about *someone else*. Time, it seems, ultimately purges passions, and posterity can only undertake the examination of a work if there is no longer anyone taking a personal interest in the results. And then, despite what Sartre says when he conjures up the artificial superiority of critics over deceased writers by comparing it to that of "living dogs" over "dead lions,"[4] there is a kind of deference we grant those who have left us, the esteem that we normally reserve for an old enemy long hated, and who dies leaving us with a serene respect for qualities that we finally agree to acknowledge publicly. It is as if we were signing a posthumous truce with those who have lost their life: they are out of the running, poor people; they pressed their advantage as far as they could; may they rest there where we will soon join them. In the meantime, there are, among those who remain, many other rivals whose preeminence in this world threatens the one we still hope to gain in the eyes of posterity.

A Court of Opinion

This posthumous calm is, however, only momentary and soon gives way to violent quarrels. Muffled for a moment by the disappearance of the writers, the hate of which they were the victim is revived by posterity, within which groups of antagonists clash with a fierceness just as intense as it was during the period in which the author that divides them was still living. More serious: this battle is apt to turn to the definitive disadvantage of writers, the panegyric that posterity was devoting to them mutating into a litany of criticism. This fear runs through the last work of Diderot, the *Essay on the Reigns of Claude and Nero* (*Essai sur les règnes de Claude et de Néron*), in which the philosopher returns to the problem of posterity that he had discussed a decade prior with Falconet. While Diderot displayed in *The Pros and Cons* a strong confidence in the warm reception he expected posterity to accord him, the *Essay* betrays the new ambivalence he felt concerning the posthumous evaluation of individual merit: "Our enormous libraries, the common repository of both works of genius and literary garbage, will preserve indiscriminately the one and the other. A day will come when the pamphlets published against the most illustrious men of this century will be dragged from the dust by nasty individuals driven by the same spirit that dictated them; but there will arise, have no doubt, *some indignant good man* who will detect the turpitude of their slanderers, and by whom these famous authors will be better defended and avenged than Seneca is by me."[5]

In *The Pros and Cons*, the great man listened to the future praise of posterity, which helped him to suffer patiently the hostility of his contemporaries. He was able to take refuge, mentally, in a later period in which he would only meet praise commensurate with his virtues. On the other hand, the *Essay* expresses Diderot's concern that future generations would undergo the influence of "pamphlets" (*libelles*) written during his life. Whereas posterity was an impartial judge before whom the philosopher expected to appear like a believer before his creator, it now embodied a court of opinion in which the memory of an author appears without his being able to defend himself in person. On the stand, nonetheless, he may delegate a defender who will speak in his place.

Diderot had no need to imagine this posthumous helper in the period of *The Pros and Cons* owing to the privileged and transparent relationship he envisaged between the author and posterity—with an optimism that, as I will explain, will be greatly diminished a decade later. Referred to as an "indignant good man" in the *Essay on the Reigns of Claude and Nero*, this ally has become indispensable to denounce the slander directed at the writer's memory. His adversary—one could say "his evil double"—is the "villain" who is striving to damage the memory of the author after being made hostile by the "pamphlets" of the past. In this combat between the spokespeople of two opposing parties we discover an early version of the contemporary problems linked to public relations. Faced with a "villain" who is generating bad publicity about the author after his death, the "good man," responsible for what we would call today "damage control," works to restore his image.

Diderot is all the more familiar with this redemptive function of the indignant good man since he assumes it regarding Seneca in the *Essay on the Reigns of Claude and Nero*.[6] The role of the villain is played by a philosopher from the preceding century, Charles de Saint-Évremond (1613–1703), whose criticism targets one after the other the life of Seneca, his literary and philosophical oeuvre, and the relationship between his thought and action. Saint-Évremond accuses Seneca in fact of not exhibiting in his actual behavior any sort of consistency with the elements of his doctrine: "It is ridiculous for a man who lived amidst abundance and took such good care of himself to preach nothing but poverty and death."[7] Unlike Socrates, whose existence and suicide were in accord with the teachings he offered to his disciples, Seneca apparently enjoyed an opulent lifestyle in total contradiction with the Stoicism professed in his works. This attack made Diderot's blood boil, and he retorted indignantly, "Seneca was frugal; although rich, he lived as if were poor because he could become so in a moment; his fortune was his charity fund; his luxury, the inconvenient decor of his social status: it was his friends who benefited from his wealth; all he got was the aggravation of preserving it and the difficulty of making good use of it" (25:303).

Diderot responded just as vigorously to Saint-Évremond's additional criticism concerning Seneca's texts rather than the relationship between his works and his life. When Saint-Évremond included in the same denigration the literary and philosophical production of Seneca—"Whether it be the philosopher or the writer, I don't think much of him"—he receives this scathing repartee from Diderot: "There is more healthy morality in his writings than in any ancient author, and more ideas in one of his letters than in the fifteen volumes of Saint-Évremond" (25:301).

Pleasure of Slander and Escalation of Criticism

Diderot based his defense of Seneca on the familiarity he cultivated over a long period of time with the oeuvre and life of this philosopher. On the other hand, Saint-Évremond, according to him, only had a superficial knowledge of these two subjects: "Someone who speaks thus has never read Seneca's works and scarcely knows anything but the titles; he is completely ignorant of his private life" (25:303). But nevertheless, despite the superior expertise of Seneca's defender, his accuser is most likely to win the battle in the court of posterity. To this ineluctable phenomenon, Diderot attributes two causes: the pleasure of slander and the escalation of criticism.

At the beginning of the *Essay*, Diderot notes that the accusations leveled against a deceased writer are eagerly listened to, while praise is normally met with indifference. The public derives some obscure satisfaction from the revelation of the personal shortcomings of authors and the criticism of their works that, on the other hand, the tales of their good actions and aesthetic successes fail to elicit: "The real or supposed fault radiates brilliantly; the reproach goes from mouth to mouth with feigned pity; it spreads throughout the city. If slander disappears at the death of an obscure individual, celebrity acts like its vehicle and carries it to the most distant ages; peering into the great man's funerary urn, it continues to stir the ashes with its dagger" (25:39–40).

The pleasure of *desecration* reinforces that of slander. It is indeed possible that the revelation of the moral turpitude of an author helps us to bear more easily the otherwise crushing grandeur of his or her artistic productions. We may thus be able to console ourselves over the insolent intellectual fertility of certain writers by emphasizing the egoism they exhibited in their relations with their friends: failing to match them with our works, at least we may consider ourselves *better* than them as a person. Likewise, emphasizing the defects of some of their works reassures their detractors as to their own creative talents. While a genius who shined through everywhere, from the works of youth to those of maturity, would be the sign of an incomparable superiority, the failed attempts of an author reveal a progressive apprenticeship that anyone is capable of undertaking: the failed work shows that there is no basic difference, just a question of improvement, between the talents of a great writer and our own. In short, whether the criticism targets the individuals themselves or their creations, its ultimate effect is to make more tolerable the proof of a talent that incites the jealousy of both contemporaries and successors. The latter do not, of course, have to bear the company of these geniuses nor the displeasure of comparing the successes of the latter to their own failures, their unbounded activity to their own tendency to procrastinate. But the living share with these famous dead men and women an identical condition, and they may always ask what they had accomplished at the age of ten, twenty, thirty, or forty before comparing what they, themselves, were able to produce during this time and what they had done with their own life. To sum up, the frantic race to recognition that sets individuals against one another is also capable of transferring its competitive logic to the examination that the living reserve for their predecessors.

The sympathy for the revelation of the ethical and aesthetic errors of an author combines with another phenomenon—the *escalation* of criticism—to explain the ultimate and necessary triumph of the detractors over the supporters in the trial underway. The former are tormented by a desire for distinction that sets them against all those who have produced diatribes before them. Inspired by the nasty pamphlets of the past, they choose to be still more trenchant in order to demonstrate their ability to formulate a personal evaluation of the merit of an author. Diderot observes in this respect: "The goal of the ignorant is to *outdo* the invective of the nasty critics for fear of sounding like echoes. The modern detractors of Seneca have been far crueler than the ancients: the twelve lines of a Suilius have engendered volumes of atrocious insults" (25:304; my italics). Saint-Évremond is less guilty of pure malevolence toward Seneca than of simple vanity: if he denigrated the memory of the latter in terms that were more violent than those of his predecessors, it was to show that his criticism was not limited to repeating theirs. Seen from this angle, the evaluation of the merits of a writer becomes less and less objective as the years pass, given that the critical evaluation produces a competition whose stakes are less the accuracy of the judgment than its uniqueness in relation to all those that have already been rendered. While the supporter goes to great lengths to draw posterity's attention to the virtues of authors, posterity itself is fascinated by the slander that their denigrators spread in vying to be the most vicious. And far from reaching a consensus on the merits of deceased writers, posterity tends to exaggerate more and more their defects.

Based on the example of Seneca, Diderot concludes that there is no phenomenon of progressive purging of the passions that authors provoke, but rather the constant production of new debates whose stakes are posterity's image of those authors. Instead of arriving at a terminal point where writers are sufficiently known, in both their grandeur and their errors, their talents and their inadequacies (as regards both personal ethics and literary aesthetics), posterity constantly reinvents their image and risks taking a caricatured vision for a faithful portrait under the influence of ignorant, foolish, or malicious individuals, such that the intervention of the "indignant good man" is both indispensable and, in all probability, doomed to failure. Thus an oeuvre is never inscribed in the network of memories without having to face new critical judgments: with each new generation, a book that endures is once again challenged by yet another evaluation.

Ethical Consistency and Morality of Adaptation

The reconfiguring of the idea of posterity in the *Essay* compared to *The Pros and Cons* cannot be explained solely by Diderot's conclusions when he reflects on the example of Seneca and his posthumous denigrators. It can only be fully understood when related to the personal drama that is being played out in this campaign in favor of the Stoic philosopher. In the text's very foreword, the question of the motivation of the good man in coming out in favor of a predecessor is explicitly posed: "Alas! It was owing to my action that the philosopher Seneca could have said to me also: 'My name has been sullied by slander for nearly eighteen centuries, and I find in you an apologist! What am I to you? And what connection, spared by time, has survived between us? Might you be one of my descendants? And what difference does it make to you if people believe me to be depraved or virtuous?" (25:39).

Although he justifies it by a kind of solidarity across the ages between learned individuals,[8] Diderot's intervention in favor of Seneca would not be so passionate if it did not at the same time play the role of a *pro domo* plea. Through the defense of a philosopher who lived under a corrupt and corrupting reign, it is his own refusal of the autarky exemplified by Rousseau that Diderot strives to justify. The *Essay* should in fact be read in the context of the famous quarrel of Diderot with the author of *The Confessions*.[9] Without entering into the details of this well-known episode of literary history, we can at least note that through his defense of Seneca, it is himself, anticipating the reproaches of the citizen of Geneva, that Diderot seeks to defend.[10] The two men did in fact clash over the position a philosopher should legitimately adopt toward political power. According to Rousseau, marginality alone is appropriate for philosophers who wish to preserve their independence. Refusing to compromise oneself with the reigning power is the way to avoid any interference between the duty of an individual and her or his personal interest, given that in the end the former may always yield to the latter. Demonstrated notably by the refusal of a royal pension, the insistence on independence constantly reaffirmed by Rousseau forced him to copy music to survive at the same time as it allowed him to proclaim loudly and clearly his refusal of moral compromise.[11] Far more than his success as a writer, it is the coherence between his thought and his acts that, according to the author of *The Confessions*, attracted the hostility of those who did not have the courage to accomplish the equivalent of his "personal reform."[12] There was, therefore, at the origin of the quarrel between Rousseau and Diderot, an "example of ethical consistency that, by contrast, condemned all of the philosophers to appear to be hypocrites, slaves and prostitutes."[13] Whereas Rousseau denounced the world such as it was in adopting a position of martyr, both *witness* of the vices of his time and *victim* of a virtue that forced him to stay apart from his fellow creatures, Diderot chose to adapt to it by favoring a sort of moral flexibility. For him, the problem did not consist in determining if it was necessary to compromise his moral integrity—everyone "adopts postures," as he brilliantly states in *Rameau's Nephew*—but rather how far.[14] Diderot substitutes a question of measure to

Rousseau's uncompromising approach: at what moment must people refuse to bend further to the demands of the society to which they necessarily belong? Rejecting Rousseau's stubborn position, in part based on his own exemplary nature, and convinced that no one is conceivable other than as the embodiment of multiple roles before diverse publics, Diderot preached a morality of adaptation. Criticized by Rousseau's partisans in their quarrel because he had chosen not to claim publicly the paternity of a number of his books, because he had cultivated highly placed officials in order to obtain favors for his friends, and because he became a courtesan of Catherine of Russia, Diderot found in his defense of Seneca the means to justify what, in his own career, was a form of moral prostitution in the eyes of the author of *The Confessions*. In doing so, he did not choose an easy task, since the Stoic philosopher had accumulated a considerable fortune in Nero's service: far from using his influence to moderate the behavior of a tyrant, Seneca seems to have done everything he could to benefit personally from his eminent position.

One of the strategies adopted by Diderot to defend the Stoic philosopher consisted in highlighting the existence not of one Seneca but of multiple Senecas, the individual being divided into various functions whose respective demands soon proved to be incompatible. All at once moralist, husband, teacher, playwright, friend, minister, and so forth, Seneca is caught "in a series of interacting networks that could prove to be perfectly irreconcilable with one another."[15] Of course, after the death of Agrippina, Seneca could have fled Nero's court, and he certainly should have if we judge the question solely on the personal integrity of "Seneca the moralist." But by doing so, we forget the interests that "Seneca the citizen," "Seneca the husband," "Seneca the brother," and "Seneca the friend" had to take into account as well: "By his refusal and his death, Seneca would have been the murderer of all those whom he would have abandoned to the ferociousness of Nero. Who would have been the first victims of a reckless resistance? His wife, perhaps, his brothers, his friends, a mass of honest and brave citizens" (25:401). These networks of interactions must be taken into account in their entirety, Diderot reminds us, when posterity judges the behavior of others. Nonetheless, certain of them are simply abandoned by Rousseau in order to preserve the harmony between his principles and his conduct. If the refusal of the royal pension permitted him to keep clear of the court, it nonetheless deprived him of the financial resources that would have allowed him to support his wife and their children much better than his work copying music. In *The Confessions*, Rousseau observes that Diderot urged him to accept this pension in the interest of his family, and that their disagreement over this led to the first of their disputes:

> He told me that if I was disinterested for myself, I had no right to be so for Mme Levasseur and her daughter; that I owed it to them not to neglect any

possible and honest means to provide them with sustenance, and since it couldn't be said, after all, that I had refused this pension, he maintained that since it seemed likely that I would be offered one, I should solicit and obtain it at any cost. Although I was touched by his zeal, I was repelled by his principles, and we had on this subject a very sharp argument, the first that I had had with him; and we have only had quarrels of this sort, him prescribing for me what he thought I should do, and me refraining from doing so because I didn't believe that I should.[16]

Beyond the apparently anecdotal character of this quarrel, in which we see Rousseau accuse Diderot of interfering in a matter that did not concern him, it is the relationship with the other and, more specifically, with the family that is at stake here. It is significant that Diderot justifies Seneca's position at the heart of imperial power by the necessity to protect his friends and family; likewise, Diderot served vigorously and tirelessly the interests of his daughter, "the being whom he loved the most passionately."[17] It was, in fact, in order to provide Angélique with a dowry that he sold his library to Catherine II, the empress with whom he curried favor during their correspondence before visiting her in Russia. It was again for Angélique, to avoid her moving to the provinces and thus far from him, that he entreated a series of influential people to help him find his son-in-law a position in Paris. The persistence of his efforts was such that it provoked "the surprise and disapproval of Grimm, who no longer recognizes Diderot in these unsavory maneuvers."[18] Never mind austere faithfulness to oneself: for Diderot everything yielded to his love for Angélique, the intensity of which is revealed in their epistolary relations, and the contrast with Rousseau's abandoning of his children is so stark that it needs no commentary. While Diderot demonstrates that the individual is caught in an intricate network of duties, not only toward himself but also toward others, and the members of his family in particular, Rousseau's moral reform led him to acts that, from the viewpoint of those around him, exhibit the egoism inherent to a rigid definition of virtue.

Horizontal Axis, Vertical Axis

What influence did this quarrel have on the recomposition of the idea of posterity in Diderot's mind? And, more broadly, how does this dispute reveal how the contemporary passions of authors may be communicated to their most distant successors? One of the key elements in the conflict between the two philosophers is the writing of *The Confessions*, a work whose posthumous publication haunted the last years of Diderot's life by posing an intolerable threat to the image he wished to pass on to future generations.[19] *The Confessions* and their author are explicitly evoked in a long passage of the *Essay on the Reigns of Claude and Nero*:

> We can agree that it is insane, that it is atrocious to sacrifice, in dying, one's friends and one's enemies to serve as the procession of his shadow; to sacrifice gratitude, discretion, faithfulness, decency, and domestic tranquility to the arrogant rage to be remembered in the future; in short, to wish to drag his whole age into his grave with him to enlarge his pile of dust.... What should we think of a man who leaves, after his death, memories in which several people are clearly mistreated, and which include the odious precaution to only permit its publication when he, himself, will no longer be there to be attacked, nor the one whom he is attacking be there to defend himself. *May Jean-Jacques disdain as much as he likes the judgment of posterity; others may not share this disdain.* (25:121; my italics)

These reproaches to Rousseau by Diderot contain a paradox. Jean-Jacques is accused of having been obsessed with a burning desire for posthumous celebrity while affecting indifference to the "judgment" of posterity. The citizen of Geneva thus appeared both to desire that people speak of him and to be indifferent to what they might say. This paradox disappears, however, if we distinguish between the abundance of the discourses (the "noise" they are going to provoke) and the public esteem they will bring him. According to Diderot, Rousseau's destruction of friendships may be compared to Herostratus's destruction of the Temple of Artemis in Ephesus, both intended to lead to posthumous existence. In contrast to Jean-Jacques's project—conceived as an effort to colonize the conscience of others at the risk of attracting negative appraisals of himself—Diderot proposes a form of control, in advance, of posthumous discourse. Certain secrets should disappear with those who had discovered them so that posterity would never suspect their existence. Acting as the curator of his own memory, Diderot would have preferred to transmit to future generations only the reasons for esteem that he knew he deserved. Well, it was precisely the control of his posthumous identity that Rousseau was taking from him with his autobiography, a veritable time bomb that would go off after his death. Awaited and discussed well before their publication, *The Confessions* threatened to reorient the image the future would form of Diderot, or at least that was the fear that tormented him. Thus what Diderot found the hardest to pardon the intractable Rousseau was to compromise the place the father of the *Encyclopedia* hoped to occupy in posterity by communicating to it these final revelations that he should have taken with him to his grave. The recourse to "the indignant good man" whose proper activity he illustrated in his works on Seneca—less perhaps out of admiration for the latter than to give an example to his future allies of the passion he expected them to display to his benefit when the moment came—may be understood as a way to give the floor to a posthumous defender in the face of attacks that would be all the more intolerable in that they would come when the accused would no longer be there to testify against them. By promising to deform his image in the network of memories, Rousseau added an element of anguish to the belief that Diderot held in symbolic immortality: what good was it to be remembered by future generations if your memory risked being tainted by the slander spread by an "enemy brother"?[20] There is thus something poignant in this final darkening of Diderot's thoughts on posterity: while he was preparing to leave his existence in the hands of the latter, he began to doubt not the inscription of the trace of his person in the collective memory but the very esteem of his distant successors.

If we go beyond the individual cases of Rousseau and Diderot to envision the general conclusions we may draw from their quarrel, we may note the manner in which the passions of the literati are transmitted to posterity. Indeed, it is not difficult to observe in the specialists of the eighteenth century a kind of polarization that reproduces the opposing positions of the two philosophers. Studying the Enlightenment involves necessarily an encounter with these two indispensable thinkers and finding oneself both judge and jury of a quarrel in which they appealed to posterity. Whatever may be the intellectual efforts to reconstruct objectively the causes and implication of their differences, their posthumous audience is called on to decide in favor of one or the other. Whether we declare ourselves "Rousseauian" or "Diderotian" in this quarrel reveals something about the ethical positions we adopt over the course of our life. The Rousseauian virtue appears admirable to some people, untenably rigid to others; likewise, the Diderotian flexibility may pass for a necessary adaptation to the practical demands of social life or for a convenient justification of any questionable moral compromise.

In short, the quarrels between authors of the past do not die with them. On the contrary, they require future generations to make a judgment about them and to embrace one position to the detriment of the other. Of course, literary quarrels are not the only ones that involve members of posterity: there are, in historical figures that we are accustomed to oppose, a similar injunction to favor one over the other. Alexander the Great or Julius Caesar; Maximilien Robespierre or Georges Danton; Napoleon Bonaparte or George Washington; Ronald Reagan or Barack Obama: we are called to choose between the parallel lives of these famous men. And this choice is not only the declaration of an intellectual preference; it ultimately involves the identity of the people who make it by suggesting to them a model for their conception of their relationship to the world, to which they may refer before making decisions that concern the course of their own life.

The relationship between the members of posterity and their predecessors is thus developed as a propagation, and not as a dissolution, of the passions driving their contemporaries. The relationship we will call "horizontal" (that between a writer and the audience contemporary with his or her existence) may be projected onto the vertical relationship (that between writers and their successors).[21] As Laurence Mall observes concerning this double relationship, "The mediocre, jealous, and vicious critics form among themselves historical families as closely knit as those that unite the illustrious creators, the good men, and the philosophers of all time."[22] What the *Essay* demonstrates through the double example of Seneca and Diderot himself is the perpetuation of the debates around the memory of authors, debates that involve the image posterity is called to construct of their work, of their person, and of the consistency of their thought and behavior. This image, variable according to the familiarity of each individual with the texts of the past, is subject to the twists and turns of the disputes that continue to excite their successors.

While it is spontaneously conceived as a court in which a definitive judgment is rendered on the merits of an author, posterity would be more accurately compared to an appeals court where the pleading is constantly resumed by the self-appointed spokespersons who, like Diderot with Seneca, identify with the person whose defense they undertake. We can thus say that posterity is incapable of rendering an irrevocable verdict on the merits of an author, since the passage of time, instead of allowing the formation of a consensus, leaves ever more space to the incessant production of contradictory and passionate evaluations. The example of the posthumous reception of Diderot's oeuvre itself exhibits a troubling instability. The central place in the philosophy of the Enlightenment that is granted him by the readers of the twenty-first century is but the most recent reconfiguration of the reflection on his subject. Immediately following his death, "Diderot was placed at the second rank, less brilliant than Montesquieu, less stylish than Rousseau, less clear than Buffon. His death didn't cause much of a stir, infinitely less, in any case, than that of Voltaire and Jean-Jacques."[23] Over the following years, Diderot's successors hardly showered him with unanimous praise, reproaching him for his "disorganized bombast," his "obscure metaphysics," the excessive complications of *Jacques the Fatalist*, or the anti-Christian sentiments of *The Nun*.[24] Who knows if what we take today to be a universal consensus on Diderot's genius is anything more than the temporary stabilization of the reception of his oeuvre? As Bernard Le Bovier de Fontenelle did before him, Diderot warned against judgments that are rendered without taking into account the modifications that the passage of time may bring: "In the memory of a rose, no gardener has ever died."[25] Similarly, what we take for the immortality of an oeuvre is perhaps only a "sophism of the ephemeral," the result of our propensity to confuse the conclusions drawn from a limited viewpoint with the statement of an eternal truth.[26]

With this third paradox of identity, it now seems clear to me that the image of authors formed by posterity in no way proceeds toward a more and more accurate evaluation of their individual merits, their artistic merits, and the coherence between the two. In taking the literary figure as the object of their commentary and the pretext for their discord, the members of posterity become collectively the authors of the authors, and the memory left by the creators, disseminated into the vast network of memories in constant reorganization, is the canvas on which incessant variations are embroidered and the terrain on which implacable quarrels are fought.

THE PARADOXES OF MEDIATION

SEVENTH PARADOX
The Rosetta Stone and Agrippina's Thrush

The study of the paradoxes of belief and the paradoxes of identity led us to the examination of crisscross images: to the images of posterity by authors, then to the images of authors by posterity. I come now to a new series of paradoxes that are formed around works and, more precisely, around the modes of their transmission to future generations. For this transmission to take place, three mediations are indispensable. The first is *cultural*: future generations must be able to master the language used in the writing of the oeuvre to be capable of spreading it in the network of memories. In addition to this, another mediation is essential: the *material mediation*, which includes a *tangible mediation* and a *technical mediation*.[1] An oeuvre is only known through the agency of a format whose perishable nature threatens the permanence of the inscriptions it is intended to preserve. Finally, we need to take into account an ultimate mediation: the *human mediation*, the posterity of texts assuming as a last recourse the existence of a readership capable of remembering them. The present chapter is devoted to the first of these three mediations and, more precisely, to the examination of the following problem: What sense does it make to produce an oeuvre destined for posterity if the language in which it is written is doomed to meaninglessness? Are we speaking of an undertaking that is *absurd* or *paradoxical*? The example of the Egyptian language will help us attempt to formulate an answer to this question through a distinction that will be employed throughout this chapter: that between silent, closed, and open languages.

The Trinity of Languages

Jean-François Champollion was only seven when Bonaparte and his troops tread upon the soil of Alexandria. In July 1798 thousands of soldiers marched beside the dashing general, accompanied by the scholars of the Sciences and Arts Commission: historians, botanists, illustrators, astronomers, and architects who were preparing to gather and inventory the marvels of Egypt. While the military campaign accomplished nothing lasting, only bequeathing to the collective memory a famous maxim uttered beneath the pyramids and some visions of glory, plague, and savagery recorded by Jean-Léon Gérôme, Antoine-Jean Gros, and Léon Cogniet, the scientific expedition founded French Egyptology. This failure and triumph are identified with two areas located a few miles apart. Not far from the port of Aboukir where Bonaparte's fleet was destroyed by Admiral Horatio Nelson is located el-Rashid (i.e., Rosetta), a village where the soldiers of Lieutenant Pierre-François Bouchard discovered at the corner of a dilapidated fortress a stone covered with mysterious signs. A year later, in 1800, the French surrendered to the English and yielded to their enemies innumerable treasures, of which the "Rosetta Stone" was the crown jewel. It took up residence in the British Museum, where Champollion would have gone to study it were it not for the continental blockade that prevented him from crossing the English Channel. He had to be satisfied with a copy that his compatriots had the foresight to bring back from the Middle East. Traced in successive strips, the first two texts inscribed in the stone were undecipherable. The last, on the other hand, was written in ancient Greek, a language that Champollion had been studying since childhood. Through sheer perseverance, the miracle happened. On September 14, 1822, Champollion rushed to his brother's home, shouted "I've got it!" and fainted: thanks to him, a silent language had become a closed language.

With the term "silent language," I am referring to the state of a language that one cannot declare "dead." As Claude Hagège observes, with death being a state of no return, it is incorrect to refer to as "dead" a language that continues to exist, be it only in the form of a series of mysterious characters.[2] Even when it has regressed to this stage, a language remains, within each document that preserves it, a system in a waking state, with its grammar and vocabulary, its particular manner of organizing the world. In short, it is in a situation similar to that of a language expressing the thoughts of an injured person who has lost the use of speech. In her mind, the language has not changed; it is nonetheless incapable of reaching the ears of others.[3] Still, despite this momentary impossibility, a potential resurgence can never be completely ruled out: just as the injured person may recuperate and recover the ability to speak, the silent language is capable of recovering its meaning for others. The metaphor of the "dead" language is thus inappropriate to designate this latency of meaning within an intact system, and I will prefer to use that of silence: the silent language lies dormant while awaiting its Champollion.

The term "dead language" is also inadequate to describe the group of intelligible languages that have lost their speakers, as in the case of Akkadian and ancient Greek. Indeed, a language that is no longer used to express spontaneous individual thoughts is no less capable of communicating across centuries what was formerly a free combination of linguistic possibilities. Provided that I have learned to read it, a "dead" language resonates in my mind in a manner strictly identical to my own language or a language called "living." When his poem is read by Hellenists, Homer is just as meaningful as the words pouring out of a radio or printed in the morning newspaper. As soon as Hellenists concentrate on the *Odyssey*, their mind is entirely occupied with the adventures of Ulysses: it is indeed living words that capture their thought during their reading. Thus, rather than employing the vitalist metaphor and adopting artificially the opposition it assumes between "dead" and "living" languages, it is more productive to replace this metaphor by another, that of "opening," in order to distinguish between "closed" and "open" languages.

"Closed languages" and "open languages" are marked by clear *tendencies*, as Alexis Philonenko observes.[4] Of course, they have in common the possibility of being both written and spoken, such that the *spoken word (la parole)*—in the Saussurian sense of the term—serves in both cases to actualize the latent possibilities in the system from which they stem. However, while the closed language does not receive new terms, its whole structure being long maintained intact without the addition of any exogenous elements, the open language is being constantly recomposed, not only by foreign influences but also because new objects appear in our reality and require the invention of new terms to designate them. The tendency of one is toward contraction and stability; that of the other toward enrichment and evolution.

The number of speakers of closed and open languages play a dominant role in the consolidation of their respective tendencies. It is in fact logical that a language mastered only by a small group of initiates will scarcely be enlivened by new additions that, on the contrary, abound when it has millions of speakers. However, an additional factor comes into play in the accentuation of the tendency that is proper to closed languages: the specific use that is made of them. Although they may serve as the intermediary of a thought that is directly expressed through them, closed languages have in common the fact that they are destined primarily to be translated into an open language. It happens, of course, that the reverse practice is encouraged—that is, a translation from an open language to a closed language. However, it is not an exercise whose ultimate goal is to get rid of the open language (as children put away the training wheels of their bikes that had helped them to keep their balance at the beginning) but, on the contrary, to master more perfectly the rules of grammar of the closed language in order to be able to transpose it with its meaning intact into the open language over the course of subsequent exercises. Of course, this practice is not inherent to closed languages, which, after all, were originally open languages. On the other hand, it is directly linked to the goals related to its learning, a language with a "closed tendency" not involving a free use of thought that would be expressed in its own vocabulary and structures.

One may conclude from this distinction between silent and closed languages that an evolution from the first to the second is an entirely conceivable phenomenon, as is demonstrated by the deciphering of the hieroglyphics through the mediation of the Rosetta Stone. Do we know if, in the sands of another desert, a miraculously intact document will not be exhumed, revealing to us the existence of a language that will remain inaudible while awaiting the Champollion who will remove the seal on the lips of the people who formerly spoke it? Conversely, the regression from a closed language to a silent language is also theoretically possible. One only has to imagine a closed language whose specialists are so few that at the disappearance of the last of them there would only remain grammars that, for lack of interest, the following generations would cease using to interpret signs that have returned to silence. Once again the signs constituting this language would become as mysterious as the Egyptian hieroglyphics were for Napoleon's troops. But what may we say about the transition from closed languages to open languages? If I refused to call them "dead languages" and "living languages," was it not to deny the existence of a definitive break between them?

The evolution from a closed to an open language is theoretically possible if we envision the intervention of a state establishing a new linguistic policy, supporting its implementation, and, if need be, punishing any violations of the norm that it is trying to impose. One may indeed imagine, on the part of a government, an extreme proactiveness that would consist in establishing as the national tongue a closed language whose teaching would no longer be designed to translate it into an open language but rather to acquire sufficient mastery for the spontaneous expression of individual thoughts. Although this scenario irresistibly evokes that of a dystopia such as *Nineteen Eighty-Four* in which the use of "newspeak" is imposed on citizens, it is still possible to imagine an ancient and closed language becoming an open language, adopted by a vast group of speakers and, little by little, completed by new terms and expressions. A historical example of this phenomenon may be found in Israel, where the revival of Hebrew shows the possibility of re-creating, from written texts, a spoken language that has been adopted by an entire national community.[5] Thus we may see a language cycle, in one direction then in the other, through three successive states (the open, the closed, and the silent), although the regression from an open language to a silent language is much more probable than the reactivation of a silent language into an open one.

Although the deciphering of the hieroglyphics is a major event in itself, something even more universal was brought into play when Champollion succeeded in deciphering the Rosetta Stone. Indeed, he was not only restoring the voice of *one* buried culture; he was offering a reason for optimism to all languages by demonstrating that the decline that threatened them may be reversed. In other words, the Rosetta Stone permits us to confront the perspective of the silencing of languages with that of their reemergence in the form of closed languages. It is thus a symbol of a faith in the resiliency of languages and of their capacity to transmit to posterity, despite possible parentheses opened in the course of several centuries, the voices of vanished peoples.

The importance of the rediscovery of the hieroglyphics by Champollion was not lost on one of his contemporaries and countrymen, Chateaubriand, who salutes him in the following terms: "The sacred languages have now shared their lost vocabulary; Champollion deciphered these hieroglyphics, up to the very granites of Mezraïm, that seemed to be seals placed on the lips of the desert, a guarantee of their eternal discretion."[6] This event attracted the attention of the famous writer owing to its resonance with a recurring question in his works: what use is it to write if, in a distant but inevitable future, the language in which I am expressing myself no longer means anything to anyone? And would Chateaubriand's memoirs truly be "from beyond the grave" if the writer's audience, after his disappearance, were a readership that was incapable of understanding him? The doubt that this reflection provokes concerning posterity has nothing to do with literary value (will my work be judged worthy of being remembered?) but, much more radically, everything to do with linguistic sustainability: will people even be able to read it? The theme of the fragility of languages appears obsessively throughout Chateaubriand's entire body of works, and we find traces of it in the *Memoirs from Beyond the Grave* (*Mémoires d'outre-tombe*) (1848) as well as in the *Journey in America* (*Voyage en Amérique*) (1827) and the *Essay on English Literature* (*Essai sur la littérature anglaise*) (1836).[7] I am going to turn now to this latter text, for it develops a vigorous meditation on the symbolic survival of authors by means of a language whose horizon is closure, silence, and oblivion.[8]

Chateaubriand and the Decline of Languages

In Chateaubriand's *Essay on English Literature* we see the irruption of a curious bird that will reappear a few years later in the *Memoirs from Beyond the Grave*: Agrippina's thrush. Originally, this winged creature takes off from a page of *Natural History* where Pliny speaks of birds capable of imitating human language: "Agrippina, wife of Claude, had a thrush (a thing unheard of until then) that reproduced people's words. The young Caesars also had a starling and nightingales that could learn Greek and Latin words."[9] Here is the use Chateaubriand makes of this anecdote through an ingenious and surprising rearrangement:

The tribes of the Orinoco no longer exist; all that remain of their dialect are a dozen words squawked from the top of trees by parrots who have regained their liberty; Agrippina's thrush chirped Greek words on the railings of Latin palaces. Such, sooner or later, will be the fate of our modern jargons: some starling of New Place will whistle on an apple tree verses of Shakespeare, incomprehensible to the passersby; some crow escaped from the cage of the last Franco-Gallic priest will say to foreign peoples, our successors: "Enjoy the accents of a voice you once knew"; you "will put an end to all these speeches." Be Shakespeare or Bossuet so that in the end your masterpieces may survive—in the memory of a bird—both your language and your memory among men.[10]

At the beginning of the chapter from which this passage is taken, Chateaubriand announces the order of the subjects he intends to treat. The last of them is "the death of languages," and it is precisely this phenomenon that Agrippina's thrush is supposed to illustrate. Accordingly, we must understand that the thrush is nothing less, for Chateaubriand, than an anti–Rosetta Stone— that is, the symbol of the reversal of the optimistic perspective of the resiliency of languages when we consider their inevitable decline. From his journey in America, Chateaubriand brought back an acute consciousness of the fragility of civilizations. In the *Journey in America*, he had already emphasized the annihilation of numerous Amerindian languages and gave the example of an unfinished dictionary: "We also have the manuscript of an Iroquois-English dictionary; unfortunately, the first volume, from the letter A to the letter L, has been lost."[11] A language full of holes, partially forgotten, Iroquois is the victim of a phenomenon of progressive erosion that, far from being an isolated case, foreshadows the destiny of "modern jargons" like English and French.

There is lacking in this poetic evocation of the future of languages an identification of the causes of the phenomenon that Chateaubriand describes, as well as an analysis of their respective mechanisms and their interactions. However, two details help us identify the reasons why, according to Chateaubriand, languages are all annihilated sooner or later. On the one hand, the disappearance of the Christian faith is directly associated with that of the French language. It is from the cage of the "*last* Franco-Gallic priest" that escapes the crow that is the custodian of the French language before perching on top of "the ruined tower of an abandoned cathedral."[12] There is no doubt possible: the genius of France and that of Christianity are inextricably bound together, and the decline of the faith can only announce the death of France itself. Without the cause-and-effect relationship being clearly explained, it is a major geopolitical phenomenon that the author seems to ascribe to the decline of his homeland, which is itself the consequence of the progressive abandonment of Christianity. Indeed, the future inhabitants of the territory occupied by France are not "successors" in the sense that they would belong to a series of generations passing on a common heritage; it is "foreigners" that Chateaubriand imagines in place of his compatriots. After the destruction of Christianity, of France, and of its people, it will be the turn of the language of Jacques-Bénigne Bossuet to disappear.

To describe the terminal stage of the death of languages, Chateaubriand takes his inspiration from the pictorial treatment of the classical vanities, whose semiotic system is characterized by the juxtaposition of conflicting signs. The painter of a vanity embeds in the same canvas the symbols of worldly pastimes (the dice refers to gambling, the crown to the desire for power, the empty cup to sensual pleasures), next to signs that express by their contiguity the futility of the foregoing (the hourglass refers to the limited time of human life, the soap bubbles to its fragility, the skull to death). A third group of signs transcends, however, the confrontation of the former two groups: those that refer to the eternity promised to the faithful, such as the sacred text or the floral symbols of the Virgin and of Resurrection. A sort of dialectic is presented in these pictorial works. If the antithesis of worldly distractions is the fragility of human existence, at least the Christian faith offers a way to transcend the anguish caused by that existence through a promise: eternity.

On the closely related subject of the death of languages, Chateaubriand also draws a vanity in which the conflicting signs are opposed. The first group refers to the highest degree of literary glory one can attain, Anglophones and Francophones having, in his opinion, found their supreme reference in the works of Shakespeare and Bossuet. The second group is composed of these winged creatures, starling and crow, whose brain is the ultimate recipient of English and French. The extreme disproportion between the creative genius of Shakespeare and Bossuet and the purely imitative faculty of these birds that are incapable of understanding what they repeat, moreover, for inattentive ears has the effect of emphasizing the *vanity* of literary glory. The obliteration of the French language is rendered still more striking by the choice of the linguistic sample that survives it: for this uttering of empty sounds announces nothing less than "the end of all speech." Famous for his funeral orations, Bossuet, the eagle of Meaux, offers the posthumous eulogy of the French language through the intermediary of a crow.

But contrary to the pictorial vanity that, after all, recalls the existence of eternity to those who stray into worldly pleasures, this conclusion is devoid of hope, since it describes the curious survival in the skull of a bird as the "last result" that the principal illustrations of the English and French languages can hope to obtain. Through this projection to a time in which modern languages will disappear, it is in fact his writer's vanity that Chateaubriand seeks to humiliate: the passage to posterity of literary works is inextricably linked to the intelligibility of the language in which they are written. Lose that language, and you have lost everything.

Closed Languages and Classical Languages

The symbol adopted by Chateaubriand is nonetheless endowed with an involuntarily paradoxical dimension that reverses the meaning. It is not the "death of languages" that Chateaubriand illustrates in this passage but, on the contrary, a kind of permanence. As Denis Hollier remarks, "Chateaubriand intends to speak of the death of languages. Taken literally, however, the lesson dispensed in this scene goes in the opposite direction insofar as it shows, in a strange manner, languages surviving those who speak them."[13] As the author of *Memoirs from Beyond the Grave* imagines them, French and English are not dead languages (obliterated, disappeared) but *silent* languages, in a situation that resembles that of Egyptian before its rediscovery: they are sets of signs that have stopped holding meaning for those that perceive them but are not devoid of meaning for all that.

The supposedly definitive character of the disappearance of languages for which Chateaubriand serves as harbinger is, in addition, contradicted by the specific idiom to which he refers to predict the fate of English and French. In fact, it is Greek words that Agrippina's thrush chirps "on the railings of Latin palaces" (493). Far from being a language whose ability to carry meaning is irremediably lost, the language that the bird remembers is, with the language of Cicero, the one that served for the writing of the founding texts of Western culture. Consequently, the phenomenon that Chateaubriand describes is not the slow erosion of open languages that, gradually losing their speakers, finally disappear, never to return; we are dealing here, on the contrary, with the progressive fossilization of open languages into classical languages.

Although all closed languages are not classical languages, all classical languages are indeed languages whose principal tendency is toward closure. For a closed language to belong to the subcategory of classical languages, it must be taught in classes—that is, convey by way of the schools a cultural heritage invigorating the modern cultures. Further on in the *Essay on English Literature*, Chateaubriand discusses the transmission through the centuries of the major works of classical culture thanks to the combined efforts of the church and the university: "The glory of Homer and Virgil was religiously transmitted to us by the monks, the priests, and the clerks, the teachers of the barbarians in the ecclesiastical schools, the monasteries, the seminaries, and the universities. A hereditary admiration was passed down to us from race to race by the lessons of a professorship whose chair, established fourteen centuries ago, constantly confirms the same judgment" (495).

Chateaubriand brings in this passage an additional element to the definition of classical languages: they are languages whose literary products have received a *definitive* evaluation. Classical languages are not only completed languages, such that no use will ever change a grammatical norm forever engraved in manuals;

they are also the material of a corpus whose aesthetic value is established and will never be enriched with new works. Such as we know them, Greek and Latin literatures are fragments of an infinitely larger set of texts: among all the works that have not reached us, a tragedy by Sophocles, a letter by Epicurus, or an elegy by Horace could eventually resurface and be recognized as new masterpieces, or the text of a Latin poet whose name alone is known to us could, in reappearing, reveal an author equal to Virgil. But apart from these rediscoveries—every day more improbable—nothing threatens the permanence of a hierarchy of texts written in a language that has for centuries no longer been used for literary creation. In short, a classical language is a language in which the die is cast, a language where the competition for the symbolic preeminence of the authors is over, a spherical language in which nothing new—neither variation in usage nor modification of the pantheon of its authors—will ever happen. Despite the twilight imagery that he summons to depict the destiny of languages, Chateaubriand recognizes in the classical languages a fundamental superiority over the "modern jargons": predating the division of languages, they are the vehicle of a posterity whose universality has become inaccessible.

The Division of Languages

In his lifetime, Chateaubriand experienced personally the geographical relativity of literary fame. Four decades after his return from America, when he was approaching the conclusion of an existence that was the subject of both the conversation and the admiration of his countrymen, he met on the road to Lugano a foreign student who spoke to him without recognizing him and soon disappeared: "The student didn't know my name; he will have met me and will never know it: this idea gives me joy; I hunger after darkness more eagerly than I formerly desired light: the latter disturbs me either by shining on my miseries or by showing me objects that I can no longer enjoy: I can't wait to pass the torch to my neighbor."[14] In reading the account of this episode, we are tempted to paraphrase Blaise Pascal: "Fame on this side of the Alps, incognito on the other side." While Chateaubriand declares that he was happy with this anonymity, the reader intuits that the indifference of the young traveler nonetheless nettled him. This anecdote suggests that even if you are one of the major writers of your time, there are always strangers who have no idea of your existence.

The fifth part of the *Essay on English Literature* explores the problem of the division of languages and its effect on the concept of posterity, to which it brings a major enrichment by distinguishing two categories: *universal* posterity and *localized* posterity. This distinction is remarkable in that we have up to now used a unified concept of "posterity," designating by this term the future public that will judge works and be charged with transmitting their memory to succeeding publics. Chateaubriand invites us now to clarify this concept by demonstrating that the posterity of a work is not evaluated solely with respect to its inscription in an unlimited temporality: he emphasizes the importance of the spatial criterion as well. In other words, the passage into posterity does not only imply the uninterrupted remembering of an oeuvre by the succession of human generations; to be complete, it must be defended against oblivion outside the borders of the linguistic community to which it was assigned by its birth. Consequently, universal posterity is one that retains the memory of a work in an unlimited time *and* space. On the other hand, since the temporal criterion is not negotiable (a posterity with an expiration date would be a contradiction in terms), it is the spatial criterion that determines localized posterities, those of oeuvres that, celebrated through the centuries, are nonetheless only famous within the linguistic community in which they were born. For Chateaubriand, works produced in the modern era can only pretend to localized posterities: the time of universal posterities, according to him, is definitively past. He attributes this situation to two causes I will analyze: the division of languages and the extension of the democratic ideal to literary life.

Just after describing Agrippina's thrush, Chateaubriand reflects on the following: "The multiplicity and diversity of modern languages must lead men tormented by the thirst for life to ask this sad question: are universal reputations in literature, like those that have come to us from antiquity, still possible today?" (494). Chateaubriand does not identify the historical moment that provoked this break, the time at which the obtaining of a "universal reputation" became an inaccessible ideal. In fact, the disappearance of universal reputations cannot be attributed to an event that took place at a precise date but rather to a slow evolution that led modern languages to dissociate themselves gradually from Latin and distinguish themselves from one another. This development of languages that were more and more distinct led progressively to the elaboration of separate literary traditions within linguistic communities whose members are, according to him, incapable of judging competently works written in a language that is not their mother tongue. We cannot fail to appreciate the paradox of a French writer composing an *Essay on English Literature* in which he confesses that he may be incapable of evaluating correctly the texts that constitute this literature: "I've just given my opinion on a raft of English authors: it is quite possible that I've been mistaken, that I've gotten it all wrong in my admiration and criticism, that my judgments will seem impertinent and grotesque on the other side of the English Channel" (495).

Chateaubriand is in fact convinced that no linguistic apprenticeship, no immersion—no matter how long—in a foreign language is capable of replacing the experience of a virgin mind whose first relationship to the world is effected through his or her mother tongue: "You may think you know a foreign language perfectly, but you do not: you lack the nursemaid's milk, as well as the first words that she taught you at her breast with you in your diaper: certain accents can only be learned in the country of your birth" (495). We are only capable of judging with authority, he says, authors whose works were written in the language that we learned during the first years of our life; as for the others, we run the risk of praising and criticizing contradictory to the judgments rendered by the true experts—that is, the fellow citizens of the foreign writer in question.

It is obvious that learning a language helps us to acquire over the years an adequate familiarity to appreciate the interest, the aptness, and the originality of the expression of sentiments and ideas by an author, and it is precisely this familiarity that translators share with those who discover a foreign body of works through their labors. But literature cannot be reduced to sentiments and ideas; it is also a matter of linguistic substance whose beauties are only open to native speakers of a language. The reasoning of Chateaubriand reveals the primacy he grants to what he calls *diction* (the rhythm) and *style* (understood as the expression of a uniqueness that is both individual and national)—that is, the carnal and extra-discursive character of the use of a language: "When the merit of an author consists especially in the diction, a foreigner will never understand this merit well. The more intimate, individual, and national this talent is, the more its mysteries escape a mind that is not, so to speak, a *compatriot* of this talent. . . . Style is not like cosmopolitan thought; it has a native soil, a sky, a sun of its own." Impossible to reverse, the separation of languages enclosed individuals in linguistic communities whose members can only hazard blind conjectures on works composed outside of them: "It's a joke to think we can know who are our great writers in London, Vienna, Berlin, Saint Petersburg, Munich, Leipzig, Göttingen, and Cologne, that we can know what is being read there passionately, and what is not being read there" (495). Conversely, this Europe whose modern masterpieces vary from nation to nation is in agreement in its appreciation of the works of antiquity: no one will put Propertius above Virgil nor Homer beneath Epaminondas.

According to Chateaubriand, this unanimity concerning the Latin and Greek authors is the combined result of the passing of the centuries and the disappearance of peoples whose works interest us: "We admire the Greeks and Romans without question; our admiration stems from tradition, and the Greeks and Romans are no longer there to mock our barbarian judgments" (495–96). All in all, it is quite possible that we are mistaken in our evaluation of the classical authors (as we are mistaken in our judgments of foreign authors), but contrary to the French who may be indignant that Racine is unknown outside of his homeland, Romans and Greeks are no longer there to point out the ineptitude of our opinions concerning their literature. In other words, the judgments on the works of antiquity have only reached a consensus because of the consolidating effect of time and were formed in the absence of any authentic familiarity with the "diction" and "style" of the authors concerned. In the absence of minds that are "compatriots" of Aeschylus and Catullus, the Europeans judge the Latin and Greek works the best they can, but they are like teachers of a foreign language who have never met native speakers: they transmit a norm that may well appear erroneous to the latter group. The risky character of the judgments issued by the moderns on antique literature is, moreover, reinforced by the disappearance of a considerable part of the texts of which it is composed. Let us imagine that in twenty centuries French theater is represented only by the plays of Houdar de la Motte and not those of Pierre de Marivaux; French poetry by the poems of Léon-Paul Fargue and not those of Charles Baudelaire; the French novel by Roger Nimier and not by Honoré de Balzac: what would be the value of the literary judgments rendered by our distant successors faced with a sparse corpus that they would nonetheless consider to be *French literature*?

Chateaubriand thus admits that the judgments on antique literature are made in the absence of a true capability of appreciation of the materiality of the Greek and Latin languages and are influenced by a tradition that is difficult to contest given the revered character that its age confers on it. The writers of antiquity have nonetheless a considerable advantage over modern authors: they alone have access to a universal posterity, whereas localized posterities await, in the best of cases, the writers of a linguistically divided world: "Thus, there will never again arise these colossi of glory whose grandeur is recognized by all nations and centuries.... We great men, we expected to fill the world with our fame, but whatever we do, it will scarcely reach beyond the limit at which our language expires. Isn't the time of supreme dominations over? Aren't all aristocracies finished?" (496–97). As the melancholic reference to the decline of the aristocracy indicates, the division of the modern languages is not the sole cause at the origin of localized posterities: the expansion of the "democratic principle" to the literary sphere also plays a decisive role in this progressive reduction.

The Expansion of the Democratic Principle

Chateaubriand defines the "democratic principle" as the assertion of the legitimacy of individual judgment and the concomitant challenge to a social order structured by the existence of unquestioned authorities: "People no longer recognize masters and authorities," he frets, "people no longer accept rules or informed opinions; unfettered examination is admitted to Parnassus, just as in politics and religion, as a consequence of this century's progress" (498). Before this progressive invasion of the democratic principle into the literary realm, people of letters, Chateaubriand writes, formed an autonomous world and tended to their respective labors without the rest of society showing much interest in their debates. However, the development of the press permitted the dissemination of opinions on literature whose legitimacy is founded neither on institutional membership (notably in an academy), nor on any particular expertise, but solely on the right of each individual to issue a judgment. This criticism of speech that asserts its own validity by referring to the liberty of expression alone, without its author bothering to support it by a competence (in particular, the ability to produce books before judging those of others) identifies the birth and exponential development in our time of a phenomenon facilitated by new technological avenues. Without losing sight of the criticism of the democratic principle proposed by Chateaubriand, I would like to make a short detour by our own era in order to show the development of tendencies that were just beginning to dawn in his time, and that, nonetheless, already appeared aberrant to him.

While the publication of literary criticism in the press assumes another form of external recognition (be it only the confidence of an editor-in-chief), the blogs published today on the internet by individuals whose sole demonstrable competence consists in knowing how to read has provoked an explosion of texts far superior to that which the growth of the press could generate at the time of Chateaubriand. In addition, digital platforms that solicit, preserve, rank, and calculate the statistical average of opinions produced by the consumers of a book offer new technical means to the public expression of personal opinions and establish themselves as either a form of "countervailing power" or, at least, as an alternate evaluating authority whose activities are carried out parallel to those of professionals who sign their articles in the specialized press. Amateurs and voluntary contributors, these new judges of works are treated with growing respect by publishing professionals who see in them forces that they must take into consideration, since they are capable of arousing or dampening the desire to acquire a new book by sharing their views with their own readers. The democratic logic combines with that of the marketplace to legitimize their discourse and ultimately encourage other individuals to speak out in turn: readers being consumers, their opinion on the literary product is capable of influencing other potential buyers for whom the work in question is likewise intended.

Indeed, the *publication* of a book—the result of a purely material process of fabrication that permits authors to offer their personal thoughts to an unlimited public, both contemporary and future, compatriot and foreigner—turns everyone into a potential recipient of the work and consequently a judge who is competent to evaluate it, if not as an expert in literature, at least as a consumer. In short, the general leveling that Chateaubriand attributes to democracy is exhibited not only in the legitimization of all individual judgments concerning literature but also, simultaneously, in the lowering of literary products to the level of market values. Their desecration is recognized by the adoption of rating methods generally used by consumers to evaluate the rest of their purchases: we give digital stars and leave commentaries on the websites of online sales outlets, whether it is a matter of sharing our opinions on the qualities of a novel or the performance of a vacuum cleaner. What Chateaubriand identifies in the *Essay on English Literature* is thus the origin of a process of multi-polarization of the sources of literary consecration whose contemporary manifestations would have frightened him. Therefore, all of his reflections on the condition of the literary figure in the era of the expansion of the democratic principle are valid a fortiori for the writers of our age, during which each reader is a pole of evaluation whose right to give her or his opinion on literary works is treated as equal to that of anyone else.

If this extreme liberalization of the right to speak out is met by Chateaubriand with bad humor and condemnation, it is not only because he is accusing a legacy of the French Revolution, among other ills, of desecrating the Catholic religion, reducing to nothing the traditional authorities, and assassinating several members of his own family; it also seems deplorable to him because, when all is said and done, it is the very passage of writers to posterity that it seems to put into question.

In the first place, Chateaubriand accuses it of limiting celebrity to ever decreasing spaces: "Each person judges and believes he has the right to judge, based on his own enlightenment, taste, system, hate, or love. This produces a crowd of immortals, confined to their street, enclosed in the circle of their school and friends, and who are unknown or jeered at in the neighboring district" (498). The division of languages reduced the fame of writers to the sphere of their linguistic community; the democratic principle reduces it still further by enclosing it within social circles comprising scarcely a handful of individuals. As narrow as they are, these circles engage in a merciless battle for recognition owing to the constant conflict of egos that cannot suffer the exaltation of a writer without interpreting it as an injustice toward all the others, revealing by this fact a subconscious zero-sum logic according to which collective recognition exists in a finite quantity and can only be bestowed at the expense of those it ignores: "We cannot tolerate reputations; it seems as if what people admire is being stolen from us: our vanity takes umbrage at the slightest success, and if it lasts a while, it is a torture for it" (498).

Nonetheless, it is not only the geographical sphere of the expansion of celebrity that the democratic principle progressively reduces; it also threatens the inscription of works in an unlimited time span owing to the frantic rhythm with which the authors are successively raised to the skies and then dragged in the mud: "Now that denigrating or admiring newspapers *sound their attack or victory*, you would have to be pretty unlucky not to know during your life what you are worth. With these contradictory judgments, if our glory begins earlier, it is over faster: in the morning an eagle, in the evening a bittern" (498). The multiplication of the vectors of opinion on literary works, the legitimization of everyone's words, the irreconcilable emulation and opposition of egos, all of these phenomena converge to refuse to authors a lasting fame during their life and explain the haste, if not the satisfaction, with which their works are discarded after their death: "They hasten to package the famous deceased in three or four newspaper articles, then they speak of him no more; they no longer open his works; they seal his fame in his books like they seal his cadaver in its coffin, sending it all off to eternity through time and death" (499). Deceased, the writer makes way for all those who aspire to interest their fellow mortals in their person, and who will not succeed any more unanimously or permanently than did their predecessors.

Consequently, if we relate the posthumous destiny of writers to the two evaluation criteria that Chateaubriand distinguished—time and space—we are left with an alarming conclusion: in the modern period, it is impossible to inscribe the memory of an oeuvre in either an infinite space or an unlimited time span. "In the era in which we live," Chateaubriand concludes, "each period is worth a century; society dies and is reborn every ten years. So, adieu any sustained, *universally* recognized glory. Whoever writes in the hope of making his name famous is sacrificing his life to the most stupid—and most vain—of illusions" (499–500). Chateaubriand thus presents himself as the contemporary of an age in which the posterity of writers is threatened by the democratic principle, such that the spirit of leveling that he attributes to the latter appears, to him, to preclude even the posthumous elevation of authors.

"You Will Put an End to All These Speeches"

The *Essay on English Literature* is a prodigious meditation on the destiny of languages whose most pessimistic consequences are not what you may think. Indeed, Chateaubriand demonstrates that all languages are subjected to a slow process that leads them to silence. Those that dispose of the largest contingent of speakers, those that are supported by a military and political power strong enough to impose them on new peoples, however great their momentary expansion may be, will ultimately end with their Rosetta Stone: if not dead, they will become at least silent. Paradoxically, the intermediate term of this evolution— the closed language—is more favorable to the symbolic immortality of writers. Indeed, open languages are the material of a growing corpus in which future masterpieces will perhaps arise, whereas works that were unheralded in their time patiently await the day of their recognition. Thus the hour of the evaluation of modern works does not ring as long as the language in which they were written has not withdrawn into itself. Only then, when the egos unleashed by the democratic principle have fallen silent; when, barring the improbable exhumation of a forgotten text, nothing more can modify the corpus of existing works, the time for judgment will have come, and the titles to recognition by posterity will finally be distributed.

As a result, closed languages do not deserve this adjective only because of the closure of their vocabulary and the definitive state of their rules of grammar: they are languages in which no new work may enter and, consequently, upset the status quo of the literary hierarchy. It is true that the consensus on the intrinsic and relative value of the works that compose its literature could have been different in other circumstances: notably had other works had survived into our era. Likewise, we will in all probability continue to admire the works written in these closed languages despite our inability to judge the stylistic qualities that the native speakers of these languages alone were able to appreciate. But with what remains of these literatures, we have done our best, we who are the posterity of Ovid, Horace, and Lucretius, we who are also the posterity of Sophocles, Aesop, and Plutarch; we have done our best to preserve, understand, and evaluate a literature whose principal illustrations have acquired a *universal* posterity.

Chateaubriand, we have seen, cites in the *Essay on English Literature* the famous quote from Bossuet: "You will put an end to all these speeches." In its original context, this phrase referred to the funeral oration that the Eagle of Meaux was finishing in honor of the Prince de Condé. The "speeches"—a term with a pejorative connotation, since we detect therein the hint of a criticism of verbosity and vacuity, if not vanity—is set in opposition to the piety of the victor of the Battle of Rocroi, this piety being his only veritable claim to glory. Included in Chateaubriand's reflection on the destiny of languages, this sentence takes on additional meanings. On the one hand, it alludes to the death of the French language through this last audible fragment, already devoid of meaning. On the other hand, it implicitly confronts the "speech" to the "work"—that is, the ontologically second word, dependent on the first, creative word. By "speech" we can understand all the *commentaries* that come to bear on the works—that is, all the linguistic productions that set out to evaluate the literary texts in order to produce praise or criticism.

If the speeches stop when the literature is just as closed as the language in which it is composed, it is because the conflict of egos among the living leads the latter to denigrate neither the works of contemporaries nor those of deceased authors whose posthumous glory nonetheless seems usurped to them. If the speeches stop, it is because there are no longer any reasons to hold forth on the works when their intrinsic and relative value has had all the time it needed to be evaluated, definitively set, and handed down from one of those "chairs" from which the same judgments perpetually fall. If the speeches stop, it is because the inventory of works is complete within a language whose form will no more change than the corpus of works it includes. To sum up, Chateaubriand invites us to imagine a last judgment of literature, when the truth of the works—beyond fashion, misunderstanding, jealousy, and bad faith—will be as transparent as the truth of hearts in the eyes of He Who sees all. The price to pay for these works, however, is identical to that which people in general must pay: for them, the great paradox consists in dying before entering eternity; for works, in being buried in a closed language before entering into the memory of posterity. A work must thus survive the use of its language and become a contradictory symbol, both a sign of the disappearance of its culture of origin and a sign of its own immortality: a monument that is the gravestone of the world to which it bears witness and on which, nevertheless, is inscribed a text just as enduring as the one on the Rosetta Stone. Chateaubriand's meditation on the destiny of languages thus brings us to this new paradox: authors are only admitted to posterity if they write in a language that no one speaks any longer, a closed language succeeding the extinction of "all the speeches."

EIGHTH PARADOX

The Manuscript and the USB Key

As an "allographic art," literature has the singular characteristic that we may distinguish its products from the medium in which they were created.[1] While a copy of a painting cannot be put on the same level as the original, it is always the same work that we read in a paperback edition or a deluxe edition, provided that the letter of the text has been respected during its production: it makes no difference if we read Proust in a coffee-table book or in a Penguin Classic. Of course, a particular value is attached to manuscripts, but this involves the value we attach to things that are irreplaceable: we cherish in them the unique evidence of an intelligence at work, although they may no longer control access to the work of which they are the original manifestation. Thus literature is an artistic form whose products are represented by a variety of material objects without the aesthetic value of the work being altered in the process of this proliferation.

It is accordingly in the form of a set of signs traced on a perishable medium that a text is presented to its readers. Traditionally, these media have been paper, papyrus, parchment, clay, and stone. While it is true that oral poetry is transmitted without it being necessary to translate the thought and emotion into visible signs, it is not an abuse of metaphor to say that the recitation of poems, legends, and tales is a means of *transcribing* them in the memories of others: in speaking of "engraving" a text in the memory of a listener, ordinary language reveals that speech is another stylus, and that the mnemonic faculties are like tablets on which it is inscribed. There can, of course, be a loss or alteration of meaning in the course of these transmissions, but, everything considered, there is no difference with the manual copying of texts, and the goal of philology is precisely to analyze the competing versions of the same work. Thus any transmission of a work to the successive reconfigurations of posterity is dependent on its material media, such that the disappearance of the last of them leads to its definitive annihilation, whether it concerns the last human memory to preserve the memory of a myth or the final copy of a book to transcend the passage of time.

Since the end of the twentieth century and the advent of computer science, a technical mediation has been added to this material mediation. Digital technology makes the access to texts and their modification dependent on the use of a player that gives access to a coded content.[2] Contrary to material mediation, which permits the immediate reading of a text by any individual who has mastered its linguistic code, technical mediation requires the use of an apparatus without which the text remains indecipherable.

This chapter will concern material mediation, technical mediation, and the reasons why the transmission of texts to posterity is dependent on the capacity of these intermediaries to prolong the access they give to the works. While an optimistic conception of digital technology leads us to consider it to be a possible solution to the fundamental fragility of the material formats of texts, I will ask if technical mediation does not lead, in another form, to the same difficulties of conservation that are inherent in material mediation—unless it actually adds an additional series of obstacles to the permanent inscription of texts in the future network of memories.

An Art of Incarnation

In *The Confessions*, Rousseau relates that he occasionally spent nights awake composing a sentence that he would not write until the morning: "It is during walks, among the boulders and the woods, or during my sleepless nights in bed that I write in my mind; you can imagine how slowly, especially for a man absolutely devoid of verbal memory, and who could never in his whole life learn six lines of poetry by heart. There are certain of my sentences that I turned around and around in my head five or six nights before they were ready to be put on paper."[3] From this example I would like to draw a series of conclusions concerning the relationship between writing and its material mediation.

On the one hand, a literary work exists in the mind of its author before being embodied in a medium. Indeed, authors possess at the minimum a general idea of what they are going to write before getting down to work: novelists know where they left their characters in their story and to what stage of the narrative progression (itself conceived before the actual writing) they wish to lead them when they begin to work; fragments of arguments may have come to the mind of an essayist in the course of a walk or while daydreaming. Writers know very well that there is no distinction between the time for writing and the time for leisure: the thought develops in them, whether they set about transcribing it on a medium or become involved in an activity apparently unrelated to writing. In short, a work possesses a prior partial state as regards its material appearance in the form of characters traced on any medium.

Nonetheless, if the work precedes its material embodiment, it is in the form of fragments whose contents and organization will be modified in the act of writing. With the possible exception of brief texts, such as haikus or quatrains, a work is never *completely* composed in the mind of its author, with the sequencing of all its sentences and the definitive selection of all its terms. On the one hand, the length of a literary or philosophical text discourages a priori an undertaking that would consist in composing it mentally in its totality before committing it to paper by writing or dictation. On the other hand, the fact of conceiving a thought at the moment of writing it down transforms its expression in unforeseeable ways, new thoughts occurring to the author and unknown obstacles arising during the formulation in words: an unfortunate assonance may determine not only a changing of terms but an intellectual deviation as well.

Literature is thus an art of *incarnation* in two complementary senses. First, the texts are obviously only knowable by others in the material form of a series of characters. Second, the act that consists in translating thought into words that can be interpreted by others and by oneself is not an act of transposition (I set on the page what already existed *in the same form* in my mind) but an act of invention that reveals to me what I did not know before trying to render it communicable, and that, in the process, leads me to alter my thought at the very moment I am attempting to express it.[4] Consequently, literature is inextricably linked to the material media that permit its physical incarnation: the intense activity exhibited by the majority of manuscripts demonstrates that thought works itself out as it is being recorded, and that the formulation ultimately retained by an author is, as a rule, the result of a series of failed beginnings. "My manuscripts, lines struck out, smeared, messy, indecipherable, attest to the effort they cost me. There isn't a single one that I didn't have to transcribe four or five times before turning it over to the press," Rousseau observes in this respect.[5] This physical dimension of literature is directly related to the problem of posterity and gives rise to a paradox whose examination will be the goal of this chapter. For if there is no literature without material mediation, there is no imperishable physical medium. While literary posterity implies the unlimited survival of texts, the latter are inevitably preserved in media whose life span is limited. In other words, writers are forced to entrust to a corruptible and fragile substance this intellective part of their person that they hope will remain accessible to the successive incarnations of the network of memories. In what follows I will briefly describe three obstacles that compromise the sustainability of texts by threatening the material media in which they are recorded: the passage of time, religious beliefs, and political ideology.

Three Obstacles to the Permanence of Texts

Stephen Greenblatt borrows from Ovid's *Metamorphoses* the expression "the teeth of time" to designate the set of phenomena that imperil the transmission of texts to posterity by attacking the substance of the material media on which they are inscribed.[6] Greenblatt reminds us, in fact, that with rare exceptions, it is not the manuscripts of ancient texts that have come down to us but copies of the latter.[7] "But where did all the books go? The actual material disappearance of the books was largely the effect of climate and pests. Though papyrus and parchment were impressively long-lived (far more so than either our cheap paper or computerized data), books inevitably deteriorated over the centuries, even if they managed to escape the ravages of fire and flood" (82).

Materials, the media of the texts, bear in themselves a principle of degeneration: paper falls apart, ink pales, and the richest works, the best-bound books, all become viscous heaps from which thought streams. It is thus on a minute portion of the literary production of antiquity that we base our judgments. Aeschylus may have written ninety-nine plays: we only know seven of them; of the ninety-two works signed by Euripides, there only remain eighteen. Despite the considerable losses within the production of these playwrights, they had far greater luck than the majority of the writers of the ancient period. Greenblatt gives the example of Didymus of Alexandria, a contemporary of Augustus, whose frightening work ethic earned him the nickname "Bronze-Ass" (literally "Brazen-Bowelled"): of the over 3,500 books he wrote, absolutely nothing, with the exception of a few fragments, has reached us (81–82). However, it is quite conceivable that at some point in this stupefying intellectual production, Didymus expressed the wish, allusively or perhaps with a self-assurance comparable to that of Horace in the conclusion of the *Odes*, that his enormous labors be recognized by future generations. This tendency toward annihilation characterizes the intellectual and artistic production of the period: of the 1,400 quotes compiled by Jean Stobée, a doxographer of late antiquity, 1,015 of them were taken from works that have been lost.

In order to fight the teeth of time and, in particular, the stubborn vandalism of mites and worms, protective measures have long been tested: cedar oil applied to texts has notably proved effective in combating the ravages of these voracious enemies. But since antiquity it is by the proliferation of copies that men have sought to save texts: "A well-trained slave reading a manuscript aloud to a roomful of well-trained scribes could produce masses of text" (86). According to Greenblatt, hundreds of thousands of copies were produced and sold for centuries, such that this solution to the problem of the disappearance of works ultimately generated new challenges. Whereas we tend to associate the excess of available knowledge with the modern period, and particularly with the capacity of the internet to make accessible a mass of digital texts that far outstrips our capacity to read, in ancient times the accumulation of works owing to copies had already brought about difficulties in the management and classification of knowledge:

There was a time in the ancient world—a very long time—in which the central cultural problem must have seemed an inexhaustible outpouring of books. Where to put them all? How to organize them on the groaning shelves? How to hold the profusion of knowledge in one's head? The loss of this plenitude would have been virtually inconceivable to anyone living in its midst.

Then, not all at once but with the cumulative force of a mass extinction, the whole enterprise came to an end. What looked stable turned out to be fragile, and what had seemed for all time was only for the time being. . . . The fate of the books in all their vast numbers is epitomized in the fate of the greatest library in the ancient world, a library located not in Italy but in Alexandria, the capital of Egypt and the commercial hub of the eastern Mediterranean. (86–87)

With the principle of degeneration at the heart of the material media of thought, the elements and accidents capable of destroying them are joined by religious beliefs that brought to bear an additional threat to the transmission of texts to posterity, as is demonstrated by the example of the famous library of Alexandria. Greenblatt recalls one of the available theories to explain its ravaging: it consists in attributing it to the Christians of the fifth century CE who may have burned this marvel to the ground at the time of the massacre of the female philosopher Hypatia (93). Over the course of the following centuries, the destruction of texts considered incompatible with the teachings of the Bible brought new purges of available knowledge. Emboldened by a criticism of the fundamental immorality of books, the "hate of literature" distinguished itself by its virtuous ardor: in the "bonfire of the vanities" that burned on February 7, 1497, in Florence, how many works were reduced to ashes?[28] While copying texts is an effective way to counter the erosive action of the passage of time; while the ubiquity of books it produces permits the preservation of certain copies at same as others are swept away by a natural catastrophe or some kind of accident, religious beliefs are capable of encouraging the irremediable destruction of texts that promote thought that is contrary to the values they defend.

The body of thought found in the books of the past did not come into potential conflict with religious beliefs alone: it also provoked the hostility of political ideologies. The auto-da-fé of May 10, 1933, in which the Nazis burned books by the armful is a sadly famous example of these concerted destructions of works by a political power that seeks to stifle any contestation, including that propagated by authors long dead. In describing human memory as the ultimate receptacle of books that a special police force is charged with burning, Ray Bradbury emphasizes in *Fahrenheit 451* the vulnerability of works when they become the target of a political authority that mobilizes the resources necessary for their methodological eradication. Whereas the mechanization of the reproduction of texts through the printing press could be considered the definitive solution to local accidents that risked destroying the last copy of a work, the twentieth century produced, in reality and in the dystopian imaginary, the nightmare of a concurrent systemization of the destruction of books.

It is because literary products must be produced within artifacts in order to be accessible to others that they fall prey to the passage of time and become the potential victim of those they offend. Literature is, in fact, a spiritual creation that is embodied in a variety of physical objects whose function is to assure collectively its transmission to posterity, but whose fundamental fragility condemns it nonetheless to disappear; without this transfusion of life that the manual copy or reprinting communicate, the work expires, and the thought of the author is definitively lost. Pierre-Marc de Biasi brings to light the paradox of paper in calling it a "fragile medium of the essential," with the major part of our historical, scientific, and cultural tradition being dependent on this ephemeral material. If we only take the example of texts produced on paper made from industrial wood beginning at the end of the nineteenth century, the majority of them are eaten by acid and condemned to an irreversible disintegration.[9] While the spiritual principle designated by the word "soul" refers to what is unique and survives the disintegration of the body to which it was momentarily united, a literary work is inscribed from the beginning in a perishable, tangible medium; while it can be reproduced an unlimited number of times, the work has no possible existence outside of these incarnations: there is no beyond in which books take refuge while awaiting their resurrection. Is digital technology, by dematerializing texts, a way to confer on them a permanent existence and, consequently, guarantee them continuous access to posterity?

Digitization and Posterity

A process effecting the formalization of a given reality in an arithmetical system, digitization converts the material existence of an object into images. The digital novel is made available on the internet, and it is solely this virtual double that I may alter—by leaving virtual notes in its margin, for example—an edit that nevertheless leaves intact the material original from which the copy came. While printing generates a finite number of copies that must be sent to readers by physical means, the digitizing of texts increases the ease and speed of the production of copies as well as their distribution: once a work has become a computer file, it takes but an instant to create a copy of it on a hard disk and send it through the internet to a reader who, in turn, will store it on another memory device hundreds or thousands of miles away. Thanks to these appropriately named "saved" copies, the same work may exist at distant and multiple points throughout the world. Such ubiquity increases the statistical probability that there will always exist an intact copy in the event that, elsewhere in the world, its other copies are destroyed, on purpose or by chance.

The digitizing of texts has the additional advantage of offering a solution to the problems created by the storage and preservation of printed works. While the technologies of storage of digital data are accompanied by a continual increase in the ability to save them, the preservation of printed texts quickly confounds its agents with an insufficiency of infrastructures. "A digitized page of text," Claude Huc observes, "may require around ten kilobytes. A document of one hundred pages (a centimeter thick) occupies a megabyte. Consequently, a terabyte allows the storage of a million documents of one hundred pages that correspond, in paper form, to ten linear kilometers."[10]

As I have already noted, the responsibility that falls on posterity grows heavier by the moment: in disappearing, each generation bequeaths a new contingent of texts that is added to the crushing mass of all those that preceding generations have already transmitted. It seems nonetheless that the constant increase of technologies for the storage of digital data is capable of accommodating this exponential production of texts that humanity passes on to its successive embodiments. Digital technology would thus seem to offer a solution to the problem of transmitting texts to posterity. By dematerializing them, it permits them to escape the ravages of time; by giving them the gift of ubiquity, it guarantees that in some space on the globe there remain virtual copies protected from efforts at systematic destruction that may target printed copies; by converting linear miles of pages into digital data, it reduces the costs of construction, maintenance, and enlargement of physical libraries. And by guaranteeing to *all* those who produce texts that a scrap of digital memory will be devoted to them, this technology is capable of dissipating the anguish of the definitive disappearance of texts. Nonetheless, the *sustainable* preservation of digital texts assumes the resolution of multiple problems that may, I will now speculate, re-create in another form difficulties that are ultimately equal to those presented by the preservation of printed texts.

Migration and Philology

The creation and maintenance of a virtual space are dependent on real efforts that people make in the physical world. While the digital file seems to have acquired a kind of eternity because it is the image of a book and, as such, escapes the law of the progressive disintegration of material objects, the sustainable access to this image depends on a very long chain of intermediaries that contrasts with the immediacy of access to printed texts. In the case of material mediation, the text is directly readable by any individual who masters the language in which it is written: other than this cultural prerequisite, nothing more is necessary for her or him to access it. On the other hand, digital technology interposes between a text and its reader a chain of indispensable intermediaries including the format, the player, the operating system, the software application, and the peripherals.[11] Digital conservation thus requires the preservation of the medium where the information is recorded as well as the proper functioning of each of its intermediaries in their original or equivalent form.[12]

Since the probability that a chain of intermediaries will be broken is in direct proportion to the number and complexity of these elements, digital technology makes the sustainable access to texts more fragile, with each link in this chain being separately doomed to obsolescence. The storage medium itself has a limited lifetime: magnetic disks or CD-ROMs are not eternal, and their destruction leads to that of the information they contain. To this material obsolescence of the intermediaries of digital mediation is added the technical and commercial obsolescence. Not only is the device that allows us to access the information stored on a memory medium no longer available on the market after a few years, but the operating system of a computer is regularly updated. Even if we were to dispose of storage media whose life expectancy were equal to that of high-quality paper (which is far from the case), they would cease to be readable well before reaching obsolescence, since their technical characteristics would no longer be recognized by the other intermediaries of the technical mediation.[13] In a word, "The technical/commercial life expectancy is shorter than the physical life expectancy."[14]

Consequently, the sustainable preservation of texts assumes that we must choose between two possible solutions: "constantly migrating all media and hardware and software chains, or creating living IT museums in which these intermediaries are kept in working condition."[15] Although this second possibility is in fact conceivable, it removes from the digital world the practical advantages that we have recognized in it and tips the balance in favor of the material mediation of texts. Indeed, we would have to visit one of these "living museums of computer science" to consult works stored in the memory of computers, while digital technology has accustomed us precisely to accessing knowledge from the location of our choice. Moreover, the maintenance costs of these museums would be prohibitive compared to those occasioned by the preservation of printed copies of the same texts and would prevent them from becoming economically viable alternatives to the traditional repositories of knowledge in printed form.

The migration of digital documents would thus seem preferable to guarantee their access in the long term. Contrary to emulation, this practice concerns the digital objects themselves and not the computer environment in which they may be consulted. It consists in modifying the digital documents such that their representation on more recent computer devices and software is not different from their original representation: "By converting the format of an object, it is possible to make it readable by a system currently in use."[16]

If we wish to make the digitizing of texts the means of preserving them for posterity, we must envision a succession of migrations: a new migration will have to be carried out each time a format is no longer in use. This necessity produces a paradox that is inherent to digital mediation: the preservation of digital texts through migration implies altering what one intends to preserve, an obligation that leads to yet another, which consists in documenting the successive changes that the text undergoes. As Bruno Bachimont remarks, "The goal is not to guarantee the original state of the object, which is impossible, but to allow us to examine its authenticity by following the course of the transformations it has undergone."[17]

Digital obsolescence, like technical-commercial obsolescence, thus leads us, in another form, to the planned obsolescence of material media, so that a digital text that remained unchanged would quickly become inaccessible. In changing in order to remain identical, however, digitized texts risk being altered in the course of their successive migrations such that in the long run—and a fortiori when we conceptualize the problem of digital preservation in the unlimited time span of posterity—we also risk preserving texts that are different from their original version. To surmount this obstacle, Bachimont suggests an adaptation of the techniques of classical philology to the challenges created by the digitizing of texts: "Like philology, which examines manuscripts and copies saved from the destruction of time in order to reconstruct the original text, the version that will become authoritative, the goal of digital archiving will be to define the criteria and genealogical rules in order to extract the content from the different material objects that had contained it in the various stages of its transformations."[18]

Thus the preservation of digital texts requires, in the long run, a conceptual innovation and the return to a very old practice. From a conceptual point of view, digitizing invites us to think of the preservation of texts as the implementation of a systematic and regular undertaking of migrations toward new formats. While the preservation of tangible media necessitates a permanent and rigorous control of the environment in which they are stored, so that the humidity, temperature, and light do not accelerate the process of disintegration of the texts, digital preservation requires the adaptation of the latter to changing digital environments. From a practical point of view, the necessity of documenting these successive migrations invites the digital archivists of today and tomorrow to return to the methods of classical philology. Their task consists, in particular, in creating a system of "documentation of transformation"[19] whose goal is the exhaustive description of the changes undergone by a document in the course of its migrations and the analysis of the eventual alterations, degradations, and improvements to which it has been subjected.

Considering digital technology in relationship to the transmission of texts to posterity thus involves plunging into problems of preservation that, at the present time, remain unresolved. Owing to the relatively recent character of this technology, we lack the hindsight necessary to anticipate the distant future of virtual libraries in which literary works will come to rest. What is nevertheless in no doubt is the inability of digitization to render texts automatically accessible to all the successive reorganizations of posterity. This accessibility assumes on the contrary a series of migrations accompanied by a documentation of the changes the texts have undergone. At this time, all we can do is note that the difficulties created by the preservation of digital texts bring into the virtual world the same problems that are related to the conservation of printed texts and require the adaptation of similar solutions. Digital obsolescence echoes the obsolescence of physical materials, digital migration is comparable to the copying of a manuscript in that it transposes a text to another material environment with the risk of altering it along the way, and "digital archiving" derives its principles and objectives from classical philology.

Nonetheless, the adoption of a given technology does not depend on the complete absence of limitations but on the existence of a greater number of advantages than problems in its use. In the area of the preservation of texts, the ideal solution would consist in identifying an absolutely sustainable medium that would not require any human intervention to be maintained in its current form. The digitizing of texts does not offer this possibility, but at least it brings numerous other advantages that justify its adoption. Digital technology facilitates, in particular, the availability of texts whose physical copies only exist in a limited number of collections, thus increasing the probability that they will be rediscovered by future generations who will not have to exhume them from the depths of an archive. From a practical point of view again, the research carried out by literature specialists is greatly facilitated by digitization, which enables them to identify, by means of a "search" function, the place of a passage in a work or to find the origin of an unknown quotation in a database. By encouraging the digitizing of texts, do these numerous advantages not risk, however, leading in their turn to new difficulties? By proliferating, does digitizing not threaten to provoke a phenomenon of memorial explosion? I will now ask what one still remembers when it becomes possible to forget nothing.

The Digital and Memorial Overload

There is a price to pay for the preservation of texts by means of the digital, namely the appropriation of the memorial faculties of posterity. The quantity of information that can be retained by each person is always limited, and the space occupied by literary works from the past is never more than a small fragment of what individuals remember. To say it differently, the global memory of posterity is finite, since it is only ever composed of the sum of individual memories. With the disappearance of texts that were not passed on to posterity, a phenomenon of memorial selection was formerly accomplished blindly by "the tooth of time." Place was made for others in the memories of tomorrow, and what was not remembered by posterity at least restored to it a space to devote to others. Today, the sum of published works is staggering: during the year 2016 alone, the National Library of France added 77,986 books and 262,199 periodicals to its official collection. As Pierre-Marc de Biasi had already observed in 1997, "This ocean of papers that we call the written patrimony is on the verge of submerging the libraries and blowing up all material capacity of preservation."[20]

All these books—a number of which appear simultaneously in digital and paper format—are the work of individuals who claim, in person or through their websites, a fragment of the collective attention that they fail in their overwhelming majority to obtain, the number of published works being far too great in relation to the available readers.[21] Simultaneously, these authors have pretentions with regard to future generations and hope to occupy a fragment of the collective memory where they will not only compete with one another, as they did during their life, but will also join the immense cohort of writers from the past: "The old collections are colossal: the National Library and the municipal libraries hold some forty million books or manuscripts prior to the twentieth century; the National Archives contain nearly three billion documents prior to 1789."[22] The network of memories is already overwhelmed, excessively solicited by calls for the posthumous recognition of deceased authors. Thus the current risk consists in preserving, through digital technology, a quantity of information that far exceeds the memorial capacities of humanity. While literary works indeed risk less than ever being irretrievably lost, each can only dispose of an infinitesimal fragment of the collective memory.

Unless, of course, the internet becomes a complementary memory, a colossal, infinite memory that will be added to the memorial faculties held in common by humanity. This memory will not be permanently solicited, and certain works will never receive the slightest attention from human minds, but they will continue to exist in this additional memory, a dormant potential awaiting the day when a future reorganization of the members of posterity will lead to a renewed interest in these texts. Such rediscoveries will be the work of new "scholars" that Bruno Bachimont suggests we call "digital men of letters":

> While the scholar must combat ignorance, which we may characterize here as the absence or shortage of knowledge, the digital man of letters must combat the abundance of information made accessible by digital means. The digital man of letters must orient himself to find his way and make his choice among this abundance. In case of failure, he is not faced with ignorance but loss of meaning; he is not ignorant, just disoriented. This is the reason why the digital man of letters is not a scholar but simply a clever man, that is, one who knows how to get his bearings and make decisions when faced with a multitude of possibilities.[23]

The figure of the scholar is characterized by the absorption of a body of knowledge of which she or he becomes a valuable custodian in a context marked by the rarity of receptacles of knowledge. This figure is embodied notably by Poggio Bracciolini, who conducted tireless research across fifteenth-century Europe before rediscovering Lucretius's poem *On the Nature of Things*. The story of this humanist reminds us of the considerable effort it was necessary to expend for centuries to navigate between the scattered cultural islands and to constitute by correspondence networks of scholarly sociability.[24] Thus the prestige of the scholar stems from his identity as a "library man" in whom knowledge is gathered and organized. On the other hand, the "digital man of letters" bears witness to a renewed relationship to knowledge. Immediately accessible on the internet, there is no longer any need for it to be memorized: erudition loses its prestige from the moment that a connection to the internet allows us to remedy any gap in our knowledge. However, its accessibility requires on the part of the digital man of letters the mastery of competencies distinct from those of the scholar, beginning with the development of a form of "sagacity" that consists in finding one's bearings in a plethora of ever ramifying information and, furthermore, in mobilizing critical tools that help us identify the source of the available data in order to evaluate their coherence and degree of reliability.

Of course, the subjective impression of being crushed by the weight of available knowledge is far from being a novelty engendered by the appearance of digital technology. In *Too Much to Know*, Ann Blair argues that the overload of information is a phenomenon that occurred even before the invention of the printing press, but which the latter nonetheless reinforced, necessitating the creation of new techniques of selecting, organizing, and saving knowledge.[25] Although the impression of an excess of knowledge has pestered humanity since the Renaissance at least, it is produced in our period by a mass of information that has no objective equivalent in human history: never before the digital age has available knowledge been so extensive. To take the example of HathiTrust alone, a digital collection comprising the collections of 120 libraries throughout the world, visitors have at their disposal 17,181,540 digitized volumes, for a total of 6,013,539,000 pages and 770 terabytes of data.[26] It thus clearly appears that the authors who today aspire to posthumous recognition no longer need address their prayers to a patient scholar who will find the last copy of their work, unjustly ignored, on the dusty shelves of an abandoned library. The digital man of letters is their new Saint Peter; the key to their symbolic immortality is in that person's hand, for it is he or she who, amid these immense catalogs of digitized works, this overabundance of available titles, will save them not from nothingness but from indifference, not from destruction but from burial.

We thus arrive, at the end of this reflection on the relationship between digital technology and posterity, at a new paradox that is tainted by bitterness. In granting to authors what they all hope for—that is, a form of memorial permanence—digital technology may offer them a situation that, in all truth, no one wants: a minimal inscription in the digital memory while awaiting an improbable rediscovery by future generations of people who will be solicited by legions of authors from the past and who will, in addition, work to create the beauty of their own time. The very form of these potential rediscoveries, of these "literary revivals" occurring at the end of a period of more or less prolonged eclipse, will have a deceptive dimension, given that a chapter in a collective work will be the highest form of posthumous recognition to which men and women of letters will be able to aspire.[27] Devote your entire existence to the construction of an immortal oeuvre, and perhaps there will be a university professor who, fifty years after your death, will compose, on your efforts, fifteen pages that will be read and then forgotten by two hundred readers ... These revivals of an oeuvre are indeed difficult, for it is delicate to manipulate the network of memories; you cannot inscribe in it the memory of a writer like you transfer data in a computer's memory, and for these grafts of renewed interest to succeed, you still have to assume the sustained devotion of readers preaching, amid a cacophony of ever more numerous voices, a message long forgotten.

The curse attached to the obtaining of what one desires is thus the same for symbolic immortality and literal immortality. While an increase of indefinite existence is generally considered desirable by individuals, the condemnation to survive all of one's close friends and relatives would nonetheless stain immortality with an intolerable bitterness that would ultimately be suffered in melancholy and regret, as the myth of the vampire demonstrates in its allusive way. It is the same for digital eternity: by granting to authors what they desire—that is, a place in the future network of memories—this technology leads to the reciprocal occultation of each by the others.

NINTH PARADOX

The Comet and the Astronomer

Beyond the problems created by the cultural, material, and technical mediations of works, an even more radical threat hangs over their transmission to posterity: the survival of the members that compose it. Symbolic immortality is only ever bestowed by others, so it is necessary for generations to be linked to one another for the memory of works to continue to exist. The present chapter is devoted to the contradiction between the testamentary undertakings of authors and the potential annihilation of their heirs. To study the consequences of this final mediation—the *human mediation*—on the transmission of texts to posterity, I will return to the *Dialogue* of Diderot and Falconet in which the correspondents develop a stimulating thought experiment concerning the destruction of humankind by a heavenly body. In this chapter, we will reflect on the notion of a scheduled apocalypse and the effects we may anticipate on humans in general and on artists in particular.

I could have envisioned, however, some intermediate cases, just as likely to break the chain of memorial transmissions that posterity implies, without going as far as the annihilation of the world, which will perhaps appear to be an overly spectacular and somewhat gratuitous supposition. Literary dystopias, in particular, have sought to imagine scenarios that make such a rupture plausible. In George Orwell's *Nineteen Eighty-Four*, it is the concerted action of political power and the control of language that account for a generalized loss of cultural products accumulated by previous generations. In Boualem Sansal's *2084*, a despotic religion orders the systematic eradication of works that are in conflict with its doctrine.[1] Of course, the conclusions of these dystopias leave scarcely any hope as regards the future overthrow of the totalitarianisms they depict. Arrested and tortured, Winston repudiates his convictions and rejoins, broken, the society against which he had revolted for a time. Likewise, Ati disappears at the end of the novel of which he is the hero: if nothing allows us to fix definitively the meaning of this final vanishing—has the character crossed the "border" beyond which the possibility of a free community still exists?—at least the epilogue of *2084* does not describe any collective liberation. The rest of humankind remains the prisoner of Abistan, after losing even the memory of the period that preceded the submission to which it is subjected.

Nonetheless, the very energy deployed by the temporal and religious powers in these works to crush any form of contestation demonstrates that the order they maintain by violence and intimidation is never assured of its own permanence: one day the systematic falsification of the past that they orchestrate will be denounced, and the individual rebellions that are brewing separately from one another will perhaps triumph by uniting their forces. Totalitarianism is perhaps laboring under an illusion when it proclaims the end of history: another world is always possible, as is demonstrated by Ira Levin's *This Perfect Day*, a dystopian novel whose hero succeeds in destroying the artificial intelligence that was holding humankind in its thrall. My own contribution to this genre envisages a period of chaos and, with the revival of a civilization badly battered for a time, a new cultural flowering.[2] In dystopian literature, the main character is often prompted to contest a tyrannical power by the resurgence of a cultural artifact that predates its establishment. In the backroom of Toz, Sansal's hero makes the stupefying discovery of objects and pamphlets predating the birth of Abistan; in *Fahrenheit 451*, Guy Montag's life is changed forever when he decides to save a book instead of reducing it to ash.

While depicting a systematic eradication of the cultural patrimony of humankind by intransigent totalitarianisms, dystopian works regularly include an exception whose consequences are staggering for their main characters: the reappearance of a work that the authoritarian power wished to destroy is comparable to the return of the repressed in Freudian psychology. It conveys a whole world of secret desires and thoughts that threaten the equilibrium imposed by the law and remind us that, by tortuous paths, despite obstacles and adversaries, the words of past centuries may always make their way to posterity. Beginning with the end—with the irremediable destruction of humankind—allows us on the other hand to put to the test the thesis discussed in this chapter, the principle that there is no artistic creation without the underlying hope to transmit its products to future generations. Would people continue to write books and paint canvasses if it were *certain* that in the future those works will disappear along with posterity?

Falconet's Comet

This question is precisely the subject of a debate between Diderot and Falconet in their *Dialogue on Posterity*. The sculptor asks the philosopher to imagine a comet still far away but *certain* to collide with Earth: "Imagine that when you were twenty you were told, Monsieur, that it has been proven that in a thousand years our globe will meet a comet that, with no respect for posterity, will send into eternal night the Homers, the Apelles, the Phidias, the parades on the boulevards, the beautiful women, and the puppets. Until then, everything will go on as usual. Those who make good books will make them, those who tear them to shreds will continue to do so. The makers of paintings, statues, et cetera, will continue to make them."[3]

According to Falconet, the certainty of this apocalypse, albeit deferred by a millennium, would change nothing in the work of artists—nor, moreover, in the manner in which the rest of humankind would lead its existence. Painters, sculptors, writers, and musicians would all pursue their respective activities in exactly the same manner. Through the scenario of an inevitable cataclysm, Falconet seeks to demonstrate that the image of praise reserved for artists by posterity has no impact on the pursuit of their work, which is inspired by goals that are distinct from posthumous recognition. What are these alternative goals, and are they capable, as he asserts, of encouraging artistic activity despite the promise of the complete destruction of humankind?

"I seek to do my work well for the pleasure of doing it well; this idea would alone guide me were it not for a few contemporaries whom I wish to please as well. It doesn't matter what posterity will think."[4] This declaration by the sculptor distinguishes between two tribunals that persuade him to surpass himself, current courts of opinion that have no relationship to that of posterity. The first of them is that of his own conscience that urges him to "do well" in order to derive a pleasure inherent in the act of creation itself. This act is, consequently, endowed with an intrinsic goal: it brings to the person who performs it a satisfaction that is simultaneous with its achievement, rendering by this fact any reference to the judgments of future generations entirely superfluous. The second tribunal is composed of the small number of contemporaries that he wishes to please because he recognizes their superior competence, based on their familiarity with the products of the art they are judging. Falconet's superb indifference to posthumous judgments is thus combined with a deference toward the opinions expressed by an elite. Accordingly, Falconet does not play current public recognition against that of Sartre's "great nephews" but delineates within the former a more restricted circle whose opinions alone seem legitimate to him.

Falconet denies to posterity the right to take its place as a competent judge alongside himself and a few colleagues. The sculptor offers the example of works of antiquity that, now destroyed, are only known through ekphrasis: such is the case of Polygnotos's *Departure of the Greeks*, whose composition he criticizes caustically based on a description by Pausanias.[5] Falconet is convinced that these paintings and sculptures, generally considered to be matchless models because a poet had described them as such centuries before, would merit his disdain if they were to reappear. The art of antiquity is not unsurpassable, he thinks, and everything leads one to think that the moderns would be capable of showing a thing or two to the ancients as regards composition and technical virtuosity.[6] Thus the judgments of posterity are immaterial, Falconet declares, insofar as they reflect the praise and criticism of a man of letters who is no more qualified to award the one than to level the other. Since, in the past, posterity has transmitted erroneous judgments on works, there is no reason to hope that it will be any different in the future: among its members, there will undoubtedly again be incompetent judges who will pass judgment brashly on artistic products whose technique is beyond their understanding and will ultimately only utter "nonsense."[7]

It is thus logical that Falconet only exhibits indifference toward the comet that, a millennium from now, will destroy the human mediation between posterity and his works: in the latter he only sees an activity for its own sake and in no way the means to obtain a form of transcendence. It is precisely the refusal to attribute any metaphysical purpose to art that provokes Diderot condemnation, equivalent to the revolt of a believer against an atheist because the latter seems to exhibit disturbing moral dispositions in refusing to recognize the existence of a supreme being. That Falconet is deaf to the call of posterity appears first to him as a proof of bad faith (*"The worst of all deaf people are those who do not wish to hear,"* he declares to the sculptor);[8] then, as he becomes convinced of his sincerity, as a veritable scandal. "Can one think highly of an individual who is indifferent to what will be said of him after his death?" the philosopher wonders, a question that is scarcely different from asking what confidence one may legitimately have in a person who does not fear the tribunal of God. Although we detect in Falconet a kind of stiffening of his argumentation owing to the necessity to defend himself from the vigorous attacks by Diderot, the sculptor remains faithful to his initial thesis: the thought of posterity is not necessary for the pursuit of creation, and it is useless to look so far ahead to find an adequate incentive to produce works. Thus the comet that would destroy the world in a millennium would change nothing in the activity of a person for whom posterity no more possesses the truth on the value of works than it is indispensable to the desire to create them.

The Astronomer's Error

Diderot holds an opinion that is diametrically opposed to Falconet's on the immediate and future effects of this devastating comet:

> And what are you telling me about this comet that is coming to strike our globe? If it ever happened that the course of comets could be known well enough to predict that a thousand years from now one of these bodies will

collide with our earth, goodbye poems, speeches, temples, palaces, paintings, and statues. Either no one would make them anymore, or they would make very bad ones. Each person would go into retirement, you along with everyone else. If people still painted galleries, it would only be because they thought that the astronomers had miscalculated. What a waste of time to embellish a house that would be gone in a moment.[9]

According to the philosopher, Falconet's comet would produce two cataclysms: a cataclysm by collision and another by anticipation. At the moment of its collision with our globe, it would reduce to eternal silence the call of all men and women who, since the beginning of time, hoped for a form of survival in the memory of their successors. No more humankind, therefore no more symbolic immortality: the inscription of the memory of works in the network of memories would be annihilated at the same time as the planet and its guests. The examination of the first two paradoxes of mediation revealed localized interruptions in the chain of transmission between a work and the successive publics that embody posterity, interruptions produced by the destruction of a material medium or by the silencing of a language formerly open. But the thought experiment to which Falconet invites Diderot allows us to imagine the possibility of a complete and irremediable destruction of everything that had been accomplished and created by mankind, up to and including the final memory of its very existence: a pure and simple disappearance of posterity.

Well before it occurred, this cataclysm would have anticipatory effects on human activity. Provided that scientists could establish the exact date of the end of the world, any creative work would come to an end instantly, since art—this is Diderot's thesis—only subsists in the hope of being an exception to the law of universal mutability of beings and things. A millennium of survival of an oeuvre does not suffice for artists, who, through their works, are striving to transcend their own finiteness: it is not a reprieve before complete oblivion that they need but countless centuries and inscription in the network of memories, with no expiration date. In the absence of this eternally open perspective, creators would stop producing works in which they could not find any remedy for the anguish of their own disappearance. Perhaps they would continue to preserve works completed prior to the announcement of the end of the world until it actually came, but surely no one would have the energy necessary to create new ones. What the philosopher emphasizes is the existence of an indissoluble link between artistic creation and the transcendence of our mortality: art only exists because of the desire to go beyond the limits of our human condition. Dispossessed of this metaphysical justification by the announcement of an apocalypse, men would lose the desire to create a millennium before the disappearance of their species, for ten centuries of memories are not eternity.

Diderot goes so far as to suggest that the desire to leave a trace in the network of memories is at the origin of progress in the arts and sciences. This is what is implied by his reflection on galleries that one would only bother to paint if one believed that the catastrophe predicted by the astronomer would not come to pass. Through this remark, the philosopher intimates that men might well continue to build shelters to protect themselves from the weather—that is, that a minimal industry would be pursued to respond to their basic needs—but the desire to embellish their personal living environment would disappear with the hope of being honored in the memory of future generations. Likewise, instead of looking up at the sky that will bring their inevitable death, individuals would prefer to keep their eyes to the ground and, like François Rabelais's Panurge, plant their cabbages. The very people who would never experience the apocalypse foreseen centuries after their disappearance would nonetheless see their existence defined by an event situated outside their sphere of experience: all of them would give up the arts for lack of the motivation necessary to produce works that, all things considered, would only, like themselves, have a limited existence.

These reflections by Diderot on the indissoluble relationship between the development of the arts and the desire for eternity suggest a parallel with the efforts of Rousseau to imagine a theoretical scenario accounting for the birth of social life that, itself, allows us to imagine the conditions that led to artistic activity. After depicting a solitary individual who only associates intermittently with others, on one of these "rare occasions where common interest forced him to count on the help of his fellow men,"[10] Rousseau describes in the second *Discourse* the progressive establishment of human groups whose growth and interdependence are ever increasing. Evolving henceforth in communities whose members are in permanent contact with one another, individuals develop new forms of leisure:

> People became accustomed to gathering before the huts or around a large tree: singing and dancing, true progeny of love and leisure, became the amusement or rather the occupation of the idle men and women assembled there. Each one began to look at the others and to wish to be looked at in his turn, and public esteem became valued. The person who sang or danced the best; the most handsome, the strongest, the most skilled, or the most eloquent individual became the most respected, and this was the first step toward inequality and, at the same time, toward vice: from these first preferences was born on the one hand vanity and scorn, on the other shame and envy; and the fermentation caused by these new yeasts ultimately produced compounds that were fatal to happiness and innocence.[11]

Rousseau describes in this famous passage the birth of a new sentiment—"self-love" (*amour-propre*)—and proceeds to demonstrate that it leads individuals to employ a form of violence toward their fellow creatures. For self-love, or pride, is this desire that another prefer me to him- or herself (in recognizing that I am *more* talented, *more* worthy), a desire that they can only satisfy to the detriment of their own aspiration to be preferred and, consequently, with a feeling of hate toward me since they are granting me what I expect from them. The imperious demands of *amour-propre* give rise to violence between individuals who may, for example, be indignant at not receiving from others the tokens of esteem they are convinced they deserve. But if we are to believe Rousseau, pride is also at the origin of the emergence and improvement of the arts: it is in order to obtain applause from their fellows that individuals strive to sing, dance, and speak better than anyone else.

To return to the terms of the debate between Diderot and Falconet in this dispute to which I have invited Rousseau, it is thus the "current concert" of praise that individuals seek, according to the philosopher from Geneva, when they attempt to stand out in the eyes of their fellow creatures. On the other hand, the "distant melody" emanating from posterity in no way explains the drive to create, whose origin is to be sought in an immediate competition, that which involves artists trying to outdo one another in front of the tribe. Consequently, Rousseau and Falconet both find in the esteem of the artists' contemporaries a sufficient incentive for the development of their faculties. Falconet is certainly more selective than Rousseau in the identification of the members of this public, since it is solely the judgment of the experts, along with his own, that he considers legitimate. As for Rousseau, he considers collective admiration to be the fuel of an insatiable *amour-propre* without it being necessary to identify a category of individuals whose admiration would be particularly desirable, an analysis that seems to be confirmed by the form celebrity has taken in our time, where the adulation of an anonymous mass, the fans and other followers on social media, is the measure of a largely quantitative notoriety. Despite this difference in their point of view, the author of *The Social Contract* would agree with the sculptor that an apocalypse a millennium away would change nothing in the practice of the arts: during this interval of ten centuries, it would still be necessary to respond to the needs of an imperious pride.

There is thus complete disagreement between Diderot on the one hand and Falconet and Rousseau on the other concerning the subjective motivations that drive individuals to cultivate and perfect the arts. By declaring that the latter would be anticipatory victims of a cataclysm in the event that the apocalypse were announced a millennium in advance, Diderot asserts that there is no creation without an underlying quest for symbolic immortality. The gratifications of pride obtained by artists through the praise of their contemporaries, the satisfaction inherent in the very act of creating, the material and symbolic advantages of the sale of works and of the prestige attached to the status of artist, all these potential justifications may well contribute to the desire to create. Diderot does not deny it, he who, after all, counts among the pleasures he enumerates that of having "written a good page," independently therefore of the idea that it will be read when he can know nothing of it.[12] These possible motivations are, however, secondary, subsumed as they are in the true goal of artists—to assert their power to transcend oblivion—given that said motivations are incapable of inciting them to pursue their activity when they learn that posterity, like all beings and things, is condemned to disappear one day.

Posterity in the Nuclear Age

Falconet's comet shoots across the pages of the *Dialogue* and is only the pretext for a brief passage of arms between the two letter-writers: it soon disappears, sweeping away with it the threat of a cataclysm that, all in all, seems quite improbable to them. It was only summoned up, of course, as an experiment, because it was the only way they had to give any kind of plausibility to the scenario of a complete destruction of the world and to reflect on its anticipatory effects on human creativity. Since their quarrel, the invention of the atomic bomb has nonetheless enriched the list of our nightmares by giving some substance to the scenario of a planned apocalypse. This extreme experience, which the two Enlightenment correspondents were free to push back a millennium, has become since the Second World War a specter that has never ceased to haunt us. That we are able to annihilate all of humankind, and with it the memory of all those who composed it, is no longer just an improbable scenario but a conjecture that international political tensions give rise to periodically. It will soon be a century that we have lived with this sword of Damocles, always in danger of falling.

In an article published at the end of 2016 by the *New Yorker* whose principal subject is the American nuclear arsenal, Eric Schlosser analyzed the potential causes of a nuclear war in the twenty-first century.[13] He emphasized in particular the aging of the infrastructure and the obsolescence of the software used to control nuclear arms: "Most of the launch complexes were built during the Kennedy Administration. . . . The command centers feel like a time capsule of late-twentieth-century technology" (12–13). In the course of his investigation, Schlosser discovered in a command center an IBM computer from 1976 whose replacement parts were nowhere to be found, and whose storage capabilities were a thousand times inferior to those of a cell phone you can buy in a store around the corner. The obsolescence of this technology renders it vulnerable to digital attacks using means—spyware, viruses, logic bombs, and other Trojan horses—that did not yet exist when it was put into service.

Strategically speaking, the atomic bomb is a weapon of last resort, a paradoxical weapon that is intended never to be used. As a classified Pentagon report explained, "What deters is not the capabilities and intentions we have, but the capabilities and intentions the enemy thinks we have" (9). The nuclear weapon serves first of all as a means of dissuasion, for all the actors involved in the decision to use it are—in principle—capable of calculating the apocalyptic consequences. The balance of terror, of which the military strategist Bernard Brodie is one of the theoreticians, presupposes that the agents involved in the use of this technology are likely to formulate the following reasoning: "The enemy may take revenge with weapons of mass destruction that will annihilate me in my turn." It is thus the prospect of the reciprocal annihilation of the warring parties that dissuades them from attacking one another. Unbeatable in appearance, this logic nonetheless imposes a balance that is difficult to maintain in the long term. Unless they agree to a simultaneous disarmament, the adversaries must keep a nuclear capability sufficiently strong, operational, and dispersed to preserve their ability to respond. Reducing their arsenal would upset the balance of power by giving an advantage to the enemy. But by preserving for decades a murderous technology that slips progressively into obsolescence, the statistical probabilities increase regularly that a human or technical error may involuntarily lead to its use. The doctrine of "mutual assured destruction" implies the permanent maintenance of a paroxysmal yet controlled tension: it anticipates neither the aging of the arsenals nor the blunders that may be committed by political leaders responsible for their use—in particular when the democratic process charged with selecting them has revealed itself to be incapable of dismissing those who have neither the competence nor the mental equilibrium required to discharge the highest functions.

"A war between two countries with nuclear weapons, like a Wild West shootout, might be won by whoever fired first" (8). Owing to the decisive advantage gained by the utilization of a nuclear weapon, the decision to use it must be made in scarcely a few minutes. In the event that nuclear missiles were launched from Russia, the president of the United States would have around twenty minutes to come to a decision on the response; she or he would only have five if the missiles originated from a submarine in the Atlantic Ocean. The dilemma to solve would be the following: assuming that the threat to the U.S. territory was a false alarm, a hasty retaliation could lead by mistake to the death of millions of people; delaying a reaction, on the other hand, would give the enemy the opportunity to completely disable the American ability to respond and to sweep away the civilian and military elites. Consequently, the logic that governs the use of a nuclear weapon has reduced to the extreme the interval of time available to decide how to respond. This narrowing of the window for action increases the possibility of miscalculations and places an excessive responsibility in the hands of a single individual whose analytical abilities and temperament are subjected to a test on which depends nothing less than the fate of the planet. In 1980, in the middle of the night, the American Secretary of Defense William J. Perry received a call that has haunted him ever since: his subordinates warned him of an imminent Soviet attack. "A catastrophic nuclear war could have started by accident" (22).

In addition to human errors that may result from a hasty decision based on erroneous information, a technical defect may likewise lead to a nuclear war. The first generation of American nuclear missiles—the "Minuteman I"—was plagued with a flaw that could cause them to be launched automatically: a simple variation in the electrical current registered by the command center could be interpreted as a signal to fire the missile. But it is not necessary to return to the period of the cold war to find an incident whose potential consequence would have been a nuclear holocaust: on October 23, 2010, at one thirty in the morning, fifty Minuteman IIIs located at an air base in Wyoming remained out of control for more than an hour. Slightly displaced by the combined effect of heat and vibrations, an electrical circuit had created a cacophony of signals and blocked communication with the missiles. When it was reestablished, one could hear a sigh of relief from the military personnel: the missiles had not left their silo, which was not at all sure a second before. To what global war would we have been led if they had hit a foreign target?

It is no doubt superfluous to recall the alarming number of circumstances where we have been on the verge of the end of the world because of nuclear arms. The example of the Cuban Missile Crisis alone, during which the fate of humankind was briefly in the hands of a Soviet submarine captain whom an officer—Vasily Arkhipov—dissuaded in extremis from launching a torpedo with a nuclear warhead against an American vessel, is enough to leave us with this certainty: the destruction of the planet may occur at any moment because of a technical failure or a simple error of judgment.[14] The fifteen thousand nuclear weapons scattered around the globe today threaten its existence, and the risk they represent is never so great as when we think they are under control. As Schlosser observes, "The 'Titanic effect' is a term used by software designers to explain how things can quietly go wrong in a complex technological system: the safer you assume the system to be, the more dangerous it is becoming" (47).

Consequently, the facts of the problem debated by Diderot and Falconet between 1765 and 1767 have changed fundamentally since the invention of the atomic bomb. Contrary to Falconet's comet, whose collision with the earth was presented as a certainty based on the calculations of an astronomer, the detonation of a nuclear bomb is put off to a possible future that may never come to pass. The cataclysm imagined by the two correspondents was distant and expected; ours is imminent and unforeseeable. The uncertainty that surrounds the nuclear apocalypse is sufficiently great that the thought of it does not trouble the development of artistic activity: indeed, human creativity does not seem to have been curbed since the irruption of the nuclear threat during the Second World War as it would inevitably be, according to Diderot, with the promise of an unavoidable cataclysm. Much to the contrary, this invisible risk has enriched the repertory of artistic works by becoming a motif embraced by the imagination of writers, musicians, and artists: among a thousand examples we might offer to show the pervasiveness of bomb imagery in twentieth-century art, just think of Robert Merle's *Malevil*, the Rolling Stones' "Gimme Shelter," or Katsuhiro Otomo's *Akira*.[15]

Nonetheless, humankind's ability to bring about its own destruction adds an additional threat to all those that were already hanging over the permanence of artistic productions and demonstrates the fragility of the dream of symbolic immortality through the transmission of works to posterity. The paradox of cultural mediation has already revealed that this transmission is involved with the unpredictable destiny of the languages in which the texts are written. In its turn, the paradox of material mediation demonstrated that the transmission of works to future generations is dependent on the constant renewal of the media that contain them. The thought experiment that Falconet invites Diderot to carry out reveals, for its part, the paradox of human mediation: the survival of artists in the network of memories is contingent on the problematical survival of our species. In the context of this entirely secular conception of the future of human beings, for which there exists no beyond where one can take refuge after death, the posthumous existence of artists and of those to whom they give life through their works is entrusted to the collective memory of future generations.

Through the examination of the paradoxes of mediation, it appears that the distribution of texts to posterity is constantly hindered by the opposing force exerted by the impermanence of everything that is related to the human species. Thus it is only owing to the masking of the threats of destruction produced by this impermanence that it is possible to *believe* in posterity. Those who, on the contrary, are not satisfied with voluntary blindness will accept that the quest for symbolic immortality by the transmission of works to future generations assumes an exception (an exception ever more improbable, statistically speaking, as time passes) that allows us to overcome the inevitable fragility of human productions and of humanity itself. And rather than fighting in vain against this essential dimension of our finiteness, perhaps it would be preferable to ponder these words of Buddha: "Do not cherish the unworthy desire that the changeable might become unchanging."[16] Following the path they indicate is not tantamount to *renouncing* posterity—a voluntary abandonment that, as we have seen with Casanova and Sartre, dissimulates diverse strategies of recuperation—but to *desiring* that, in the end, it simply forget us, a possibility I will examine in the conclusion.

CONCLUSION
Why Do People (Still) Write?

At the end of a lecture that an American novelist had just given, and whose purpose was to demystify the writer's profession by revealing some of its least flattering realities—such as the mediocrity of the income it normally generates—a member of the audience raised his hand and stated, "You've just given excellent reasons *not to write*. Being a writer, according to you, means working for months on the writing of a book that will probably only reach a handful of readers and will allow you at best to make a half-decent living. So, *why write?*" It is to the credit of the writer that, called out in such a fashion, he did not take the slightest offense at the materialism underlying this question. He was speaking to fellow countrymen and -women, and the fact that they might judge an activity in terms of the money it brought in was hardly surprising to him; nor, moreover, did it cause him any regret, since the second career he was leading parallel to his writing afforded him a comfortable existence. Instead of taking the easy way out, which would have consisted in disqualifying the question by attributing it to vulgar pragmatism, he offered an idealistic response. He brought up the parable of the talents and spoke of the duty of each person to make the most of those that had been bestowed upon him or her; he suggested, finally, the existence of "superior ideals" that are at the origin of the most admirable things that humankind has accomplished. His interlocutor nodded at the mention of "superior ideals" and seemed satisfied. As for me, I was not. The question remains: why write or, more precisely, why *still* write when the justifications that we are inclined to give to this strange activity, when examined closely, all vanish one after the other?

The "superior ideal" analyzed in this book consists in the metaphysical goal attributed to literature. Literature is intimately involved with death: if we write, it is because we refuse to disappear *entirely*. The chapters of this work have described the paradoxes involved in the search for symbolic immortality and demonstrated that the latter never deserves its name, the inscription of a work in the network of memories always being in danger of eradication. Through the paradoxes of belief, I tried to show that posterity is conceived by authors as a form of divinity whose final judgments are both unforeseeable and revocable. The paradoxes of identity revealed, for their part, that it is never the creators themselves that posterity remembers but the fictitious doubles with which it confuses them. The paradoxes of mediation emphasized, finally, that the eternity of works is dependent on intermediaries whose intrinsic fragility threatens the transmission they are responsible for with respect to the successive members of posterity. So, why do people continue to write if they have understood that posterity is temporally as well as geographically limited, the inscription of an author in the future network of memories varying according to the national and linguistic communities? Why still write when posterity, far from being an infallible tribunal with eternal judgments, is troubled by the same passions that already perturbed the contemporaries of the author whose worthiness it is evaluating?

The answer lies in the indestructible hope, in each person's heart, of being the exception to the rule. Even if there were only one successful transmission out of ten billion failures, there would still be hundreds, thousands of candidates trying their luck in this "lottery." For the adults that nourish it, this belief in the exception is probably a faint echo of the exalted place they once enjoyed at the center of the universe when they were small children. If we continue to think that we will be the exception to the rule of disappearance and oblivion, it is because there was a time when reality itself was organized around our person and obeyed our desires. We retain the memory of this childish omnipotence, as well as the shameful hope that it will once again be granted to us.

While it is a historical consequence of our development from an early age to the age of writing, this belief in exception, upon examination, has a much longer genealogy and is rooted in an ancient past. The process of natural selection is congruent with an instinct that disposes living beings to transmit their genes to the next generation. Subject to the adverse circumstances of practical existence, this instinct leads each person to collaborate with others when their respective interests converge but to put oneself before anyone else when they are opposed—with the exception of offspring, perceived as an extension of oneself and a vehicle of those same genes that we are striving to safeguard. Without realizing it, we are obeying the silent exhortation to consider ourselves more important than all the others: "The feeling of being a special person is not far from the heart of this system of values conveyed by natural selection."[1] Consequently, what leads us to believe, despite overwhelming proof to the contrary, that we alone will elude the general law of annihilation of beings and things is the ultimate manifestation of the impulse to consider ourselves exceptional beings, a state we have achieved by virtue of the process of natural selection. Tending naturally to place ourselves at the center of the network formed by our fellow creatures, we spontaneously expect to occupy a special place in the network of memories.[2] Nonetheless, just as we have to recognize that each of us cannot have interests that supersede those of all the others, it is important to accept that in all probability, we will, like everyone else, be swallowed up by the multitude of those who came before us, without leaving any more traces within the collective memory than a stone cast into the sea. So, what are we to do with our desire for eternity when we have a *nearly* absolute certainty that it will be in no way satisfied?

To begin with, it is useless to attempt to destroy entirely the yearning for posthumous praise, for people of letters cannot give this up—as the first paradox demonstrated—without at the same time losing the justification that it gave their existence. It is, however, the excessiveness lent to it by Diderot, its most ardent defender, that we may first question:

> The sphere that surrounds us and in which we are admired, the length of time we exist and hear the extoling, the number of those who give us directly the praise we have deserved, all that is too small for the capacity of our ambitious soul; perhaps we do not consider ourselves sufficiently rewarded for our labors by the genuflections of the current world; alongside those whom we see prostrated, we expect those who aren't there yet to kneel also. Only this unlimited mass of worshipers can satisfy a spirit that is always yearning for the infinite.[3]

If we are to believe the philosopher who would have liked his fame to resound all the way to Saturn,[4] this desire resembles a gas that spreads throughout the space granted to it: temporal space, that of unlimited eternity where the name of a creator echoes endlessly; and geographical space as well, whose current state of being limited to the terrestrial globe in no way prevents an expansion to the infinity of planets, in the event that the human race succeeded in reaching them. The image of the future discourse of posterity, we have seen, possesses an ethical dimension: the individual wishes to be remembered by future generations as a decent person (Diderot observes in this respect, "We wish to leave an honorable memory, we wish it for our family, for our friends, and even perhaps for the indifferent").[5] But the ethical concern does not settle the problem of the expansion of this desire for praise, for if such were the case, the desire would be limited to a small circle, that of one's descendants who cultivate the memory of the members of their line. This reduction of posterity to our progeny does not satisfy Diderot, who considers the insatiable desire for praise to be an essential source of progress in the arts and sciences. It is because the desire for praise is limitless that individuals surpass themselves and strive to outdo others in a perpetual competition: here, excessiveness carries a value because it is a psychological driving force essential to the quest for self-perfecting that is itself a means to obtain posthumous praise.

However, by aspiring to the infinity of time and space, our desire leads necessarily to its disappointment: no, nothing will ever assure us that our oeuvre and person will be remembered across the centuries and throughout the world; the excessiveness of this quest may perhaps be an encouragement to progress, but it is certainly also a cause of suffering. How many lives are worn out and consumed in the search for a symbolic immortality that nothing can ever assure the seeker of obtaining? For a handful of major philosophers, how many thinkers have pursued with the same relentlessness, the same dedication, the same madness, the construction of an oeuvre that will not even be forgotten, since for that it would have had to attract at least a hint of interest while they were living? That is how, to quote Sartre, people's lives are stolen by immortality.

Thus it is important to match our desire to the inherent limits of our human condition. Rather than considering the limitlessness of our desire as the cause of our action, we should, on the contrary, entertain a more realistic idea of what we can reasonably hope for in order to correlate our efforts with that. Let us begin therefore with this premise: that the inscription of our oeuvre in the memory of future generations will be localized, fluctuating, and, in the end, probably nil. The memory of our person will colonize a proportion of the global memory of posterity so minute that it will border on nonexistence. In all likelihood, we will be neither Miguel de Cervantes nor William Shakespeare nor Marcel Proust, those giants whose prestige is so immense that it makes us forget that they, too, will disappear one day from the memory of other humans; they who, already today, only occupy a minute fraction of the network of memories when considered globally and only enjoy, moreover, a localized posterity. Does anyone seriously believe that Swann is widely known in Malaysia and the ingenious hidalgo in Rwanda? The "universality" of Western writers is just an indication of the ethnocentric prejudice of those who think of them in those terms.

But in order to appease our appetite for eternity, we will at least have some reassuring perspectives. On the one hand, we need never exclude the possibility of a rediscovery in the future: our oeuvre may be reedited, explored again. This perspective is all the more certain since humanity has never been so replete with individuals whose profession consists in commenting on the works of the past: this industry needs to be fueled, and our oeuvre will perhaps make the career of an ambitious university professor who, working for him- or herself, will labor for the revival of our name two centuries after our death. In addition, we have, in the twenty-first century, solid reasons to believe in the preservation of the media containing our texts. Their digitizing, while far from presenting a definitive solution to the problem of obsolescence, as the eighth paradox revealed, at least increases the statistical probability of their being saved. These positions on our posthumous fate amount to an embrace of what Buddhism refers to as the "noble path," the one that takes a middle course between two extremes. In giving up Diderot's extremist notion of a celebrity that would extend to the outer limits of our solar system (if such an extension were even possible), while at the same time rejecting the perspective of an irreparable and complete destruction of our intellectual productions in toto, we opt for a more modest ambition, in accordance with the unforeseeable and mutable nature of the inscription of works in the network of memories to come.

Nevertheless, the terror caused by the thought of our disappearance—terror that, as I have tried to show, we attempt to control through artistic creation, among other ways—is perhaps only really manageable if we actually desire our disappearance. Yes, we must desire it, desire the complete annihilation of the memory of our existence and of our works, for a monumental inscription in posterity sterilizes future generations. A reflection on the beneficial effects of our mortality will reveal an analogy with those that will be engendered by the deletion of our memorial inscription. If it was infinitely prolonged, our stay on Earth would continue at the expense of other individuals: after my death, the house I occupy, the garden I cultivate, will be passed on to others who will enjoy them in their turn; if I were to occupy them for all eternity, this space would only ever provide pleasure to me and never to others. Likewise, the work I have been doing must be entrusted to others, who will accomplish it with a fresh enthusiasm, that which we demonstrate at the beginning and which, little by little, always wanes in the end. When I disappear, the place my pride induced me to demand in public opinion becomes available to others. Perhaps they will have a better claim to this collective admiration; in any case, they will solicit it by means of new thoughts. Individuals may only have, in depth, *a single* veritable contribution to humanity. Their life is often spent attempting to formulate it adequately: everything that precedes is groundwork; everything that follows is rumination. But it is there, at the center of their life—a center that is located sometimes at its dawn, sometimes at its dusk—this jewel, this formulation, as crystal clear and perfect as possible, of the *great problem* that they had dedicated their life to define and solve. A stay on Earth prolonged indefinitely would only produce the rehash of the same ideas, the disguising of an old discovery in the trappings of new inspiration. We thus must die to leave to others the opportunity to discover their great problem and prefer the general interest of the species—its progressive enrichment through the treasure brought by each—to the interest of individuals who cling to being while discovering nothing more and at the risk of disfiguring their original contribution through the desperate desire to produce an original idea of which, without wanting to admit it, they are no longer capable.

This disappearance that we must not only accept but actually desire also extends to our inscription in posterity. An omnipresence in the future network of memories would be at the expense of other writers: by holding the attention of our successors excessively, we prevent them from devoting their efforts to deceased thinkers whose contribution is equally worthy. Still more serious, the great name of an artist who has disappeared is apt to discourage those who wish to express themselves in their turn: after hearing you repeat over and over that the genius of so-and-so is unsurpassable, how does one dare speak after him or her? If the concert of praises Diderot dreams of genuinely corresponded to the excessive expectations nourished by the artist, its repercussions would threaten to suspend the creative impulse of future generations: in wishing for too much for ourselves, we deprive others of the motivation to write.

It is thus to another form of existence—secret, disembodied, and anonymous—that we should aspire. As I have shown through the examination of the paradoxes of identity, it is never the artists themselves that posterity remembers: it is the collective fiction that it substitutes for them that is durably inscribed in its memory, a fiction partially orchestrated by the authors through various representations of their person in their work and portraits, a fiction founded in truth on authentic materials but nonetheless, as time passes, more and more independent of its referent and always more simplified, reduced to formulaic features. When Lautréamont calls Chateaubriand a "melancholy Mohican," he is not only expressing the irreverence of a young, ambitious writer toward his famous predecessor; he is anticipating the very work of posterity by reducing a vast and contradictory identity to a concise turn of phrase.[6] In the network of memories there is no room for vast expositions: one is put away in a corner like a mummy in a sarcophagus, the organs scattered, the orbits empty. There are, of course, exceptions within this vast public, explorers who have pierced the darkness of our tomb, deciphered all of our hieroglyphics and unrolled our bandages like long strips of papyrus in which the story of our existence is inscribed. But as for what we call "posterity" in its broadest sense, we are nothing or almost nothing: words, the vague memory of an acquaintance we had for a time then forgot; and our successors hasten toward their pleasures, for it is for them alone that the sun has ever shone.

Likewise, intertextuality maintains our existence after our death in a similarly disembodied form, completely different from the complex individuals that we know ourselves to be. If my work, minor, forgotten by nearly everyone, is read by a great writer who leaves, through an allusion, a trace of knowledge of it, who evokes just one beautiful feature, perhaps some rigorous scholar will grace me, from beyond the grave, with a few commemorative words like we see on the front of historical buildings in cities. In this footnote that he (supposing the scholar is a man) will have devoted to me at the bottom of the page, he will observe that the great writer (supposing that it is a woman), in a moment of fatigue and boredom, was entertained by the reading of my work, in which she found this idea, this formulation, that she did me the honor of borrowing from me—and it is doubtlessly an honor, since I am only remembered through her. Or one of my richest finds, the rhythm of one of my sentences, may be engraved in the memory of this famous author before she models one of her graceful sentences on my own, setting it then in a text that, unlike my own, will be admired by posterity. As Paul Valéry showed, in a famous commentary on one of his masterpieces, literary creation puts into play disembodied forms, rhythms devoid of content; it takes root on the margins of language: "As for 'The Graveyard by the Sea,' this intention was at first only an *empty rhythmic figure*, or *filled with empty syllables*, that became an obsession for a time. I observed that this figure was decasyllabic, and I reflected a moment on this type of line so little used in modern poetry: it seemed poor and monotonous to me. It wasn't much compared to the alexandrine, that three or four generations of great artists have prodigiously developed."[7]

The "decasyllabic figure" referred to by Valéry is a pure form; the poet describes it as an abstract rhythm, with no reference to its use in a particular work. However, that is not how he came to experience it, but rather through its embodiment in language: although the ten syllables that obsessed him have only a limited existence in modern poetry, that of past centuries made good use of it. Valéry does not indicate the work in which the use of the decasyllable struck him: was it in Charles Baudelaire, Victor Hugo, or François Villon that he discovered a particular use of this rhythm that haunted him, or is "Ce toit tranquille, où marchent des colombes" (This quiet roof where doves walk) a distant reminiscence of Joachim du Bellay's "Pâles esprits, et vous ombres poudreuses" (Pale spirits, and you, powdery shadows)? It is not a matter of relating all original creation to a prior reading, nor of the investigation of the authors' "sources" that, as a rule, reveals little other than their erudition and their superiority over those whom they remember. It is rather to emphasize that for writers, reading is not only a collecting of ideas and images—that is, of contents—but also an impregnation by rhythms, syntactical forms that strike them without their being able to say why a particular beautiful line makes more of an impact on them than another, a line that, by mysterious pathways, after a slow maturation in darkness, comes back into the light by digging the furrow into which their words flow. Sometimes the exact origin of this inspiring rhythm will remain unknown to the authors themselves, who will be incapable of saying in what work they first discovered it; in other cases, they will know very well and keep the secret to themselves. No matter, as this mysterious intertextuality that does not speak its name because it borrows the form and not the idea, the rhythm and not the words, is another mode of posthumous existence for works: certain authors exist in this manner through the texts of others, humble, anonymous, forgotten, and nonetheless necessary, like the ancestor who bequeathed us her or his gaze, through whom we see and of whom we know nothing. It is, in the realm of thought, an exact equivalent of genetic transmission, given that it exhibits the permanence of character traits borrowed from others, the recurrence of traits that were another's and henceforth belong to you constitutively.

And just as a mother looks at you and recognizes her nose in yours, in the irregular form of your mouth that of her spouse, in this mixture of gray and green in your eyes those of her father, then dies in her turn carrying away with her the key to all this deciphering, such that your visage is henceforth yours alone—in the same way, readers will display a complicit smile in recognizing in your sentences a souvenir of Baudelaire, an involuntary allusion to a line by Beaumarchais, the mark left on your mind by an exclamation by Chateaubriand, or the epigrammatic turn of a Proustian phrase. Then they will admit that this jumble of all the great ancestors and all those they were not able to identify is *you*, uniquely and irreplaceably you, while deep within your sentences the voices of all these dead people continue to speak.

These ancestors, like yourself, would never have spoken out without the hope of being awarded the crown of symbolic immortality. Well, this is only a delusion, an empty hope: the only real thing is the inner thought I offer to my fellow men and women, its ability to help them live and tolerate their condition, this "education that substitutes for experience"[8] that they will also profit from, whether they remember its author or know nothing of her or him. Thus we may speak of a kind of *ruse of posterity*: what I would not have the generosity and compassion to do solely for others, in the end I accomplish for them. Of course, I would not write without the hope that this being I call "me" will be inscribed in the network of memories, but if I succeed in giving up my self-love, my *amour-propre*, and replacing it with love for the species, I will *still* write, because my work has something to give it, something that I desire for it, without remuneration of any kind. The practice of writing thus represents a differed altruism: I write for those who will come after me, and I have to accept that they will forget me in return or will only be grateful to a fictional reinvention of my person. "What remains of the will to write when one has lost all hope of symbolic immortality?" To this question I will answer that what remains is the love of others. There remains the will to speak to those who will come after us, even if they were to know nothing of the beings we have been, in order to say to them, "Do not repeat our errors" or "Here is what we have understood."

The two possible meanings of posterity merge in this final erasure. My children preserve the memory of the person I was, just as their children after them, but as generations pass, I am no longer anything but a branch on the genealogical tree; reduced to my position relative to the person who is conducting the study of his origins, I am a "great-great-maternal grandfather" or a "great-uncle by marriage." But over the years I both disappear and remain, for the biological characteristics of my person are transmitted to my progeny, while this example of love and generosity that I embodied is perpetuated through those who succeed me and adopt it in their turn. If there are heritages of violence and bloody atavisms, there exist also legacies of affection. And if one asks to what more, to what better, a writer may aspire, the emphatic answer is: nothing. To understand that one only writes, in all truth, in the interest of others, whereas the posthumous recognition we think they owe us is but a sublime deception whose goal is to extract from us what, otherwise, would risk being lost, is a dangerous awareness: will we be like Diderot's painter, idle in his gallery, refusing to finish the work because we know that no one will be grateful to us for it in the future?

I believe, on the contrary, that once freed of this illusion, people will write better because they will be writing for better reasons. How many works are only undertaken by *amour-propre*, gratuitous works whose only goal consists in obtaining the applause of one's contemporaries and, perhaps, the praise of future centuries? But if the current concert is slow in coming, the wound is deep: one must write again, hurry to produce another book in the hope that this one will bring immediate and posthumous recognition. In this impatience to create that is in fact a frenzy of pride, it does not take long to produce failed works one after the other while life passes you by, constantly put off to later. Of course, we may think that an illusion must be cultivated as long as it is profitable: what does it matter if we are mistaken as regards symbolic immortality if our error leads us to work for the benefit of posterity? But there is no authentic truth that does not bring a liberation. To write with full knowledge of the facts—that is, to become aware that we only ever write in the interest of others while we think we are writing for ourselves—will dissuade no one from composing works that must really be written, those whose "origin judges them" and that, while being indispensable to the people who undertake them, are also necessary for their readers.[9]

Liberated from the obsession of our posthumous existence, we will gladly give up these labors that are only useful to the satisfaction of our vanity: series of "publications" that no one reads, "contributions" to an intellectual dialogue with twenty participants, all these "discourses" that stifle literature more than they encourage people to discover it. Perhaps we will even come to ask this question before beginning a new book: How will it serve others? What will it be able to teach them that they did not know already by themselves or through a predecessor? And beyond the exposure of my inner world, what comfort, what wisdom, what pleasure will it afford them, even if they are never grateful to me for it? I am quite aware that in destroying a certain naïve and spontaneous conception of posterity, my action appears sacrilegious: I feel it by this sadness that invades me, I who believed, as so many others, that a life only had meaning if it was remembered, and who have nonetheless shown that this memorial inscription is neither certain nor lasting nor universal; that, in short, it gives us nothing that we hope from it. But when Lucretius, reiterating Epicurus's lesson, declares to us that the gods do not exist, it is not despair that he is trying to propagate but rather this intolerable and magnificent lesson: we have this life and nothing more. A similar effort is rendered necessary by the beyond that creators yearn for, subordinating their current existence to it: the inscription in the network of memories to come will never bring them what they expect of it, and more than just paradoxical, it is downright absurd to sacrifice a life to this fantasy.

NOTES

Introduction

All translations from French by Alan J. Singerman, unless otherwise noted.
1. Albert Camus, *The Myth of Sisyphus and Other Essays*, trans. Justin O'Brien (New York: Vintage International, 1991), 3.
2. Claude Lanzmann, *The Patagonian Hare: A Memoir*, trans. Frank Wynne (New York: Farrar, Strauss and Giroux, 2012), 1.
3. Sheldon Solomon, Jeff Greenberg, and Tom Pyszczynski, *The Worm at the Core: On the Role of Death in Life* (New York: Random House, 2015), x. The title of this work is borrowed from a passage in William James's *The Varieties of Religious Experience*.
4. The authors of *The Worm at the Core* identify this age as that of the emergence of the consciousness of death in the child (23).
5. Roland Gori, *La fabrique des imposteurs* (The imposter factory) (Paris: Les liens qui libèrent, 2013), 37.
6. An earlier version of this section was published in March 2017, under the same title, in the "Atelier de théorie littéraire" of *Fabula*. http://www.fabula.org/atelier.php?Empreinte_des_oeuvres.
7. Ovid, *The Metamorphoses*, trans. F. J. Miller, rev. G. P. Goold, Loeb Classical Library 43 (Cambridge: Harvard University Press, 1916), 2:427.
8. Potential posterity is situated one notch above oblivion: it consists of the material preservation of a work in the absence of any existence in a human consciousness. Such is the situation of a work in a library where no one comes to borrow it and whose location is only known by a computerized classification system. On the other hand, the registration of a work in one individual memory—at the very least—is the instrument of its actualization. There exists, consequently, a vast range of activated posterities, the whole bundle going from the work that is known by a single reader to those (such as *The Odyssey* or *Hamlet*) whose reading may in fact be viewed as superfluous as regards mastering the content, given the great variety of indirect means by which one can access the latter. On this distinction, see the eighth paradox, "The Manuscript and the USB Flash Drive."
9. On this subject, see Stephen Greenblatt, *Will in the World: How Shakespeare Became Shakespeare* (New York: W. W. Norton, 2004).
10. C.-F.-A. de Lezay-Marnésia, *Letters Written from the Banks of the Ohio*, ed. Benjamin Hoffmann, trans. Alan J. Singerman (University Park: Pennsylvania State University Press, 2017).
11. One has only to think of the contemporary interest in Sinclair Lewis's novel *It Can't Happen Here* (1935) that was fostered by the candidacy and subsequent election of Donald J. Trump for the presidency of the United States.
12. On this subject, see A. Y. Kaplan. "Guy, de Man, and Me," in *French Lessons: A Memoir* (Chicago: University of Chicago Press, 1993), 147–74.
13. On this question, see the seventh paradox, "The Rosetta Stone and Agrippina's Thrush."
14. On this question, see Heather J. Jackson, *Those Who Write for Immortality: Romantic Reputations and the Dream of Lasting Fame* (New Haven: Yale University Press, 2015), 6–12.
15. On the posthumous rediscovery of William Blake's works, see Jackson, "Raising the Unread," in *Those Who Write for Immortality*, 167–216.

16. On Borges's accident on Christmas Day in 1938 and its effect on his subsequent works, see Pierre Bayard, *Demain est écrit* (Tomorrow is written) (Paris: Éditions de Minuit, 2005), 73–81.

17. Jackson, *Those Who Write for Immortality*, 228.

18. On the successive rewritings of a literary text until the author signs off on it, see Benjamin Hoffmann, "La relecture des épreuves" (Proofreading), *Les écrits* 150 (2017): 33–42.

19. I borrow this example from Albert Camus: "If I see a man armed only with a sword attack a group of machine guns, I shall consider his act to be absurd." *Myth of Sisyphus*, 29.

20. On this question, see Alain Séguy-Duclot, "Nouvelle solution pragmatiste du paradoxe du Menteur" (A new, pragmatist solution to the liar's paradox), *Dialogue: Canadian Philosophical Review* 53, no. 4 (2014): 671–90.

21. Michel Delon, "Le nom, la signature" (The name, the signature), in *La Carmagnole des muses: L'homme de lettres et l'artiste dans la Révolution* (The Carmagnole of the muses: The man of letters and the artist in the Revolution), ed. Jean-Claude Bonnet (Paris: Colin, 1988), 280.

22. On the debates over the immateriality and the immortality of the soul in the eighteenth century, see Ann Thomson, *L'âme des Lumières: Le débat sur l'être humain entre religion et science; Angleterre–France (1690–1760)* (The soul of the Enlightenment: The human debate between religion and science; England–France [1690–1760]) (Seyssel: Champ Vallon, 2013).

First Paradox

1. Denis Diderot and Étienne Maurice Falconet, *Le pour et le contre ou lettres sur la postérité* (The pros and cons of letters on posterity), in *Œuvres complètes* (Complete works), vol. 15, ed. E. Hill, R. Mortier, and R. Trousson (Paris: Hermann, 1986).

2. "I've had the dispute on posterity copied. If You will permit it, Madame, I'll send it to You, and if You think that this pastime of two dreamers is worth it, I'll have it printed here, with the corrections that I humbly beg You to add." Étienne Maurice Falconet, *Correspondance de Falconet avec Catherine II, 1767–1778* (Correspondence of Falconet with Catherine II, 1767–1778), ed. Louis Réau (Paris: Champion, 1921), 9–10.

3. Denis Diderot, *Correspondance* (Correspondence), ed. Georges Roth et Jean Varloot (Paris: Editions de Minuit, 1955–70), 7:53–54.

4. Ibid., 9:197. The undated fragment in which this declaration is found was probably written in 1769.

5. Ibid., 7:62.

6. On the origin of this anecdote, see by Roland Mortier, "Le 'concert lointain' et le 'compas de la raison'" (The "distant concert" and the "compass of reason"), in Diderot and Falconet, *Le pour et le contre*, x.

7. Yves Benot remarks that, instead of composing a dialogue, the letters in this correspondence juxtapose "two monologues that each participant continues for himself alone and with little concern for his interlocutor." Introduction to Diderot and Falconet, *Le pour et le contre: Correspondance polémique sur le respect de la postérité, Pline et les anciens auteurs qui ont parlé de peinture et de sculpture* (The pros and cons: Polemical correspondence on the respect of posterity, Pliny, and the authors of antiquity who spoke of painting and sculpture) (Paris: Les Éditeurs français réunis, 1958), 30. Note that all subsequent citations of *Le pour et le contre* are drawn from the previously cited 1986 edition edited by Hill, Mortier, and Trousson.

8. "You see that I'm not arguing anymore, because you are repeating yourself, and I've already answered you." "Lettre XVIII, Falconet à Diderot, février 1767" (Letter XVIII, Falconet to Diderot, February 1767), in Diderot and Falconet, *Le pour et le contre*, 237.

9. Diderot, *Correspondance*, 15:92.

10. On the history of the publication of *The Pros and Cons*, see Emita B. Hill, "Notes for a Modern Edition of the *Dispute sur la postérité*," *Studies on Voltaire and the Eighteenth Century* 201 (1982): 185–93.

11. In *D'Alembert's Dream*, Diderot alludes maliciously to his quarrel with Falconet when he proposes to crush and grind up a work by the sculptor. When D'Alembert takes exception ("Go easy, please: that is Falconet's masterpiece"), Diderot replies, "Falconet could care less: the statue is paid for, and Falconet attaches little importance to his current reputation and none whatsoever to consideration by future generations." Denis Diderot, *Le rêve de d'Alembert* (D'Alembert's dream), ed. Colas Duflo (1769; repr., Paris: Flammarion, 2002), 57.

12. Jean-François Barrière, *Tableaux de genre et d'histoire, peints par différents maîtres, ou morceaux inédits sur la régence, la jeunesse de Louis XV, et le règne de Louis XVI* (Historical and genre works, painted by various masters, or unpublished pieces on the regency, the youth of Louis XV, and the reign of Louis XVI) (Paris: Ponthieu, 1828).

13. Hill, "Notes for a Modern Edition," 185–86.

14. Jacques-André Naigeon described as "flat, insolent, and sullen" Falconet's *Observations sur le cheval de Marc-Aurèle* (Observations on Marcus Aurelius's horse), to which Diderot replied in a letter of May 2, 1773. On this question, see Herbert Dieckmann, *Inventaire du fonds Vandeul et inédits de Diderot* (Inventory of the Vandeul collection and unpublished texts by Diderot) (Geneva: Droz, 1951), 105.

15. Raymond Trousson, "Diderot, Falconet et les anciens" (Diderot, Falconet and the ancients), in Diderot and Falconet, *Le pour et le contre*, xiv.

16. Sending his translation of Pliny to Voltaire in 1772, Falconet declares, "I'm felling an idol adored for centuries, and I'm sending you both the idol and the tools I use for his destruction." Quoted in Diderot and Falconet, *Le pour et le contre*, xiv, n. 4.

17. "I take great pleasure in reading Voltaire when he speaks neither of painting nor of sculpture. May he pardon me for knowing these two arts better than he. May he pardon me also for trying to shed light where, most assuredly, he has cast shadows." "Lettre X, Falconet à Diderot, mai 1766" (Letter X, Falconet to Diderot, May 1766), in Diderot and Falconet, *Le pour et le contre*, 99.

18. Denis Diderot, *Le neveu de Rameau* (Rameau's nephew), ed. Michel Delon (1762–73; repr., Paris: Gallimard, 2006), 45–46.

19. Mortier, "'Le concert lointain,'" xii.

20. Ibid., x.

21. Marc Buffat, "Diderot, Falconet et l'amour de la postérité" (Diderot, Falconet and the love of posterity), *Recherches sur Diderot et sur l'Encyclopédie* 4 (2008): 9.

22. "Lettre I, Diderot à Falconet, décembre 1765" (Letter I, Diderot to Falconet, December 1765), in Diderot and Falconet, *Le pour et le contre*, 3–4.

23. Buffat emphasizes here, "It is for Diderot that there is often a difference in intensity between the nearby voice of contemporaries and that of posterity, which is sometimes only a far-off sound, hard to perceive because of the distance." "Diderot, Falconet et l'amour de la postérité," 10.

24. "Lettre I, Diderot à Falconet, décembre 1765," in Diderot and Falconet, *Le pour et le contre*, 4. My italics.

25. "Lettre II, Falconet à Diderot, décembre 1765" (Letter II, Falconet to Diderot, December 1765), in Diderot and Falconet, *Le pour et le contre*, 6.

26. "Lettre III, Diderot à Falconet, janvier 1766" (Letter III, Diderot to Falconet, January 1766), in Diderot and Falconet, *Le pour et le contre*, 8.

27. The theme of continuity between the mental and physical spheres is explored by Diderot in *D'Alembert's Dream*. On this text and Diderot's materialism, see Florence Lotterie, "Hybrides philosophiques: Quelques enjeux du dialogue matérialiste dans *Le rêve de D'Alembert* et *La philosophie dans le boudoir*" (Philosophical hybrids: Some issues in the materialist dialogue in *D'Alembert's Dream* and *Philosophy in the Bedroom*), *Recherches sur Diderot et sur l'Encyclopédie* 42 (2007): 27–81.

28. "Lettre III, Diderot à Falconet, janvier 1766," in Diderot and Falconet, *Le pour et le contre*, 9.

29. Ibid., 10.

30. "There is nothing that can halt my unbridled desires; I feel driven to love everything on earth, and like Alexander I wish that there were other worlds in order to be able to expand my amorous conquests." Molière, *Dom Juan* (1665), in *Œuvres complètes* (Complete works), ed. Georges Forestier (Paris: Gallimard, 2010), 2:853.

31. "Lettre XV, Diderot à Falconet, septembre 1766" (Letter XV, Diderot to Falconet, September 1766), in Diderot and Falconet, *Le pour et le contre*, 149.

32. As regards Diderot's devotion to Socrates, see Jean Seznec, *Essais sur Diderot et l'antiquité* (Essays on Diderot and Antiquity (Oxford, UK: Clarendon Press, 1957); and Raymond Trousson, *Socrate devant Voltaire, Diderot et Rousseau: La conscience en face du mythe* (Socrates before Voltaire, Diderot, and Rousseau: Conscience confronting myth) (Paris: Minard, 1967).

33. "Lettre VII, Diderot à Falconet, février 1766" (Letter VII, Diderot to Falconet, February 1766), in Diderot and Falconet, *Le pour et le contre*, 56–57. My italics.

34. Jean-Christophe Abramovici, "'Vous me tyrannisez, mon poulet': La publicité de l'intime dans les premiers *Salons*" ("You are tyrannizing me, my chickadee": The publicity of the intimate in the first *Salons*"), in *Les Salons de Diderot: Théorie et écriture* (Les *Salons* de Diderot: Theory and writing), ed. Pierre Frantz and Élisabeth Lavezzi (Paris: Presses Paris Sorbonne, 2008), 91.

35. Ibid.

36. Antoine Lilti, *The Invention of Celebrity*, trans. Lynn Jeffress (Cambridge, UK: Polity Press, 2017), 149.

37. On this text, see the sixth paradox, "Distance and Judgment."

38. Yves Citton, "Retour sur la misérable querelle Rousseau-Diderot: Position, conséquence, spectacle et sphère publique" (Return on the miserable Rousseau-Diderot quarrel: Position, consequence, spectacle, and public sphere), *Recherches sur Diderot et sur l'Encyclopédie* 36 (2004): 88. My italics.

39. "Lettre XII, Falconet à Diderot, juin 1766" (Letter XII, Falconet to Diderot, June 1766), in Diderot and Falconet, *Le pour et le contre*, 119. My italics.

40. François Quesnay, "Évidence" (Evidence), in *Encyclopédie, ou dictionnaire raisonné des sciences, des arts et des métiers* (*Encyclopedia, or a Systematic Dictionary of the Sciences, Arts, and Crafts*), ed. Denis Diderot and Jean le Rond d'Alembert (Paris: Chez Briasson, David, Le Breton, Durand, 1756), 6:146b. My italics.

41. Edme-François Mallet, "Croyance (Théologie)" (Belief [Theology]), *Encyclopédie* 4 (1754): 516b. My italics.

42. On this question, see Jean-Alexandre Perras, *L'Exception exemplaire: Inventions et usages du génie (XVIe–XVIIIe siècle)* (The exemplary exception: Inventions and uses of genius [16th–18th century]) (Paris: Classiques Garnier, 2015).

43. Denis Diderot, *Pensées sur l'interprétation de la nature* (Thoughts on the interpretation of nature), ed. Colas Duflo (1754; repr., Paris: Flammarion, 2005), 70.

44. On this question, see Lucien Nouis, *De l'infini des bibliothèques au livre unique: L'archive épurée au XVIIIe siècle* (From the infinite of libraries to the single book: The uncluttered archive in the 18th century) (Paris: Classiques Garnier, 2013).

Second Paradox

1. "And I buy a ticket for a lottery whose grand prize is reduced to this: to be read in 1935." Stendhal, *Vie de Henri Brulard* (Life of Henri Brulard), in *Œuvres intimes* (Intimate works), ed. V. Del Litto (Paris: Gallimard, 1982), 2:745.

2. Étienne Cabet, *Voyage en Icarie* (Trip to Icaria), preface by Jacques Attali (Paris: Dalloz, 2006). On this text, see Leslie J. Roberts, "Étienne Cabet and His *Voyage en Icarie*, 1840,"

Utopian Studies 2, nos. 1–2 (1991): 77–94. On Thomas More and "Christian communism," see Edward L. Surtz, "Thomas More and Communism," *PMLA* 64, no. 3 (1949): 549–64.

3. Joachim du Bellay, "La défense et illustration de la langue française" (Defense and illustration of the French language," in *Les regrets: Les antiquités de Rome*, preface by J. Borel, ed. Silvestre de Sacy (Paris: Gallimard, 1967), 237.

4. Théophile de Viau, "Élégie à une dame" (Elegy to a lady), in *Après m'avoir fait tant mourir: Œuvres choisies* (After having made me die so much: Selected works), ed. Jean-Pierre Chauveau (Paris: Gallimard, 2002), 75.

5. This position is made clear by the title of chapter 3 of the second book of the *Défense et illustration*, translated into English as "That natural talent is not sufficient for a poet to create a work worthy of immortality," 236–37.

6. De Viau, "Élégie à une dame," 75. On the relationship between imitation and spontaneity in the works of Théophile de Viau, see Alain Lanavère, "Théophile de Viau, imitateur des anciens" (Théophile de Viau, imitator of the ancients), *Dix-septième siècle* 251 (2011): 397–422.

7. Having taken refuge in Paris after his escape from the Venice prisons in 1756, Casanova introduced in France the "Genoese" lottery, a game based on wagers on the combinations of numbers that came out of drawings. His project was accepted by the Conseil d'État in 1757, and the first drawing of the lottery of the École royale militaire took place the following year. On this subject, see Helmut Watzlawick, "Casanova et les loteries" (Casanova and lotteries), in *Être riche au siècle de Voltaire* (Being rich in the century of Voltaire), ed. Jacques Berchtold and Michel Porret (Geneva: Droz, 1996), 161–71.

8. See C. J. de Ligne, *Fragments sur Casanova* (Fragments on Casanova) (Paris: Allia, 1998), 45–46.

9. Letter from Casanova to J. F. Opiz (January 10, 1791), quoted by Marie-Françoise Luna in *Casanova mémorialiste* (Casanova memorialist) (Paris: Honoré Champion, 1998), 55.

10. Casanova wrote three versions of the preface of *Histoire de ma vie*: in 1791, 1794, and 1797. The reflections that follow bear on the last version.

11. Giacomo Casanova, *Histoire de ma vie* (The story of my life), ed. Jean-Christophe Igalens and Érik Leborgne (Paris: Robert Laffont, 2013), 1:7. My italics.

12. On the reinterpretation of an existence that has run its course and the quarrels it provokes, see the sixth paradox, "The Distance and the Judgment."

13. "[I] am unable to find anything more pleasant than talking about my own doings and giving a noble object of amusement to the good company that is listening to me, that always gave me signs of friendship, and that I've always frequented. To write well, I only have to imagine that it is they who will read me: Quaecumque dixi, si placuerint, dictavit auditor [If something is pleasing in what I said, it is what the listener dictated]." Casanova, *Histoire de ma vie*, 1:7–8.

14. Ibid., 1:7.

15. Giacomo Casanova, *Ma voisine, la postérité* (My neighbor, posterity) (1797; repr., Paris: Allia, 1998).

16. On Casanova and games of chance, see Thomas M. Kavanagh, *Dice, Cards, Wheels: A Different History of French Culture* (Philadelphia: University of Pennsylvania Press, 2005), 85–109.

17. Jean-Christophe Igalens, "Casanova écrivain" (Casanova the writer), in Casanova, *Histoire de ma vie*, 1:xxv.

18. Giacomo Casanova, *Le Duel, ou essai sur la vie de J. C. Vénitien* (The duel, or essay on the life of J. C. Vénitien), trans. R. Vèze (Paris: Allia, 1998); Giacomo Casanova, *Histoire de ma fuite des prisons de la République de Venise, qu'on appelle les Plombs* (The story of my escape from the prisons of the Republic of Venice called The Leads) (1787; repr., Paris: Allia, 1999).

19. Chantal Thomas, *Casanova: Un voyage libertin* (Casanova: A libertine journey) (Paris: Denoël, 1985), 77.

20. On this episode, see Casanova, *Histoire de ma vie*, 1:96.

21. Dirk van der Cruysse, "Don Juan et le miroir: Le projet autobiographique casanovien" (Don Juan and the mirror: The Casanova autobiographical project), in *De Branche en branche: Études sur le XVIIe et le XVIIIe siècles français* (From branch to branch: Studies on the 17th and 18th centuries in France), ed. Dirk van der Cruysse (Louvain: Peeters, 2005), 95.

22. Casanova, *Histoire de ma vie*, 2:309.

23. On the role played by O'Reilly in the triggering of the writing of *The Story of My Life* in 1789, see Luna, *Casanova mémorialiste*, 53.

24. Gérard Lahouati, "Le long travail" (The long work), *Genesis* 34 (2012): 98.

25. Helmut Watzlawick, "Mémoires et thérapie: Les 'anticonfessions' de Casanova" (Memoirs and therapy: The "Anticonfessions" of Casanova), *Annales de la société Jean-Jacques Rousseau* 41, ed. Jacques Berchtold and Michel Porret (1997): 285.

26. Giacomo Casanova, *Confutazione della storia del governo veneto d'Amelot de la Houssaye* (Refutation of the history of the Venetian government by Amelot de la Houssaye), 3 vols. (Amsterdam: Presso Pietro Mortier, 1769).

27. *Istoria delle turbolenze della Polonia dalla morte di Elisabetta Petrowna fino alla pace fra la Russia e la Porta ottomana: In cui si trovano tutti gli avvenimenti cagioni della rivoluzione di quell regno* (History of the turbulences of Poland from the death of Elizabeth Petrowna to the peace between Russia and the Ottoman Porte: In which all the events of the revolution of that kingdom are found), 3 vols. (Goritz: Valerio de Valeri, 1774). On the autobiographical digressions in Casanova's historical work, see Luna, *Casanova mémorialiste*, 41–46.

28. *Icosaméron ou histoire d'Édouard et d'Élisabeth qui passèrent quatre-vingt-un ans chez les Mégamicres habitants aborigènes du Protocosme dans l'intérieur de notre globe, traduite de l'anglais par Jacques Casanova de Seingalt Vénitien* (Icosameron or the story of Edward and Elizabeth who spent eighty-one years with the Mégamicres, aboriginal inhabitants of the protocosm inside our globe, translated from the English by Jacques Casanova de Seingalt, Venetian), 5 vols. (1788; repr., Plan de la Tour: Éditions d'Aujourd'hui, 1986).

29. Marie-Françoise Luna, "Casanova et ses dieux" (Casanova and his gods), *Europe* 697 (May 1987): 65.

30. Annie Ernaux, *Mémoire de fille* (A girl's story) (Paris: Gallimard, 2016), 143. My italics.

31. François Roustang, *Le bal masqué de Giacomo Casanova* (The masked ball of Giacomo Casanova) (Paris: Éditions de Minuit, 1985), 11.

32. On this question, see Béatrice Didier, "Plaisir et autobiographie: Réflexions sur une préface" (Pleasure and autobiography: Reflections on a preface), *Europe* 697 (May 1987): 51–58.

33. See the preface to Casanova, *Histoire de ma vie*, 1:6.

34. On this episode, see Casanova, *Histoire de ma vie*, 1:27–28. On the programmatic value of this scene and the obviously intended parallels it establishes with the episode of the *Confessions* in which Rousseau steals Madame de Vercellis's ribbon, see Benjamin Hoffmann, "La scène du vol dans l'enfance de Rousseau et Casanova" (The scene of the theft in the childhood of Rousseau and Casanova), *Revue Littératures* 27 (2012): 93–115.

35. As regards the "diverse transcendencies" exhibited in Casanova's memoirs, see Luna, "Casanova et ses dieux"; and Luna, *Casanova mémorialiste*, 248–53.

36. Casanova, *Histoire de ma vie*, 1:295–96.

37. Ibid., 1:413.

38. Giacomo Casanova, *Histoire de ma vie* (The story of my life), ed. Francis Lacassin (Paris: Robert Laffont, 1993), 3:614.

39. "Extrait d'une lettre de M. de Casanova de S. Galt [à Vienne] à M. Max Comte de Bamberg à Brünn, 15 avril 1785" (Excerpt from a letter from Mr. de Casanova de S. Galt [in Vienna] to Mr. Max Count of Bamberg in Brünn, April 15, 1785), in *"Mon cher Casanova . . .": Lettres du comte Maximilien Lamberg et de Pietro Zaguri, praticien de Venise à Giacomo Casanova* (My dear Casanova . . .": Letters from Count Maximilian Lamberg and Pietro Zaguri, a Venetian practitioner to Giacomo Casanova), ed. Marco Leeflang, Gérard Luciani et Marie-Françoise Luna (Paris: Honoré Champion, 448), 87–88.

40. Denis Diderot, "Immortalité, immortel" (Immortality, immortal), in *Encyclopédie*, ed. Diderot and d'Alembert, 8:576b. My italics.
41. Casanova, *Histoire de ma vie*, ed. Igalens and Leborgne, 2:1231. My italics.
42. On the circumstances of these breakups, see, respectively, ibid., 1:650–54, 2:291–98, 2:299–301; and in the Lacassin ed., 3:314–16.
43. On this question, see Félicien Marceau, *Casanova ou l'Anti–Don Juan* (Casanova or the anti–Don Juan, 1954) (Paris: Gallimard, 1985).

Third Paradox

1. On this question, see Casanova, *Histoire de ma vie*, ed. Igalens and Leborgne, 1:78–110.
2. Simone de Beauvoir, *La force des choses* (Paris: Gallimard, 2004), 1:63–64.
3. Benoît Denis, "Politiques de l'autobiographie chez Sartre" (The politics of autobiography in Sartre's works), *Les Temps modernes* 641 (2006): 156.
4. On this subject, see Philippe Lejeune, "Sartre et l'autobiographie parlée" (Sartre and oral autobiography), in *Je est un autre: L'autobiographie de la littérature aux médias* (I is somebody else: Autobiography from Literature to the Media) (Paris: Le Seuil, 1980), 161–72.
5. *Sartre par lui-même: Le temps de la réflexion; Le temps de l'engagement* (Sartre by himself: The period of reflection; the period of commitment), directed by Alexandre Astruc and Michel Contat (1976; Paris: Éditions Montparnasse, 2007), DVD; Jean-Paul Sartre, "Autoportrait à soixante-dix ans" (Self-portrait at seventy), in *Situations, X: Politique et autobiographie* (Paris: Gallimard, 1976), 133–226; Simone de Beauvoir and Jean-Paul Sartre, *La cérémonie des adieux, suivi de entretiens avec Jean-Paul Sartre: Août–septembre 1974* (The farewell ceremony, followed by interviews with Jean-Paul Sartre: August–September 1974) (Paris: Gallimard, 1981).
6. On this question, see Geneviève Idt, "L'autoparodie dans *Les Mots* de Sartre" (Autoparody in *The Words* of Sartre), *Cahiers du XXe siècle* 6 (1976): 53–86.
7. Annie Cohen-Solal, *Sartre, 1905–1980* (Paris: Gallimard, 1985), 328.
8. Ibid., 332.
9. Beauvoir, *La force des choses*, 1:61.
10. On the history of "French Theory," see François Cusset, *French Theory: Foucault, Derrida, Deleuze et Cie et les mutations de la vie intellectuelle aux Etats-Unis* (French Theory: Foucault, Derrida, Deleuze, and Co. and the transformations in U.S. intellectual life) (Paris: La Découverte, 2005).
11. Beauvoir, *La force des choses*, 1:62.
12. Ibid., 1:63.
13. This aphorism by Nicolas Chamfort, often misquoted in a manner that reduces its paradoxical dimension ("Celebrity is the advantage of being known by people whom you do not know"), is discussed by Lilti in *The Invention of Celebrity*, 105–8.
14. On this period in Sartre's life, see Cohen-Solal, *Sartre*, 120–67.
15. Beauvoir, *La force des choses*, 1:63.
16. I will return to this problem in the sixth paradox, "The Distance and the Judgment."
17. Walter Benjamin, *Baudelaire*, ed. Giorgio Agamben, Barbara Chitussi, and Clemens-Carl Härle, trans. Patrick Charbonneau (Paris: La Fabrique Éditions, 2013).
18. Beauvoir, *La force des choses*, 1:63.
19. Ibid., 1:64.
20. Jean-Paul Sartre, "Présentation des *Temps modernes*" (Presentation of the *Temps modernes*), in *Situations, II* (Paris: Gallimard, 1949), 15. Subsequent citations in this chapter appear parenthetically in the text.
21. Bernard-Henri Lévy, *Le siècle de Sartre: Enquête philosophique* (Sartre's century: A philosophical investigation) (Paris: Grasset, 2000), 92.
22. Jean-Paul Sartre, "Qu'est-ce que la littérature?" (What is literature?), in *Situations, II* (Paris: Gallimard, 1949), 57.

23. Beauvoir, *La force des choses*, 1:63–64.
24. Jean-Paul Sartre, "Sur *L'Idiot de la famille*" (On *The Family Idiot*), in *Situations, X: Politique et autobiographie* (Paris: Gallimard, 1976), 105.
25. Sartre, "Autoportrait à soixante-dix ans," 156.
26. John Gerassi, *Sartre, conscience haïe de son siècle* (Sartre, detested conscience of his century) (Paris: Editions du Rocher, 1992), 154.

Fourth Paradox

1. Diderot, "Immortalité, immortel," 8:577a.
2. Jean-Baptiste Poquelin sometimes used his two identities on official documents. The oldest of them is dated June 28, 1644. On this question, see Madeleine Jurgens and Elisabeth Maxfield-Miller, *Cent ans de recherches sur Molière, sur sa famille et sur les comédiens de sa troupe* (One hundred years of research on Molière, his family, and the actors in his company) (Paris: Imprimerie nationale, 1963), 241–42.
3. According to the journalist Claudio Gatti, the pseudonym Elena Ferrante hides the identity of an Italian translator named Anita Raja. On this question, see "Elena Ferrante: An Answer?" *New York Review of Books*, October 2, 2016.
4. First proposed by Samuel Butler in *The Authoress of the Odyssey* (1897), the thesis according to which the *Odyssey* is the work of a woman was also espoused by Andrew Dalby in *Rediscovering Homer: Inside the Origins of the Epic* (New York: W. W. Norton, 2006).
5. Anne Dacier, "La Vie d'Homère" (The life of Homer), in *L'Iliade d'Homère traduite en français, avec des remarques* (Homer's *Iliad* translated into French, with observations) (Amsterdam. Wettstein and Smith, 1731), 1:1.
6. On forgetfulness as a type of "nonreading," see Pierre Bayard, *Comment parler des livres que l'on n'a pas lus?* (How to talk about books you haven't read) (Paris: Éditions de Minuit, 2007), 55–62.
7. On *La Henriade*, see Pierre Bayard, *Comment améliorer les œuvres ratées?* (How to improve failed works?) (Paris: Éditions de Minuit, 2000).
8. On the role of passions in the evaluation of a work after the disappearance of its author, see the sixth paradox, "The Distance and the Judgment."
9. On the evolution of the aesthetic value granted the novel in the Enlightenment, see Georges May, *Le dilemme du roman au XVIIIe siècle* (The dilemma of the novel in the 18th century) (New Haven: Yale University Press, 1963).
10. For an example of biographical fiction, see the film by Laurent Tirard, *Molière* (Culver City, Calif.: Sony Pictures Home Entertainment, 2007), DVD.
11. On this question, see André Magnan, *Dossier Voltaire en Prusse: 1750–1753* (The file on Voltaire in Prussia: 1750–1753), Studies on Voltaire and the Eighteenth Century 244 (Oxford, UK: Voltaire Foundation, 1986).
12. Pierre Michon, *Corps du roi* (The body of the king) (Paris: Verdier, 2002), 44.

Fifth Paradox

1. On this question, see Jean-Claude Bonnet, *Naissance du Panthéon: Essai sur le culte des grands hommes* (The birth of the Pantheon: Essay on the cult of great men) (Paris: Fayard, 1998).
2. On the paradoxes inherent in the definition of personal identity, see Stéphane Ferret, *Le bateau de Thésée: Le problème de l'identité à travers le temps* (The Ship of Theseus: The problem of identity over time) (Paris: Éditions de Minuit, 1996).
3. Cardinal Godfried Danneels, "La réincarnation: Une croyance qui séduit" (Reincarnation: A seductive belief), *Questions actuelles*, May 1998.

4. Cardinal Danneels refers to the survey "Valeurs européennes" (European values) conducted in 1990 and cites the following statistics: "According to this survey, 27% of the Swiss and Canadians, 24% of the French, and 13% of the Belgians believe in reincarnation. In Europe, 23% of the Catholics and 21% of the Protestants believe in it. Among the Catholics who practice 'regularly' (who go to mass at least once a month), the percent reaches 26% (as opposed to 18% of nonpracticing Catholics). Finally, 43% of the Europeans who believe in resurrection say that they also believe in reincarnation" (ibid., 22).

5. Ibid., 21–22.

6. "There is no longer here [in Buddhism] any 'self' [*soi*] or 'I' [*moi*]: everything becomes evanescent, and we only exist by a continual flow of thoughts, memories, sensations, and deliberate acts. *Such that one may wonder if we are still speaking of a true reincarnation*: there is no longer, in fact, any continuous "self" that returns to existence" (ibid., 23). My italics.

7. I will return to this question later in the chapter.

8. Matthieu Ricard observes, "In his book *Entrez dans l'espérance*, [Jean-Paul II] asserts that, according to Buddhism, 'we must cut our ties to exterior reality' and 'as this liberation grows, we become more and more indifferent to everything in the world. . . .' He likewise describes *nirvana* as 'a total indifference toward the world.' These are misinterpretations—excusable perhaps because they are due to a lack of information—that many Christians and Buddhists have regretted." Jean-François Revel and Matthieu Ricard, *Le moine et le philosophe: Le bouddhisme aujourd'hui* (The monk and the philosopher: Buddhism today) (Paris: Nil éditions, 1997), 214. Revel and Ricard remind us that the goal of Buddhism consists in developing an ultimate comprehension of the phenomenal world rather than encouraging any detachment from it, whereas nirvana implies compassion toward the entirety of sentient beings and not indifference.

9. Ian Stevenson, *Twenty Cases Suggestive of Reincarnation* (1966; repr., Charlottesville: University of Virginia Press, 1974).

10. Danneels, "La réincarnation," 24.

11. On this question, see Stevenson, *Twenty Cases*, 2.

12. Promulgated in 1964 by Pope Paul VI, the official church dogma reaffirms the uniqueness of earthly existence and reiterates the promise of resurrection brought by Christ: "Without knowing the day and the hour, we must, in accordance with the Lord's warning, remain constantly vigilant in order, when *the unique course of our earthly life* is over, to be admitted with him to the nuptials and be counted among the blessed of God" (*Lumen gentium*, 48; my italics).

13. The expression "conditioned world" refers to the Buddhist theory of the interdependence of the objects that constitute reality. The Buddhist theory insists on the fact that nothing exists independently: all physical and mental objects are born and remain a function of a series of causes and conditions whose termination brings about their own. On this question, see Peter Harvey, *An Introduction to Buddhism: Teachings, History and Practices* (Cambridge, UK: Cambridge University Press, 1990), 54–60.

14. Peter Harvey, "Buddhist Visions of the Human Predicament and Its Resolution," in *Buddhism*, ed. Peter Harvey (New York: Continuum, 2001), 75.

15. Ibid., 76. My italics.

16. Gérard Huet, "Skanda," in *Dictionnaire Héritage du Sanscrit* (Sanskrit heritage dictionary), 1994–2019, http://sanskrit.inria.fr/DICO/71.html#skandha.

17. On this question, see Revel and Ricard, *Le moine et le philosophe*, 316.

18. On the law of karma, see Harvey, *Introduction to Buddhism*, 32–46.

19. On the "discriminating consciousness," see the articles "Citta" and "Vijñāna" in the *Dictionary of Buddhism*, ed. Damien Keown (Oxford, UK: Oxford University Press, 2003), 62, 328–29.

20. Harvey, "Buddhist Visions of the Human Predicament," 79–80.

21. Harvey, *Introduction to Buddhism*, 53.

22. "From desire action follows; from action suffering follows; desire, action, and suffering are like a wheel rotating endlessly." Bukkyō Dendō Kyōkai, *The Teaching of Buddha* (Tokyo: Bukkyō Dendō Kyōkai, 2014), 87.
23. On the refutation of idealism by Chandrakirti and the convergence of his argumentation with that of Immanuel Kant in the *Critique of Pure Reason*, see Jay L. Garfield, *Engaging Buddhism: Why It Matters to Philosophy* (Oxford, UK: Oxford University Press, 2015), 193–99.
24. Revel and Ricard, *Le moine et le philosophe*, 359–60.
25. The fourteenth Dalai Lama recalls this fundamental principle of Buddhist ethics in his introduction Khandro Rinpoche, *This Precious Life* (Boston: Shambhala, 2003), ix.
26. Matthieu Ricard, "La réincarnation n'est pas la renaissance d'un 'moi'" (Reincarnation is not the rebirth of a 'self'"), November 24, 2012, http://www.matthieuricard.org/articles/la-reincarnation-n-est-pas-la-renaissance-d-un-moimoi.
27. Bukkyō Dendō Kyōkai *Teaching of Buddha*, 87–88.

Sixth Paradox

1. On this question, see Beauvoir, *La force des choses*, 1:63–64.
2. On the concept of the "distant melody," see the first paradox, "The Current Concert and the Distant Melody."
3. The expression "miserable quarrel" is borrowed from Diderot and refers to his disputes with Rousseau: "If you do not beware of your first movement, you will find yourself involved in some *miserable quarrel* that will impinge on your happiness." Denis Diderot, *Œuvres*, ed. Laurent Versini (Paris: Robert Laffont, 1977), 5:848–49. My italics.
4. Sartre, "Qu'est-ce que la littérature?" 80.
5. Denis Diderot, *Essai sur les règnes de Claude et de Néron* (Essay on the reigns of Claude and Nero), in *Œuvres complètes* (Complete works), ed. Jean Deprun, Jean Ehrard, Annette Lorenceau, and Raymond Trousson (Paris: Hermann, 1986), 25:304. My italics.
6. The *Essai sur les règnes de Claude et de Néron* (1782) is a sequel to the *Essai sur la vie de Sénèque le philosophe, sur ses écrits, et sur les règnes de Claude et de Néron* (Essay on the life of Seneca the philosopher, on his writings, and on the reigns of Claude and Nero) (1778) that constitutes volume 7 of the translation of the *Œuvres* (Works) of Seneca by La Grange. According to Jacques Chouillet in "La présence de J.-J. Rousseau après sa mort dans les écrits de Diderot" (The presence of J.-J. Rousseau after his death in the writings of Diderot), *Cahiers de Varsovie* 10 (1982), the two texts "came one from the other by means of broadening and amplification, but in different forms and with different orientations" (179).
7. This comment by Saint-Évremond on Seneca is quoted by Diderot in *Essai sur les règnes de Claude et de Néron*, 25:303. Subsequent citations in this chapter appear parenthetically in the text.
8. "Oh, Seneca! You are and will forever be, with Socrates, with all the unfortunate illustrious men, with all the great men of antiquity, one of the sweetest links between my friends and me, between the learned men of all the ages and their friends" (ibid., 25:39).
9. The publication of the *Essay* precedes by several months that of *The Confessions*. According to Jacques Chouillet, it is the very imminence of the appearance of Rousseau's autobiography that led Diderot to publish the *Essay*: "Faced with a growing threat whose nature was not yet completely known to him, and warned by a public opinion that designated him, Diderot, and his *Encyclopedia* friends, as the principle target of Rousseau, Diderot reacted by going on the offensive to defend what he considered his honor and the honor of the cause he was defending." "La présence de J.-J. Rousseau," 183.
10. In addition to the above-mentioned articles of Jacques Chouillet and Yves Citton on this subject, see the chapter of Jean Fabre, "Deux frères ennemis: Diderot et Jean-Jacques" (Two enemy brothers: Diderot and Jean-Jacques), in *Lumières et romantisme* (Paris: PUF, 1975), 19–65.

11. Rousseau refused a position as a cashier for a receiver general of finances, then the pension he could have obtained if he had agreed to meet Louis XV following the performance of his opera *Le devin du village* (The village soothsayer) on October 18, 1752, at the Fontainebleau castle. The desire to preserve his independence vis-à-vis the reigning political power is cited by Rousseau as a determining factor in his decision: "I was losing, it is true, the pension that was more or less offered to me, but I was also freeing myself from the yoke that it would have imposed on me. Goodbye truth, liberty, and courage. How could I dare speak of independence and selflessness after that? All I would be able to do henceforth, in receiving this pension, was to flatter or be silent. Moreover, who could assure me that it would even be paid? So many steps to take, so many people to beg?" Jean-Jacques Rousseau, *Les Confessions*, in *Œuvres complètes* (Complete works), ed. Bernard Gagnebin, Marcel Raymond (Paris: Gallimard, 1959–95), 1:380.

12. "It was less my literary fame than my personal reform . . . that provoked their jealousy; they would perhaps have pardoned me for writing well, but they could not pardon me for offering by my behavior an example that seemed to trouble them" (Rousseau, *Les Confessions*, 1:362).

13. Citton, "Retour sur la misérable querelle Rousseau-Diderot," 62.

14. According to "Him" (Lui), "to adopt postures" means to be in a situation of dependence in relation to others that no one—other than the philosopher—can hope to escape: "Whoever needs another person is indigent and adopts a posture." Diderot, *Le neveu de Rameau*, 148.

15. Citton, "Retour sur la misérable querelle Rousseau-Diderot," 73.

16. Rousseau, *Les Confessions*, 1:381.

17. Jeannette Geffriaud Rosso, "Diderot et Angélique à travers la *Correspondance*: Humain, trop humain" (Diderot and Angélique through the *Correspondence*: Human, all too human), *Revue Belge de philologie et d'histoire* 70, no. 3 (1992): 683.

18. Ibid., 693.

19. Chouillet notes in this respect, "There are few dead people who tormented the living more than the shadow of Rousseau did the aging Diderot," "La présence de J.-J. Rousseau," 177.

20. I borrow this expression from the chapter by Jean Fabre mentioned above.

21. I borrow this distinction from the article by Laurence Mall, "Une œuvre critique: L'*Essai sur les règnes de Claude et de Néron* de Diderot" (A critical work: The *Essay on the Reigns of Claude and Nero* by Diderot), *Revue d'histoire littéraire de la France* 106, no. 4 (2006): 843–57.

22. Ibid., 856.

23. Raymond Trousson, "Préface," in *Denis Diderot: Mémoire de la critique* (Denis Diderot: Memory of the critic), ed. Raymond Trousson (Paris: Presses Paris Sorbonne, 2005), 15.

24. On the critical reception of Diderot in the nineteenth century, see Raymond Trousson, *Images de Diderot en France, 1784–1913* (Representations of Diderot in France, 1784–1913) (Paris: Honoré Champion, 1997).

25. This phrase was invented by Bernard Le Bovier de Fontenelle in the *Entretiens sur la pluralité des mondes* (Conversations on the plurality of worlds), ed. Christophe Martin (1686; repr., Paris: Flammarion, 1998), 155.

26. According to Bordeu in *Le rêve de d'Alembert*, a "Sophism of the ephemeral" is "that of a transient being who believes in the immutability of things" (97).

Seventh Paradox

1. I borrow the concepts of "cultural mediation" and "technical mediation" from the article by Bruno Bachimont, "La conservation du patrimoine numérique: Enjeux et tendances" (The conservation of the digital patrimony: Issues and tendencies), in *Patrimoine et numérique: Technique et politique de la mémoire* (Digital heritage: Technology and politics of the memory) (Paris: INA, 2008), http://www.ina-expert.com.

2. Claude Hagège, *Halte à la mort des langues* (Enough with the death of languages) (Paris: Éditions Odile Jacob, 2000), 44.

3. I borrow this comparison from Hagège. See ibid., 43.

4. I borrow the concept of "tendency" from Alexis Philonenko, who observes, on the subject of what we traditionally call "dead languages," "A dead language will be characterized, from a very summary viewpoint, as a totality oriented toward an ultimate diversification of internal moments. To the very extent that it neither invents nor imports new elements, it exhibits *a tendency towards closure*." "Langue morte et langue vivante" (Dead language and living language), *Revue de métaphysique et de morale* 2, no. 54 (2007): 157. My italics.

5. On the historical stages of the revival of Hebrew, see Hagège, *Halte à la mort des langues*, 271–341.

6. François-René de Chateaubriand, *Mémoires d'outre-tombe* (Memoirs from beyond the grave), ed. Jean-Claude Berchet (1848; repr., Paris: Le Livre de poche, 1989), 4:604.

7. In the preface of the *Voyage en Amérique*, Chateaubriand emphasizes the fragility of the languages spoken in India. See *Voyage en Amérique* (Journey in America), in *Œuvres complètes de Chateaubriand* (The complete works of Chateaubriand), ed. Henri Rossi (Paris: Honoré Champion, 2008), 6:113.

8. The rest of this chapter is an extension of the article by Denis Hollier, "French Customs, Literary Borders," *October* 49 (Summer 1989): 40–52. I continue his reflections on the paradoxical character of the symbol of the death of languages adopted by Chateaubriand (Agrippina's thrush) and rally to the conclusion of his essay—that is, that the French language is, for Chateaubriand, a future dead language in which he wishes to "freeze" his work. My intention is to pursue the reflection on what Hollier calls a "dead language" and that I call here a "closed language," and on the manner in which the latter is the paradoxical vehicle of the passing of works to posterity.

9. Quoted by Berchet in his edition of the *Mémoires d'outre-tombe*, 1:498n1.

10. François-René de Chateaubriand, *Essai sur la littérature anglaise et considérations sur le génie des hommes, des temps et des révolutions* (Essay on English literature and considerations on the genius of men, of time, and of revolutions), ed. Sébastien Baudoin (1836; repr., Paris: Classiques Garnier, 2013), 493–94. Subsequent citations in this chapter appear parenthetically in the text. This passage is taken up again by Chateaubriand in the *Mémoires d'outre-tombe*, which, nonetheless, exclude the example of William Shakespeare and the English language, only retaining that of Jacques-Bénigne Bossuet and French (1:498).

11. Chateaubriand, *Voyage en Amérique*, 290. On Chateaubriand and the disappearance of the Amerindian languages, see Benjamin Hoffmann, *Posthumous America: Literary Reinventions of America at the End of the Eighteenth Century*, trans. Alan J. Singerman (University Park: Pennsylvania State University Press, 2018), 146–56.

12. Chateaubriand, *Mémoires d'outre-tombe*, 1:49.

13. Hollier, "French Customs, Literary Borders," 49.

14. Ibid., 4:154–55.

Eighth Paradox

1. In *Languages of Art*, Nelson Goodman distinguishes between the "autographic arts" (where the distinction between the original and the copy is essential, as in the case of painting) and the "allographic arts" (where this distinction is not significant as regards the aesthetic status of the work, in literary works notably). On this question, see the third chapter of *Languages of Art: An Approach to a Theory of Symbols* (1968; repr., Indianapolis: Hackett, 1976), 99–123.

2. I am referring to the definition of digital technology given by Bruno Bachimont: "A term designating an arithmetical system formalizing a given reality. Digital technology possesses, consequently, formal properties to which are added arithmetical operations and the

associated calculations. Digital technology corresponds to formal systems including the totality of the computable, that is, data processing that can be effected by a machine." *Ingénierie des connaissances et des contenus: Le numérique entre ontologies et documents* (The engineering of knowledge and contents: Digital technology between ontologies and documents) (Paris: Lavoisier, 2007), 257.

3. Rousseau, *Les Confessions*, 1:114.

4. On the role of improvisation and chance in the process of literary creation, see Benjamin Hoffmann, "Écrivain cavalier, écrivain géomètre" (The writer as horseback rider and the writer as surveyor), *Les Écrits* 148 (2016): 45–58.

5. Rousseau, *Les Confessions*, 1:114.

6. "And now my work is done, which neither the wrath of Jove, nor fire, nor sword, *nor the gnawing tooth of time* shall ever be able to undo." Ovid, *Metamorphoses*, trans. Frank Justus Miller (Cambridge: Harvard University Press, 1958), 2:427. My italics. The Latin expression used by Ovid, *edax uetustas*, is sometimes translated by "voracious time," sometimes by "the teeth of time." It is the second translation that is adopted by Stephen Greenblatt in the fourth chapter of *The Swerve: How the World Became Modern* (New York: W. W. Norton, 2011), 81–109. Subsequent citations in this chapter appear parenthetically in the text.

7. "Apart from the charred papyrus fragments recovered in Herculaneum and another cache of fragments discovered in rubbish mounds in the ancient Egyptian city of Oxyrhynchus, there are no surviving contemporary manuscripts from the ancient Greek and Roman world. Everything that has reached us is a copy, most often very far removed in time, place, and culture from the original." Greenblatt, *The Swerve*, 81.

8. On this question, see William Marx, *La haine de la littérature* (The hatred of literature) (Paris: Éditions du Minuit, 2015), 141–42.

9. "At the National Library of France, they estimate that of two million French books published between 1875 and 1960, 90,000 are irremediably lost, 580,000 in immediate danger, and 600,000 in danger in the midterm." Pierre-Marc de Biasi, "Le papier, fragile support de l'essentiel" (Paper, fragile medium of the essential), *Les Cahiers de médiologie* 4 (1997): 11.

10. Claude Huc, "La pérennité des documents électroniques—points de vue alarmistes ou réalistes?" (The permanence of electronic documents—alarmist or realistic points of view?), *Bulletin des Archives de France sur la conservation à long terme des documents électroniques* 7 (2001): 3.

11. A "peripheral" is a device that adds functionalities to the digital system to which it is connected. While the "input devices" (such as the keyboard and the mouse) furnish information to the system, the output devices (like the screen and the printer) permit us to obtain information from it.

12. On this question, see Christian Rossi, "From Distribution to Preservation of Digital Documents," *TUGboat Proceedings* 30, no. 2 (2009): 274–80.

13. According to Jean-Charles Hourcade, Franck Laloë, and Erich Spitz, the authors of *Longévité de l'information numérique: Les données que nous voulons garder vont-elles s'effacer?* (Longevity of digital information: Are the data that we wish to keep going to be erased?) (*EDP* Sciences, 2010), the life span of digital media does not exceed ten years or so.

14. Rossi, "From Distribution to Preservation," 274.

15. Ibid.

16. Jeffrey van der Hoeven, Bram Lohman, and Remco Verdegem, "Emulation for Digital Preservation in Practice: The Results," *International Journal of Digital Curation* 2, no. 2 (2008): 124.

17. Bachimont, "La conservation du patrimoine numérique," 3.

18. Ibid.

19. Ibid.

20. Biasi, "Le papier, fragile support de l'essentiel," 11.

21. An author's page is an internet site whose architecture and content are controlled by the person whose works are presented there. In this digital space are combined the

implementation of a commercial function (consisting in arousing the visitor's interest in the books published by the author) and of an artistic function (expressed by the production of new texts and paratexts). It is thus both a publicity tool promoting the notoriety of the author who is administering it and a space for the continuation of his work by other means. On this subject, see Benjamin Hoffmann, "Le site d'auteur: Un nouvel espace d'investigation critique" (The author's website: A new space for critical investigation), *French Studies* 76 (2016): 565–80.

22. Biasi, "Le papier, fragile support de l'essentiel," 11.

23. Bachimont, *Ingénierie des connaissances et des contenus*, 225–26.

24. On Poggio Bracciolini, see Greenblatt, *The Swerve*.

25. Ann Blair, *Too Much to Know: Managing Scholarly Information Before the Modern Age* (New Haven: Yale University Press, 2011).

26. This body of data is growing constantly. See http://www.hathitrust.org/about.

27. The expression "literary revival" (*revie littéraire*) designates the reintroduction of a work into the network of memories by the production of new editions and new critical commentaries. On this subject, see *Mémoires du roman: La revie littéraire des romanciers oubliés* (Memoirs of the novel: The literary revival of forgotten novelists), ed. Bruno Curatolo and Paul Renard (Besançon: Presses Universitaires de Franche-Comté, 2010).

Ninth Paradox

1. "It was necessary to rename everything, rewrite everything, so that the new life not be in any way stained by past history now null and void, erased as if it had never existed." Boualem Sansal, *2084: La fin du monde* (2084: The end of the world) (Paris: Gallimard, 2015), 22.

2. Benjamin Hoffmann, *American Pandemonium* (Paris: Gallimard, 2016).

3. "Lettre II, Falconet à Diderot, décembre 1765," in Diderot and Falconet, *Le pour et le contre*, 7.

4. "Lettre VIII, Falconet à Diderot, février 1766" (Letter VIII, Falconet to Diderot, February 1766), in Diderot and Falconet, *Le pour et le contre*, 89.

5. The dispute between Diderot and Falconet over the painting by Polygnotos is developed in the Letters X to XIV. Falconet concludes it in these terms: "I know that Polygnotos's painting hadn't yet found anyone who had treated it so properly; not even Polygnotos." "Lettre XIV, Falconet à Diderot, août 1766" (Letter XIV, Falconet to Diderot, August 1766), in Diderot and Falconet, *Le pour et le contre*, 143.

6. "Let no obsession lead us to put the great modern painters beneath Polygnotos and those like him. The Dominiquins, the Guides, the Carraches drew just as well as the finest ancient. They have sometimes proved to be his equal in thought, and they have surpassed him in composition, color, and chiaroscuro; they are thus superior to him." "Lettre X, Falconet à Diderot, mai 1766," 106.

7. Ibid., 104.

8. "Lettre III, Diderot à Falconet, janvier 1766," in Diderot and Falconet, *Le pour et le contre*, 10.

9. Ibid.

10. Jean-Jacques Rousseau, *Discours sur l'origine et les fondements de l'inégalité parmi les hommes* (Discourse on the origin and the foundations of inequality among men), in *Œuvres complètes*, ed. Bernard Gagnebin and Marcel Raymond (1755; repr., Paris: Gallimard, 1959–95), 3:166.

11. Ibid., 3:169–70.

12. "Sometimes, with my friends, I enjoy an evening of debauchery, even a little turbulent. But I will not hide from you that it is infinitely more pleasurable to have come to the aid of some unfortunate person, to have concluded a thorny matter, given some useful advice; read

something interesting; taken a walk with a man or woman dear to my heart; spent a few instructive hours with my children, written a good page, fulfilled the duties of my position." Diderot, *Le neveu de Rameau*, 85.

13. Eric Schlosser, "World War Three, by Mistake," *New Yorker*, December 23, 2016. Subsequent citations in this chapter appear parenthetically in the text.

14. "In perhaps the most dangerous incident, the captain of a Soviet submarine mistakenly believed that his vessel was under attack by U.S. warships and ordered the firing of a torpedo armed with a nuclear warhead. His order was blocked by a fellow officer. Had the torpedo been fired, the United States would have retaliated with nuclear weapons." Ibid.

15. Robert Merle, *Malevil* (1972; repr., Paris: Gallimard, 1983); The Rolling Stones, "Gimme Shelter," *Let It Bleed* (London: London Records, 1969). This song was written and composed by Mick Jagger and Keith Richards. The former described it as the "end of the world song"; see his interview with Jan Wenner, "The *Rolling Stone* Interview: Jagger Remembers," *Rolling Stone*, December 14, 1995; Katsuhiro Otomo, *Akira*, 6 vols. (1982–90; repr., Grenoble: Éditions Glénat, 2016).

16. Bukkyō Dendō Kyōkai, *Teaching of Buddha*, 13.

Conclusion

1. Robert Wright, *Why Buddhism Is True: The Science and Philosophy of Meditation and Enlightenment* (New York: Simon & Schuster, 2017), 230.

2. On the manner in which natural selection conveys to individuals a spontaneous certainty regarding the primacy of their personal interests, see ibid., 229–32.

3. "Lettre I, Diderot à Falconet, décembre 1765," in Diderot and Falconet, *Le pour et le contre*, 4.

4. "Lettre III, Diderot à Falconet, janvier 1766," in Diderot and Falconet, *Le pour et le contre*, 10.

5. Diderot, *Essai sur les règnes de Claude et de Néron*, 25:121.

6. Lautréamont enumerates the "great soft heads" of his time that he accuses of causing the degeneration of poetry since Racine. Famous and denigrated, these contemporaries are dressed up with ridiculous pseudonyms by the author of *Les chants de Maldoror* (The songs of Maldoror): Chateaubriand is called "Mohican-Mélancolique" (Melancholy Mohican), Edgar Allan Poe "Mameluck-des-Rêves-d'Alcool" (Mameluke of dreams of alcohol), Rousseau "Socialiste-Grincheur" (Grumpy socialist), Alphonse de Lamartine "Cigogne-Larmoyante" (Tearful stork), and so forth. See "Poésies I" (Poetry I), in *Œuvres complètes de Lautréamont et Germain Nouveau* (Complete works by Lautréamont and Germain Nouveau), ed. Pierre-Olivier Walzer (Paris: Gallimard, 1970), 268.

7. Paul Valéry, "Au sujet du 'Cimetière marin'" (About "The Graveyard by the Sea"), in *Variétés* (Varieties) (Paris: Gallimard, 1936), 3:63–64. My italics.

8. "Each fact we relate is a degree of light, an education that substitutes for experience; each adventure is a model that one can follow in life; all one need do is adjust to the circumstances in which he finds himself. The entire work is a moral treatise reduced to pleasant exercises." Antoine François Prévost, "Avis de l'auteur" (Author's foreword), in *Histoire du chevalier des Grieux et de Manon Lescaut* (History of the Chevalier des Grieux and Manon Lescaut), ed. Robert Mauzi (1731; repr., Paris: Imprimerie Nationale, 1980), 44.

9. "A work of art is good if it stems from necessity. It is judged according to the way it originates: there is no other judgment." Rainer Maria Rilke, "Lettre du 17 février 1903 à Franz Xaver Kappus" (Letter of February 17, 1903, to Franz Xaver Kappus), in *Lettres à un jeune poète* (Letters to a young poet), ed. and trans. Claude Mouchard and Hans Hartje (Paris: Le Livre de poche, 1989), 38.

INDEX

Abraham, 57
absolute, versus relative, 56
absurdity, 15–17
adaptation, morality of, 90–93
Aeschylus, 121
aesthetic merit, 85
aggregates of attachment, 76–79, 82
Agrippina's thrush, 105–6, 108
Alain-Fournier, 12
Alexandria, library of, 122
allographic arts, 164n1
amour-propre, 137, 150, 151
anonymity of writers, 109
anonymous existence, 148
antique literature, judgments on, 111–12
apocalypse
    and Diderot and Falconet's debate concerning writing texts certain to disappear, 132–38
    and posterity in nuclear age, 138–42, 167n14
    science fiction on, 131–32
Arkhipov, Vasily, 140
Art for Art, 52–53
arts
    autographic versus allographic, 164n1
    emergence of, 136–38
    judging, 167n9
atomic bomb, 138–42, 167n14
attachment, five aggregates of, 76–79, 82
authorial freedom, 38
author's name
    as common noun, 70–71
    and perception of posterity as exclusive club, 62–63
    referential transparency of, 63–65
author's page, 165–66n21
autobiographical voice, Sartre's shift of, 47
autographic arts, 164n1

Bachimont, Bruno, 126, 129, 164–65n2
Baudelaire, Charles, 50, 51
Beauvoir, Simone de, 47–49, 50, 52
belief, paradoxes of. *See* paradoxes of belief
belles lettres, and vogue of existentialism, 48–49

Benjamin, Walter, 51
Benot, Yves, 154n7
Bible, and uniqueness of the person, 74
biography, 68, 69, 70
Blair, Ann, 129
Blake, William, 12
blogs, 113
body, and five aggregates of attachment, 77
Bonaparte, Napoleon, 101–2
books
    burning, 122–23
    and cyber metaphor, 9
    increasing volume of, 128
    loss of, 122, 165n9
Borges, Jorge Luis, 12
Bossuet, Jacques-Bénigne, 106, 107, 116
Bracciolini, Poggio, 129
Bradbury, Ray, 122–23, 132
Brodie, Bernard, 139
Buddha, 142
Buddhism
    concept of "I" in, 77, 82–83, 161n6
    and five aggregates of attachment, 76–79, 161n8
    interdependence of objects in, 161n13
    and possibility of future rediscovery, 146–47
    and posterity in light of Noble Truths, 79–83
    and uniqueness of the person, 73, 74–75
Buffat, Marc, 25, 155n23

Cabet, Étienne, 35
Camus, Albert, 1, 154n19
capitalism, and fame of Sartre, 51
capital punishment, 1
Casanova, Giacomo, 37–45, 46, 57, 157 nn. 7, 13
catastrophe
    and Diderot and Falconet's debate concerning writing texts certain to disappear, 132–38
    and posterity in nuclear age, 138–42, 167n14
Catherine II of Russia, 92, 93
celebrity. *See* fame

170 • INDEX

Chamfort, Nicolas, 49, 159n13
Champollion, Jean-François, 101, 102, 104–5
chance, 14–15
Chateaubriand, François-René de
    called "melancholy Mohican" by Lautréamont, 148, 167n6
    and closed and classical languages, 108–9
    and decline of languages, 105–7, 164n8
    and destiny of languages, 115–17
    and division of languages, 109–12, 114
    and expansion of democratic principle, 112–15
Chouillet, Jacques, 162 nn. 6,9, 163n19
Christianity
    disappearance of French language and, 106–7
    and uniqueness of the person, 74–76
Citton, Yves, 30–31
classical languages, 108–9
closed languages, 103–5, 108–9, 115, 116–17
collective fiction, remembered by posterity, 148
comet, and Diderot and Falconet's debate concerning writing of texts certain to disappear, 132–38
commitment, of writers, 56
common noun, author's name as, 70–71
concert metaphor, in *Pros and Cons*, 25–26, 27, 28–29
Confessions, The (Rousseau), 92–94, 119
consciousness, discriminating, as aggregate of attachment, 78
consistency, ethical, 90–93
creative genius, Diderot on, 32
criticism, escalation of, 88–90
Cuban Missile Crisis, 140
cultural mediation, 101, 141
culture, general, 67
cyber metaphor, 8–9

Dacier, Anne, 64–65
D'Alembert's Dream (Diderot), 155n11
damned poet, 50
Danneels, Cardinal Godfried, 74–75, 161n4
dead languages, 102–3, 164 nn. 4,8
death
    awareness of, 2–3
    evaluation of authors following, 85–87
    personal solutions to, 3–5
de Biasi, Pierre-Marc, 123, 128
decasyllabic figure, 149

dedication, and probability of surviving into posterity, 35–36
"Defense and Illustration of the French Language" (du Bellay), 35
deity, posterity substituted for, 61
Delon, Michel, 18
democratic principle, expansion of, 112–15
Descartes, René, 56
desire, 78, 79–80, 147–48
Destiny, 42
de Viau, Théophile, 35–36
Dialogue on Posterity (Diderot and Falconet), 132–38
diction, Chateaubriand on, 111–12
Diderot, Angélique, 93
Diderot, Denis
    allusion to quarrel with Falconet, 155n11
    ambivalence concerning posthumous evaluation of individual merit, 87–88
    and content and publication of *Pros and Cons*, 21–24
    and debate concerning writing of texts certain to disappear, 134–38
    and debate over Polygnotos painting, 166 nn. 5, 6
    and debate precipitating correspondence in *Pros and Cons*, 25–28
    on desire for posthumous fame, 145–46
    education of, 23
    and ethical consistency and morality of adaptation, 90–93
    and gap in dispute in *Pros and Cons*, 28–33
    "paradox of the actor," 16
    on permanence of names, 63
    and pleasure of slander and escalation of criticism, 88–90
    quarrel with Rousseau and idea of posterity, 93–97, 163n19
    on sacrifice, 44
    See also *Essay on the Reigns of Claude and Nero* (Diderot)
Didymus of Alexandria, 121
digital men of letters, 129
digital technology
    defined, 164–65n2
    and expansion of democratic principle, 113–14
    and memorial overload, 128–30
    migration of, 124–27
    and possibility of future rediscovery, 146–47

and software controlling nuclear arms, 138–39
and transmission and preservation of literary work, 118–19, 123–25
See also technical mediation
disappearance, 147–48
disappointment, in search for posthumous fame, 146
disciples, and posthumous fame, 13
discriminating consciousness, as aggregate of attachment, 78
disembodied existence, 148–49
documents, staging of, 69–70
du Bellay, Joachim, 35, 36
Ducasse, Isidore, 64
dukkha, 76
Duel, The (Casanova), 39
dystopian works, 131–32

emotion, as aggregate of attachment, 78
emulation, posterity from viewpoint of, 23, 34
English language, 107, 108
Epicurus, 13
"equivocal" sensation, 26–27
Ernaux, Annie, 41
Essay on English Literature (Chateaubriand), 105–8, 109–10, 114, 115
Essay on the Reigns of Claude and Nero (Diderot), 87–88, 89, 90–92, 93–94, 96, 162 nn. 6,9
eternity, Sartre and separation of immortality and, 52–55
ethical consistency, 90–93
Euripides, 121
evidence, versus faith, 31
exceptionalism, 144–45
existence, belief in, as illusion, 72–73
existentialism, explanations for vogue of, 48–49
Existentialism Is a Humanism (Sartre), 48

Fahrenheit 451 (Bradbury), 122–23, 132
faith
 versus evidence, 31
 in posterity, 31–33
Falconet, Étienne Maurice
 and content and publication of *Pros and Cons*, 21–24
 and debate concerning writing of texts certain to disappear, 132–34, 137
 and debate over Polygnotos painting, 166 nn. 5–6

and debate precipitating correspondence in *Pros and Cons*, 25–28
Diderot's allusion to quarrel with, 155n11
education of, 23–24
and gap in dispute in *Pros and Cons*, 28–33
on Voltaire, 155n17
fame
 and anonymity of writers, 109
 aphorism on, 49, 159n13
 disjunction between posterity and, 11–14
 immediate versus posthumous, 51
 posthumous, 11–14, 27–33, 50–51, 53–54, 73, 145–47
 of Sartre, 48–50, 51–52
fear, of disappearing, 147–48
Ferrante, Elena, 64, 160n3
final value, 3, 4–5
five aggregates of attachment, 76–79, 82
Force of Circumstances, The (Beauvoir), 46–48, 50, 52
foreign languages, 110–11
Fortune, 42
Four Noble Truths, 76, 79–83
freedom, authorial, 38
French language, 106–7, 108, 116, 164n8
future rediscovery, 146–47

Gatti, Claudio, 160n3
general culture, 67
genius, Diderot on, 32
"Genoese" lottery, 157n7
Gerassi, John, 58
globalization, and fame of Sartre, 51
God, 3, 4, 31–32
Goodman, Nelson, 164n1
Graffigny, Françoise, 7
Greek works, 111–12
Greenberg, Jeff, 2
Greenblatt, Stephen, 120–22, 165 nn. 6–7

Hagège, Claude, 102
Harvey, Peter, 79
HathiTrust, 130
Hebrew, revival of, 104
Hill, Emita B., 23
History of the Turbulence of Poland (Casanova), 41
Hollier, Denis, 108, 164n8
Homer, 64–65, 103, 160n4
Horace, 11–12
Huc, Claude, 124
Huet, Gérard, 76–77

Hugo, Victor, 12, 64
human mediation, 101, 131
Hypatia, 122

"I," concept of, in Buddhism, 77, 82–83, 161n6
Icosameron (Casanova), 43
identity, paradoxes of. *See* paradoxes of identity
immortality, Sartre and separation of eternity and, 52–55
  See also fame; posterity
incarnation, literature as art of, 119–20
indifference, to posterity, 37
individual merit, 84–85, 87–88
information, overload of, 129–30
institutions of learning, and diffusion of discourse of posterity, 66–67
interdependence of objects, 161n13
internet, and expansion of democratic principle, 113–14
  See also digital technology; technical mediation
intertextuality, 148–49
Iroquois language, 106
Isaac, 57

Jackson, Heather J., 14
Jean-Paul II, Pope, 161n8

karma, 3
Keats, John, 13–14
knowledge
  discriminating consciousness and production of, 78
  excess of, 129–30

La Bruyère, Jean de, 12
Lamartine, Alphonse de, 70
languages
  Chateaubriand and decline of, 105–7
  classical, 108–9
  closed, 103–5, 108–9, 115, 116–17
  and cultural mediation, 101
  dead, 102–3, 164 nn. 4,8
  destiny of, 115–17
  division of, 109–12, 114
  foreign versus mother, 110–11
  fragility of, 10
  open, 103–5, 115
  silent, 102–3, 104, 115
Lanzmann, Claude, 1
Latin works, 111–12

Lautréamont, Count of, 64, 148, 167n6
legend, 71
leisure, emergence of, 136–38
letters, staging of, 69–70
Letters from a Peruvian Woman (Graffigny), 7
Letters Written from the Banks of the Ohio (Lezay-Marnésia), 7
Levin, Ira, 132
Lezay-Marnésia, Claude-François de, 7
liar's paradox, 17
library of Alexandria, 122
Lilti, Antoine, 30
literary being, 41–43
literary criticism, publication of, 113
literary quality, 84
literary revivals, 130, 166n27
literary work
  as "allographic art," 118
  dystopian, 131–32
  obstacles compromising sustainability of, 120–23
  transmission of, 12, 118–19
  writing and material mediation of, 119–20
localized posterity, 109–10, 112
lottery
  and Casanova's *The Story of My Life*, 37–39
  posterity compared with, 35–37, 57
Louis IV, 163n11
Lucretius, 13, 152

Mall, Laurence, 96
Mallet, Edme-François, 31
material mediation, 101, 119–20
  and memorial overload caused by digitization, 128–30
  and migration of digital technology, 124–27
  and obstacles compromising sustainability of texts, 120–23
  and transmission and preservation of literary work, 123–25
mediation, paradoxes of. *See* paradoxes of mediation
memoirist, authorial freedom of, 38
memorial imprint, 7–8
memorial overload, caused by digitization, 128–30
memories
  network of, 6, 8, 9
  transmission of, 6–8
men of letters, digital, 129

mental formations, as aggregate of attachment, 78
merit
  Diderot's ambivalence concerning posthumous evaluation of, 87–88
  posthumous fame and literary, 14, 84–85
Metamorphoses (Ovid), 43, 121, 165n6
metempsychosis, 82
Michon, Pierre, 70
minimal narrative, 65–68
"Minuteman I" and "Minuteman III" nuclear missiles, 140
Molière, 62–64, 65–66, 67
money, 3
morality of adaptation, 90–93
moral norms, violation of, 41–43
mother tongue, 110–11
"mutual assured destruction," 139

Naigeon, Jacques-André, 155n14
name. *See* author's name; surname, referential transparency of
natural selection, 144
Nineteen Eighty-Four (Orwell), 131
noble path, 146–47
Noble Truths, 76, 79–83
non-virtuous mental formations, 78
noun, common, author's name as, 70–71
novels, 69
novelty, 80–81
nuclear age, posterity in, 138–42, 167n14

obsolescence
  digital and material, 125, 126, 127
  of software controlling nuclear arms, 138–39
Odyssey (Homer), 64, 103, 160n4
open languages, 103–5, 115
oral autobiography, 39–40
oral transmission, 118
originality, 80–81
Orwell, George, 131
Ovid, 43, 121, 165n6

panache, 15
paradox, versus absurdity, 15–17
paradoxes of belief, 17, 21, 143–44
  and content and publication of *Pros and Cons*, 21–24
  and debate precipitating correspondence in *Pros and Cons*, 25–28
  and gap in dispute in *Pros and Cons*, 28–33
  See also Casanova, Giacomo; Sartre, Jean-Paul
paradoxes of identity, 17, 61–62, 72–73, 84–85, 144
  and creation of persona, 68–71, 72
  and Diderot's ambivalence concerning posthumous evaluation of individual merit, 87–88
  and Diderot's quarrel with Rousseau and idea of posterity, 93–97
  and ethical consistency and morality of adaptation, 90–93
  and five aggregates of attachment, 76–79
  and minimal narrative, 65–68
  and perception of posterity as exclusive club, 62–63
  and pleasure of slander and escalation of criticism, 88–90
  and posterity in light of Noble Truths, 79–83
  and posthumous judgment of authors, 85–87
  and referential transparency of author's name, 63–65
  uniqueness of the person and faith in resurrection, 73–76
paradoxes of mediation, 17, 101, 118–19, 131–32, 144
  and closed and classical languages, 108–9
  and decline of languages, 105–7
  and destiny of languages, 115–17
  and digitization, 123–25
  and division of languages, 109–12, 114
  and expansion of democratic principle, 112–15
  and material mediation of writing, 119–20
  and memorial overload caused by digitization, 128–30
  and migration of digital technology, 124–27
  and obstacles compromising sustainability of texts, 120–23
  and posterity in nuclear age, 138–42
  and silent, dead, and closed languages, 101–5
  and writing of texts certain to disappear, 132–38
"paradox of the actor," 16
Pascal, Blaise, 109
passage metaphor, 8
passiveness, of writers, 53

perception, as aggregate of attachment, 78
Perfect Day, This (Levin), 132
Perry, William J., 140
person
    Buddhist conception of, 77–79, 82–83
    uniqueness of, 73–74, 82
persona, creation of, 68–71, 72
philology, and preservation of digitized texts, 126–27
Philonenko, Alexis, 103, 164n4
Pliny, 24
poet, damned, 12, 47–48, 50, 84.
political ideologies, as obstacle compromising sustainability of texts, 122–23
Polygnotos, 166 nn. 5–6
Poquelin, Jean-Baptiste, 160n2
posterity
    as abstraction, 85
    chance and, 14–15
    compared with lottery, 35–37, 57
    and enjoyment of transgression, 41–43
    as exclusive club, 62–63
    faith in, 31–33
    indifference to, 37
    institutions of learning and diffusion of discourse of, 66–67
    localized, 109–10, 112
    meanings of, 150–51
    and paradox versus absurdity, 15–17
    past quarrels' influence on, 95–96
    and posthumous fame, 11–14
    potential, 6, 153n8
    ruse of, 150
    sacrifice in attaining, 44–45
    substituted for deity, 61
    and trace of works and network of memoirs, 6–9
    universal, 7, 109–10, 112, 116
    as value, 3
    from viewpoint of emulation, 34
    writing for contemporaries versus, 53–55
    See also immortality, Sartre and separation of eternity and
posthumous fame, 11–14, 27–33, 50–51, 53–54, 73, 145–47
potential posterity, 6, 153n8
"Presentation of the *Temps modernes*" (Sartre), 52, 53
preservation of literary works, 120–30
press, publication of literary criticism in, 113
Prévost, Antoine François, 167n8
pride, 137, 150, 151
progeny, 3

Pros and Cons / Dialogue on Posterity (Diderot)
    content and publication of, 21–24
    debate precipitating correspondence in, 25–28
    and Diderot's ambivalence concerning posthumous evaluation of individual merit, 87–88
    gap in dispute in, 28–33
Providence, 42
pseudonyms, 63, 64
Pyszczynski, Tom, 2

Quesnay, François, 31

Realism, 52–53
rediscovery, future, 146–47
referential transparency, 63–65
reincarnation, 74–76, 81–83
relative, versus absolute, 56
religion, as obstacle compromising sustainability of texts, 122
    See also Buddhism; Christianity
reputations, universal, 110
resurrection, faith in, 74–76, 161 nn. 4,12
Revel, Jean-François, 161n8
Ricard, Matthieu, 80–81, 82, 161n8
rivalries, 4–5
Rosetta Stone, 102, 104–5
Rousseau, Jean-Jacques, 13, 91–97, 119, 120, 136–37, 163 nn. 11–12,19
Rousseau, Judge of Jean-Jacques (Rousseau), 30
ruse of posterity, 150

sacrifice, to attain posterity, 44–45
Saint-Évremond, Charles de, 88–90
Sansal, Boualem, 131–32
Sartre, Jean-Paul
    on critics, 86
    fame of, 48–50, 51–52
    farewell to posterity announced by, 46–52, 55–58
    and separation of immortality and eternity, 52–55
Schlosser, Eric, 138–39, 140
scholars, versus digital men of letters, 129
self-love, 137, 150, 151
Seneca, 88–92, 96, 162 nn. 6,8
sensations, as aggregate of attachment, 78
Shakespeare, William, 6–7, 106, 107
silence, of writers, 53
silent language, 102–3, 104, 108, 115

skandha (aggregate), 76–77
slander, pleasure of, 88–90
social life, Rousseau's theoretical scenario
　for birth of, 136–37
Socrates, 29
Solomon, Sheldon, 2
sound metaphor, in *Pros and Cons*, 25–26,
　27, 28–29
Southey, Robert, 13
Stendhal, 35, 54, 68
Stevenson, Ian, 75
Stobée, Jean, 121
*Story of My Escape from the Prisons of the
　Republic of Venice, The* (Casanova), 39
Story of My Life, The (Casanova)
　enjoyment of transgression in, 41–45
　and posterity as reward obtained through
　　lottery, 37–41
　premeditation of, 39–41, 43
style, Chateaubriand on, 111–12
suffering, 76, 77, 78, 79–80, 146
surname, referential transparency of, 64

talent, and probability of surviving into
　posterity, 36
tangible mediation, 101
technical mediation, 101, 119
　See also digital technology
time, as obstacle compromising sustainabil-
　ity of texts, 120–22
"Titanic effect," 140

Truths, Four Noble, 76, 79–83
2084 (Sansal), 131–32

"unequivocal" sensation, 26–27
uniqueness of the person, 73–74, 82, 161n12
"universality" of Western writers, 146
universal posterity, 109–10, 112, 116
universal reputations, 110

Valéry, Paul, 149
virtuous mental formations, 78
Voltaire, 7–8, 24, 64, 68, 70, 155n17
Voyage en Icarie (Cabet), 35

Western writers, "universality" of, 146
Words, The (Sartre), 48
works, appropriation of, 68–69
writers
　commitment of, 56
　involvement of, in contemporary issues,
　　52–53, 55, 56
　posterity of, 9–11
　and posthumous fame, 11–14
　silence of, 53
writing
　for contemporaries rather than posterity,
　　53–55
　motivations for, 143–45, 150, 151
　relationship between material mediation
　　and, 119–20

www.ingramcontent.com/pod-product-compliance
Lightning Source LLC
Chambersburg PA
CBHW022013290426
44109CB00015B/1161